FIVE HOURS

HOW MY SON'S BRIEF LIFE CHANGED EVERYTHING

BY LUCINDA WEATHERBY

Published by Akashic Books
©2015 Lucinda Weatherby

ISBN-13: 978-1-61775-433-3
Library of Congress Control Number: 2015943282
First printing

Akashic Books
Twitter: @AkashicBooks
Facebook: AkashicBooks
info@akashicbooks.com
www.akashicbooks.com

For Jasper, Kevin, and Theo

PART 1

CHAPTER 1

No one will ever know when or why the chromosome splits the wrong way. It could be the sperm, but more likely, because of my age, thirty-five, it is the egg that carries faulty information. I've traveled a lot this year, several round-trips to Costa Rica and England, the radiation from airport X-ray machines blasting my body. Not long before conception, I treated the boys for head lice, pouring noxious-smelling shampoo onto my hands to kill the bugs and their eggs. Later, I will darkly recall that I disregarded the instructions cautioning users to wear gloves.

However it happens, the embryo is doomed from the start.

As its first cells begin to split neatly into pairs, the thirteenth chromosome adds an extra chromosome to each new cell, over and over again, first two, then four, then eight, then scores, then hundreds, thousands, millions, and billions of cells. All with faulty instructions on how to construct a body.

It's estimated that between 95 and 98 percent of such cases are miscarried early on. Many of the remaining embryos are detected by prenatal screening and aborted, or are miscarried or stillborn later. But against the odds, our embryo will grow to be a fetus, and the fetus will make it to full-term and survive the birth process.

We'd have better odds of being struck by lightning.

A baby girl is born with a lifetime supply of eggs, millions of them, a constellation of genetic universes waiting to mature. So the egg that would become half of Theo was already with me the day of my birth, October 24, 1969. I know a little about what was happening in the world and in my family around that time: The *Apollo 11* moon landing had taken place a couple of months before. *Sesame Street* would debut that November. The very first message on what we now call the worldwide web would be sent in five days. My mother, neither Jewish nor much of a drinker, woke with a hangover that morning, the result of a few too many glasses of Manischewitz at a friend's Yom Kippur celebration the night before. She also woke with painful cramps and told my father she thought she was getting her period. My father reminded her she was pregnant and past her due date, and drove her to the hospital, where I was born several hours later.

What I won't learn for decades is that the celestial circumstances surrounding my birth are as notable as anything happening on the human plane. Though I consider myself open-minded and have explored various spiritual traditions, I've never been a big fan of astrology, finding horoscopes merely amusing and not to be taken seriously. But in early 2008, months and months after Theo has been and gone, I cave in to a friend's strong recommendation that I see Jane, an astrologer who lives down the road from me. I'm not sure what I'm looking for exactly, but going through what I did has made me much more curious about the mysteries of the universe. I am willing to suspend judgment if there's even an outside chance of getting some answers, of making sense of the things that have unfolded.

Jane opens the door for me. "You must be Lucinda."

I nod, giving her a brief smile, and step into her bland town house.

I've decided not to tell her anything about myself; my way of testing her and her craft. She already knows my and my husband Dicken's birth dates from our phone conversation.

Jane is in her fifties, I'd guess, pleasant-looking with almost translucent blue eyes that seem to stay fixed on me until I look at her directly. Then they dart away.

"Go ahead and have a seat," she says, pointing to a round wooden table with papers spread over it. "If it's okay with you, I'm going to record this session."

"That's fine."

Jane sits down and begins to look at the colorful diagrammed charts, twisting them this way and that, frowning as she studies the images from different angles.

"Well, the first significant thing I see is that you were born under Black Moon Lilith. You've probably been told that before. It's very striking."

"I've never been told that. I've never even heard of Black Lilith Moon."

"Black Moon Lilith," she corrects me. "It has to do with the power and the terror of the deep feminine. In other words, it's a certain configuration that opens between the moon's orbit and the earth—a paradox that creates a void, a vast, empty, black hole–like area. In your particular chart this moon is in the sign of Cancer, the sign of the mother, and is on the cusp of the eighth house, which represents death."

I try not to look too interested, not wanting to encourage her in any direction, but the words *black hole, motherhood,* and *death* are achingly resonant.

"Motherhood and death, you say?"

"Yes, being born under Black Moon Lilith in this way would set the stage for motherhood and the unrelenting power of the feminine to play a hugely impactful role in your life, and it would somehow relate to death. Black Moon Lilith cycles throughout your lifetime. It takes a little under nine years to complete its course and begin again."

I think back and calculate that Theo was born three months after I turned thirty-six, which would mean I had just returned to the beginning of this dark void-like cycle for the fourth time in my life.

The astrologer continues: "The year 2004 marked the commencement of a Pluto process in your chart, which would last until the beginning of 2008. Pluto represents death and rebirth, a purification on many levels. It would have been intense, taking you to your depths, to the core, bringing tremendous soul growth. You know, you really should consider work that deals with death and dying. I would say you have a very unusual capacity to tolerate and understand the depth of pain people go through."

She doesn't know I'm a grief counselor, that I organize and run support groups and talk with grieving people every day. And she couldn't possibly have guessed that in 2004, months before Theo was conceived, I felt inexplicably drawn to the idea of death.

"Wow" is all I can say. I'm still trying not to give anything away, to stay neutral and not influence the course of the reading, but this is startling.

Jane shifts some papers around and says, "Your husband also went through this Pluto process at the exact same time, because your birthdays are pretty close. But it would have been more intense for you since you're a Scorpio, and Scorpio is ruled by Pluto."

This also rings true. Dicken lost Theo as well as his beloved brother-in-law that year, but I don't think his grief journey has changed him as profoundly as mine has changed me.

"Dicken has a wonderful chart," Jane continues, smiling. "It has the look of a very benevolent king, the kind of man who goes out of his way to take care of children. I imagine he's marvelous with kids."

Hearing these words, I feel a sense of gentle pride. Dicken and I met when we were twenty. I was depressed and lonely and heading off to spend my junior year of college in York, England. My father, who is Anglo-Irish, knew Dicken from an old family connection in Ireland and introduced us. We fell in love very quickly, and my life turned from black-and-white to color. Now, in Jane's office, I sit there thinking of my ruggedly handsome husband shepherding our boys and the nieces and nephews he loves, organizing made-up adventure games that keep them all entertained for hours, staying up late into the night to hold our kids when they're sick or scared. Having lost his own father at twelve, Dicken has enormous reserves of compassion and patience for children. I also feel sad, wondering why a man this wonderful with little ones has only one surviving birth child. My eyes fill with tears.

"You okay?" Jane asks.

I spill out the story of Theo, gushing about how everything she's said so far feels true to me and is making me happy and sad all at once.

"Would you like me to take a look at your baby's chart?" she asks. Before she's even finished the sentence, I'm saying, "Yes."

She types Theo's birth details into her computer, then studies the screen for a few moments.

"Wow," she says. "This is quite a chart, with a very standout feature. At the exact moment of his birth, the star Spica arrived on the eastern horizon. Spica is one of the brightest stars in the galaxy. The only other chart I know of that has this is Princess Diana's."

I think of Diana, who fascinated me as a child. She was radiant, the "Queen of Hearts." She died much too young. My Theo, *he moved hearts too, and he was doomed from the start.*

I walk home, barely noticing the cold air and the late-afternoon traffic whizzing by, pondering the mysterious nature of life. I feel awed, amazed that the stars and some charts printed out by a computer could give Jane a language to describe what sounded very real to me. But I wonder if I am simply a desperate, bereft mother, grasping at any story that will give meaning to what happened. And does it really help to know any of this, whether it is true or not? It won't bring him back. Yet I have a sense that he is with me right now, as I walk along in the darkening light, glowing at the thought of him, my star in the heavens.

I enter the warm house. Dicken is on his knees at the coffee table, playing the board game *Risk* with Jasper and Kevin. Tiny colored plastic pieces spread across a map of the world.

"Hi, love!" Dicken says.

"You wanna play, Mom?" Jasper asks.

"No thanks."

"Mom doesn't like games about war," Dicken explains.

"But Mom, people get hurt without guns," Jasper says. "'Member I broke my shoulder in 'non-competitive' games class?"

"Of course I do," I say, thinking back to the trip to the emergency room a few months earlier, the first time I'd been back there since the night Theo was born.

"It's ironic that an athlete like you would have your most significant injury in a cooperative games class," Dicken says.

"I hate that class!" Jasper explodes. "It's so boring and stupid. And I could kill Max for kicking me in the shoulder."

"It was an accident," I say. "He was in the middle of falling down himself."

Jasper is ten and plays competitive ice hockey. It's his greatest passion, but we send our boys to a Waldorf school that doesn't have a sports program.

"Your turn, Kevin," Jasper says. "Look, Mom, Kevin has Costa Rica."

"I want to be president of Costa Rica when I grow up," Kevin says. He is from Costa Rica and lived there until we adopted him three years ago at age eight.

"I love Costa Rica because it abolished its military," I say. "I'll play if I can have Costa Rica and Switzerland."

"I have Australia because that's where the fiercest rugby warriors are from," Jasper says, holding up his fists and making a stern face.

"You mean New Zealand," Kevin says.

Jasper's face falls.

"That's right, Kevin," says Dicken. "The Maoris are the best rugby players in the world. But New Zealand is really close to Australia, so I can see why Jasper would get them confused."

"I want to play rugby like you did, Daddy!" Jasper says. Dicken grew up in England and attended sporty boarding schools from the age of eight. Jasper has Dicken's formal team photographs on his wall. "I want to be in the scrum, I'd be so fierce."

"No rugby for you till we know how that shoulder is doing," I say.

"Oh, Mom, you're always against me!" Jasper complains. "Go away and leave us alone. I just want to be with my dad."

I head into our room and lie down on the bed. A few minutes later, Dicken enters.

"You okay?"

"Yeah, I'm good," I answer, though I'm feeling a little stung by Jasper's rebuff. Mostly, though, I'm thinking about Black Moon Lilith and Pluto and the brightest star rising on the eastern horizon. Part of me wants to tell Dicken all about the reading with Jane, but most of me wants to hold it inside for now, my own sweet secret, and digest it more fully before I share it with anyone.

"Jasper doesn't mean to hurt you," Dicken says. "He's just riled up."

"That game makes him more aggressive."

"Jasper has always been aggressive," Dicken points out, "and maybe that's why he's so attracted to war games."

"You love that game and you've never been aggressive," I say. I think about Jane's description of him as a benevolent king.

"Daddy!" Jasper cries from the other room. "Come back, come see what I just did to one of your countries!"

Dicken kisses me on both cheeks, then goes back to the living room to rejoin the boys. I'm left to ponder what it would be like to mother a quiet, gentle child, and how children get to be the way they are, and whether the stars lining up a certain way really do predispose us to certain life experiences and qualities, and what kind of child Theo would have been had he lived.

I remember moments of my Black Moon Lilith/Pluto trajectory, this strange journey through motherhood and death, pain and truth.

CHAPTER 2

A year after I graduate from college with a degree in English, Dicken and I have decided to get married. And then what? I'm drawn to the idea of having children one day, but I'm young and don't feel ready. Plus, Dicken plans to pursue a degree in naturopathic medicine, which means two years of premed sciences followed by four of full-time graduate school. I can't see having a baby while he's a student, so I'm looking at six years to focus on something while I prepare for parenthood. I need a path, a job or career of some kind, but I'm uncertain.

My family's ethic of pursuing "unselfish" work opens up two broad career categories: service-oriented or creative. It also leaves plenty of room for youthful confusion. I've often thought about becoming a writer, but I don't feel I have anything important to say. Since my teenage years, I've written a great deal, and I'm usually too terrified to share it with anyone. But listening to others is easy for me. Though I didn't take any psych classes in college, I quietly begin to consider this field as a possibility. I like the idea of learning more about myself and using that knowledge to help others. And maybe I can write about psychology one day. Creativity is too wide-open. Psychology, in writing and in practice, offers parameters.

Studying child psychology will solve everything, I tell myself. I will learn to be the ideal mother, better than my own. I'll have a fulfilling career, a way to earn income while I help others.

I won't realize the deeper source of my attraction to this

field until much later: I want to discover and heal the wounds of my own childhood, what I see as my parents' failings. And if it's too late to heal myself, at least I can ameliorate other childrens' suffering.

Dicken and I celebrate our wedding in the Adirondack Mountains of New York. Both raised Catholic, we no longer attend church and find organized religion objectionable. We have a nontraditional ceremony on a mountaintop. After a joyful week with our families, we load a U-Haul and head out west so I can start graduate school and Dicken can begin premed courses.

Further and further from home and familiar faces, we pass miles of concrete and flat gray land, fast food restaurants and suburban sprawl. Each night we find somewhere inconspicuous to park and sleep in the windowless storage area in the back of the truck. The bleak landscape and monotonous hours of driving seem to be bringing out my dark side. Given that the week before was such a high, I'm struck by the force of the negative thoughts arising in my mind. Somewhere in Nebraska, I think, *What a grim world we live in. I never want to bring a child into such a hellish place.* I figure the only thing to do in light of this is to use my psych degree to help some of the more desperate denizens of the earth. This reflects some of the privileged guilt I was raised with: we have so much, we must give back to the less fortunate. Meanwhile, I feel nauseous. *Must be carsickness,* I tell myself, though I haven't been carsick since I was a small child.

In a gritty motel in Daly City, the only place we can afford in the Bay Area while we search for a one-bedroom rental, I notice a small hole in my diaphragm.

"Oh my God, Dicken. Look at this."

"Oh."

"Maybe that's why I feel sick."

"It's only a tiny hole."

"You're right, there's no way . . ."

I can't sleep. The itchy motel blanket chafes my skin like

worry. With my super-sensitive sense of smell, I'm sure I can detect stale urine in the sheets.

A few days later, with my period now undeniably late, I take a test. I am pregnant.

I think of all the champagne I drank during the wedding week and imagine a deformed fetus growing in me. I think of the cramped apartments we've looked at so far, most above our budget. I hear again the clear thought I had on the drive out here, about not subjecting children to this world. *Was I thinking that for a reason? Was it a sign?* This is not the way I want to start a family. I am filled with gloom and fear, terrified to have a baby and terrified to end this pregnancy willfully.

Dicken's face is dark with concern for me and our situation. The more I panic, the sicker I feel, and the more overwhelmed he becomes.

Our families can't understand why we are leaning toward an abortion. "But you just got married. It's all so perfect!"

Both of our mothers were once devoted Catholics, but they no longer attend church regularly. They've both become New Age enthusiasts, going on pilgrimages to sacred sites and meditating regularly. My mother is always looking for something new to explain or deepen her life. One minute it's acupuncture, the next minute it's numerology. I'm looking for answers too, but I don't understand how such an intelligent, educated woman can be so credulous. I want a practice, a way of approaching life that's rooted in an ancient culture. I just don't know what it is yet.

My own religious and spiritual beliefs are mixed up and contradictory, with elements of rebellion against the formal church I was reared in as well as an obsession about my own morality. I view decisions as either right or wrong. In my nauseous, anxious, ungrounded state, every choice feels wrong right now. I tell myself I am bad, that somehow I must deserve this. I feel the weight of sin in the air.

As a child, I listened carefully in church and Sunday school. Desperately wanting to be good and lovable, I worked hard to be a dutiful child of God. I took the Ten Commandments literally and knew I'd broken some—I lied to my mother, I stole candy from my sister—yet I was too shy and shame-ridden to confess my sins to Father James. I could vividly picture the black spot on my soul.

Convinced I was doomed and beyond hope, I lay awake at night petrified by the thought of hell. By my mid-teens, I had stopped going to church, hoping to end my suffering and start afresh, but the guilt and dogma I'd been bathed in was already internalized.

And now, at age twenty-two, pregnant after a week of drinking, I still badly want God's approval. I secretly believe I might be able to make up for the sin of getting pregnant at the wrong time if I can do what's right. With no clear "good girl" path, I feel more doomed than ever. Though I won't articulate this, I also feel angry. Angry that things are not going according to plan. This is not how it was supposed to be. My life, our first days of marriage, the course of the world. Everything feels wrong, and I will never find my way back to grace.

Dicken's mother, Caroline, presses us to carry on with the pregnancy. "I'll help you raise the baby." I try to erase her words as I hear them. The kindness hurts too much.

My mother tells us to do what we want. "I hate to see you suffering with this," she says. She will fly out and help us through this trial.

I can't describe the desperation I feel. We are thousands of miles from home. We have no place to live, no friends, no community, no source of income other than a small monthly allowance from my father, and a trust fund I know about vaguely but have no access to yet.

Dicken, who was also raised Catholic, internalized a gentler God than mine. I've always been struck by how forgiving he is, with himself and others. His kindness is what drew me to him, his unconditional love a hearth fire that warms my colder nature. Dicken is mostly upset about this pregnancy because it's causing me pain. He doesn't see decisions in black-and-white, the way I do. His answer comes in colorful dreamscape—he dreams we catch a dolphin, my favorite animal. "We had to take it back out to sea," he tells me, his eyes filling with tears. "It wasn't our time to keep it, even though it was beautiful and we loved it."

On the table at the doctor's office, I can hear the machine whirring. I can't feel the lower half of my body, and my mind is vast, white, numb. Dicken's tears fall on me as he holds my hand. I tell myself to be happy the awful nausea will lift soon.

Two days later, I begin my graduate program in psychology and start an internship at a day treatment center for emotionally disturbed children. I love the children, I hate myself. Dicken gets a job scooping ice cream and begins a premed program on the weekends. Our sex life is dormant for months, because Dicken is afraid to get me pregnant again, and I am too numb to experience desire.

CHAPTER 3

Spring 1997

We are living in Portland, Oregon. Dicken is in his third year of naturopathic medical school. I'm a therapist in a dual-diagnosis program for teens and adults, seeing some of the most desperate, alienated people in the city. Friends ask me if I find the work depressing, but somehow the opposite is true. As I gain experience, I grow more comfortable working with challenged patients, and I'm able to see the sweet humanity in each, especially the young ones. It fortifies me to witness people at the bottom, in the darkest states imaginable, and see hope, glimmers of light, the help that good people offer them, and the help they offer each other.

All this makes me more confident about bringing life into the world. But I still have moments of doubt, especially seeing adolescents as young as twelve who are extremely violent and self-destructive. I think of myself at that age, pretending to be happy and compliant, but in quieter ways, I was just as lost. *Is anyone in this world truly happy?*

"These poor kids," I tell an older coworker, a parent herself. "How do they get messed up so young? Is it just me, or is our culture getting darker all the time?"

"No," she tells me. "Look at their parents. They're all children themselves, addicted, abusive." As if she can read my thoughts, she adds, "You don't have to worry. You're going to be a wonderful mother. You're so gentle."

Yes, I tell myself, *Dicken and I will never make the terrible mistakes these parents make.*

One evening, after a three-hour meeting with the meditation

group we've been part of for a year or so, I come home feeling open and relaxed, in touch with a rare sense of peace about myself and the world. Dicken and I make love without protection for the first time—a spur-of-the-moment decision, in a way, but also something we've been moving toward for quite some time.

I quit my job the day I find out I'm pregnant. I don't want our baby to spend its first nine months in a locked-down ward, and I don't want to have to see the results of bad parenting.

Two weeks later, I start to bleed. It's an early miscarriage.

I cry for hours. Dicken holds me, looking more concerned than tender.

"What do you want to do?" he asks.

"I want to have a baby."

"Okay."

The topic needs no further discussion. He trusts me to know how we should proceed.

We wait one cycle, try again, and get pregnant. This time, it sticks.

Again, I feel terribly ill. Though the sickness eases considerably by the second trimester, the days seem to stretch on forever. I have little to do and spend most of my time pining for the baby, wondering, wondering, *What will he or she be like? What will motherhood be like?* I try to write, not just in my journal like I always do but something more serious, some short memoir pieces. I can't concentrate, and figure all my creative juices must be going into this baby. I am aimless and lonesome by myself in the house all day while Dicken is in classes and doing clinic shifts. I long for company, but most of my friends work or go to school, or live far away.

A woman I know from our meditation group is also pregnant and doesn't work, and we visit each other. She lives in an organized spiritual community with about a dozen other families who all own apartments in the same housing complex. They have community meals and share chores. My friend tells me she is never lonely. "I can always find someone to have a cup of tea with, or do laundry with, or yoga." I look out her window at the communal gardens in the backyard, where people grow vegetables and flowers. I can't see any weeds, only neat paths and healthy flowers and a brightly painted play structure.

I decide this is how people should dwell, tribal-like, not in isolation the way most Americans do. My younger sister Maud is traveling in India for the year with her boyfriend, Tom. I know from her letters she is taken with the Indian tradition of extended-family living. I miss Maud terribly. After a rocky relationship as teenagers, she and I have become close allies. I write her, suggesting we all live together when she and Tom return from India. The letters I send take weeks to get to her; she picks them up at the post offices along their planned route. A few days after I send my letter, before mine could possibly have reached her, I get one from her suggesting we live together when they return.

Maud tells me she and Tom have decided to become farmers and grow organic produce. They've met a woman working on a traditional farming project in Ladakh who is from Ashland, Oregon, and has urged them to start a farm there. Our mother has just decided to retire to this small town of Ashland, and Dicken has been offered a job as the junior doctor in a naturopathic practice there.

I am overjoyed at the beauty of this synchronicity. How could we not go ahead? I imagine our kids having the kind of childhood I wish I'd had. Country, not city, with nature as an influence instead of the ambitious, career-driven climate of Washington, DC. A quiet life full of people and home-based activity, not nanny-supervised kids in a big, busy house and wearing starchy dress clothes to church every Sunday.

January 1998

Maud and Tom fly home from India shortly before I go into labor. The birth is long, three days. The pain is so intense I would take any drug available, but since I have decided not to go to the hospital for this, I have no choice but to deliver the baby naturally. At one point during a break between contractions, I think to myself, *Well, at least I'm not afraid of dying anymore. There's no way it could be this bad.*

When the baby is finally born in our living room, with seven of our family members and three midwives in attendance, looking like a mini-replica of Dicken, I feel as triumphant as I ever have in my life.

Two weeks after Jasper's birth, I'm on the couch nursing him, watching the Winter Olympics on TV. The long-distance cross-country skiers are sprinting for the finish line, looking exhausted. *That's not so impressive,* I think, recalling my grueling labor. I now see almost anything else as easy. I know I could climb Everest, I could swim the English Channel, but I don't need another heroic feat to prove anything to myself or anyone else. I feel relaxed and complete. I never anticipated this before childbirth, but I feel purified on a soul level, like everything I have ever done wrong in my life has been washed away, my slate wiped clean. *I am forgiven.* And having this baby in my arms is the most fulfilling way to celebrate my new state.

Late that night, Jasper is fretful; Dicken is asleep, needing rest for an exam the next morning; and I am tired, my stitches from a small vaginal tear burning. I find myself longing for a reprieve, then quickly catch this impulse: *This is what I wanted, this is the choice I made.* I stay up late rocking Jasper in my arms. For the first time in my life, I am sure I'm doing what I'm meant to be doing. My body is weary, but what serenity there is in knowing my exact place in the universe. I feel glorified.

The first year goes well. I am blissfully serene much of the time, madly in love with my baby and my husband. I am with Jasper almost every minute of the day and night, thrilled by merging my being with his, and happy to settle for the glory of being a martyr mother in the rare moments I'm not feeling content.

But year two exposes some major cracks in the foundation.

CHAPTER 4

Summer 1999

We have moved onto the land we bought with Maud, her husband Tom, and their baby daughter Grace, born just ten months after Jasper. Here in the mountains of Southern Oregon, near Ashland, the town where my mother and her husband Ralph have recently retired, the plan is to raise our small children together in a back-to-the-land utopia. Tom runs the farm, baby Grace on Maud's back while she works the soil; Dicken practices natural medicine in town; and I stay at home, being the happy earth momma I was born to be. Our lawyer father calls us "dropouts" for foregoing ambitious careers and choosing this unorthodox lifestyle, but we don't take it personally. We snicker behind his back that he's the one who's deluded and missing out on the good life.

Maud and I are sitting on the dilapidated sofa in the one-room kitchen/bathroom/living space we're sharing while we build our 4,500-square-foot, two-family house. We're sipping tea and chatting while Jasper and Grace play on the wooden floorboards. For the third time in ten minutes, Jasper, age one and a half, walks over to Grace, nine months, and whacks her on the head. Grace wails.

I run to them and grab Jasper, telling him, "No!" in a stern voice.

Maud picks up Grace. "We're out of here," she says. "This isn't working."

"Wait a minute," I say. "Why should you guys have to leave? We can go."

But she's already gone. The room is quiet. Jasper looks at the door and reaches his hands out, mournfully calling, "Gugu," his name for Grace. I turn to get a marker and piece of paper to distract him, but when I turn back around, he is gone, the door open. I run out into the yard, catch up with a giggling barefoot Jasper, and carry the squirming, protesting bundle back into the kitchen. On the way in I notice nails and scraps of wood scattered all over the ground, and remember the rattlesnake Tom found coiled up in the barn the other day, and make a mental note to find Jasper's moccasins. It's before eight o'clock, already hot out, and I am tired.

Back inside, I feel aimless and uneasy, wishing Maud was still around. It's been a few months since Jasper started lashing out at Grace for no apparent reason, and it has taken a toll on all of us. This is not turning out to be the idyllic cousin-as-companion scenario we factored into our back-to-the-land plans.

I settle Jasper in with the paper and marker, then call my mom, relieved to hear her cheerful voice answer the phone.

"Hi, Mom, it's me, Cinda," I say, and she immediately asks, "What's wrong, sweetie?"

I describe the situation to her.

"I just don't get it," she says. "Why is Jasper so violent?"

"I don't know. We've tried doing what the books say, and he doesn't seem to respond."

I read parenting books compulsively. A recent one points out how absurd it is that women so lack confidence as mothers, they would rather be told what to do by an author, usually male, whom they've never met. I heartily agree, shaking my head in pity at these mothers. When I finish the book, I move on to the next one.

"What about a therapist?" Mom suggests.

I groan inside. *I'm a therapist, I've worked with kids, I'm supposed to know how to deal with my own kid who's had every advantage we could give him.*

"Something's not right with him," she says.

Tears spring to my eyes. "I don't think he's that bad. Isn't it normal for boys to test physical limits at this age?"

"Benny never did this." I flash back to all the old home movie footage of me and my brother, a year older than me, playing as babies and toddlers, and can't remember a single violent scene.

"Well, I don't know what to do, Mom. I'm exhausted by it and can't figure out what's right. I'm trying to give him everything I can. I've devoted my whole life to him. I don't understand why he's angry or why he'd hurt anyone! No one's ever laid a finger on him."

"Maybe you're giving him too much. He's probably angry that he's so dependent on you. It must be a terrible internal conflict for him."

What am I supposed to do with that? I start to cry.

"Oh, sweetie," Mom says, real concern in her voice. I'm the daughter who very rarely breaks down. "I think you need something for yourself. Why don't I take you shopping later this week? You could use some nicer clothes. It'll help your self-esteem."

I cringe at the words "self-esteem."

My mom, a lawyer for twenty years, went back to school to get a master's degree in social work at the same time I did mine in counseling. Frustrated by the law's inability to protect the children of her disadvantaged clients, she decided to work with kids on a one-to-one basis. Despite her legitimate reasons for pursuing social work, I suspected her timing wasn't completely coincidental. She always talked about how she felt disconnected from me when I was growing up, how she couldn't seem to find a way to reach me. I didn't think she was aware of it, but I believed her return to school in a similar field was a way to find a connection. And for a while, it worked. During those two years, with three thousand miles between us, we chatted often about programs, classes, ideas. We bonded as never before.

But by now, our relationship seems to have gotten more and more complicated, with lingo my father calls "psychobabble" running rampant, the enmeshment and self/other evaluation sessions ever increasing, threatening to turn every conversation into a house of mirrors.

"I better go," I tell her. We say our goodbyes and hang up.

I look around the messy room, aware of a deep exhaustion. Everything seems hopeless and overwhelming. I feel trapped, like the walls of my life are coming in on me. I begin to cry again, then think, *Look at me! I never cry. Things must be worse than I even know.*

"Mama, Mama!"

Jasper's piercing cries snap me out of my trance and I see that he is making the baby sign for hungry, stuffing several fingers into his mouth. I rally, heading to the cramped, disorganized kitchen corner of the room to find something healthy for him to eat.

"Yogurt and banana?"

"No!"

"Carob chips?"

"No!"

"Toast?"

"No!"

I fix him a bowl of yogurt with maple syrup and set it in front of him. He begins to eat without protest. I sit back on the couch and sigh.

"Tat, tat, tat, tat!" Jasper cries, mimicking the construction noises coming from outside. *Might as well be the sound of my trust fund draining away. I hope Dicken's practice picks up so we can actually afford to live in this huge house we're building.*

What I look forward to most each day is Dicken's return in the evening, and the chance to hear about what happened at work that day. Did more patients call and make appointments? Did some well-connected community member contact Dicken and promise to refer people? Did he get invited to speak at an important conference? I gave up working when I had Jasper, determined to be a full-time mom, available to my child in a way my busy career mom never was to me. I don't regret that and have no desire to return to my career now, relieved I don't have to juggle a paid job with the very challenging work of raising a child. I wasn't expecting my choice to make life easy. But I did think it would make my life simpler than it feels right now.

Jasper climbs into my lap, covering my already dirty shirt with yogurt handprints. *Laundry time.* I run my hand over his soft blond curls, put my face in his hair, and inhale. Even through layers of yogurt and dust, I can smell his distinctive baby scent, like a strange and delicious mixture of sweat and fresh-baked cookies. I remind myself to take in his sweetness, not to miss this stage of childhood.

Jasper pulls at my hair, then says, "Gugu?" I miss my sister's company and wonder when she and Grace will return. Dicken won't be back for another ten hours. The day stretches out long before me.

February 2002

Dicken is away for two days teaching a seminar. I've been with Jasper nonstop, and I'm exhausted. Maud is around and helps out some, but I still feel responsible for Jasper around the clock and can't seem to relax. We're living in the lovely and spacious house we built, with a wing for each family and a shared main house, but communal living in relative luxury is not the happy experiment I hoped it would be.

When the phone rings and I hear Dicken's voice, I'm momentarily lifted from my gloom. "Hi, honey!" I say. "How did the seminar go?"

"Hi," he says, and instantly I know he is low. "We didn't get as many students or sales as we'd hoped. We'll be lucky to break even."

"What did you do wrong?" I ask, realizing how critical this sounds as the words come out of my mouth. Luckily, Dicken doesn't seem to take it the wrong way and answers me at face value. He is sensitive to those he loves, but not so self-critical that he takes on all my judgment.

"We probably shouldn't have picked the week before exams," he says. "Bad timing, I guess."

I am silent, reeling in the wake of this disappointing news.

"I miss you so much, love," he says. "I just want to be home, snuggling up with you and Jabu."

I know he's asking for comfort right now, but I feel cold and resentful. My side of the unspoken agreement we have is to take care of Jasper full-time, while Dicken is supposed to be providing for us financially. These last two days without breaks have been grueling for me, and there will be nothing to show for it except two exhausted parents.

"See you when you get home," I say. "Drive carefully." I hang up the phone and flop on the couch.

Maud is in the kitchen making a snack. "You okay?" she asks.

Before I can answer, Jasper runs over and jumps on my foot.

"Ouch!" I cry. "Don't do that!"

Jasper tries to jump on the other foot. I pull both feet into my lap so he can't reach them.

"Here, Jasper," Maud says. "Have some carob chips."

He goes to her, takes a handful of the chips, and says, "One for Gugu?" Grace comes over from the play area and puts her hand out.

"What do you need?" Maud asks me.

I close my eyes. I feel tired and defeated, yet there's an antsy energy humming under my skin. I haven't exercised for a few days, other than straightening up the house over and over again, and carrying Jasper around in my arms. I tell myself I'm lazy and probably getting fat.

"I think a walk would be good," I say.

"Jasper, stay with me and Grace," Maud says. "I'll read you a story, okay?"

"No!" Jasper wails. He pulls up my shirt roughly, trying to get to my breasts while I squirm and deflect him. Then Grace starts to cry, I'm not sure why. The sounds echo around the big main room and seem to magnify inside my head, a cacophony of pain and chaos.

I need to get out. I push Jasper off me and head for the front door.

Jasper runs after me and starts to grab every shoe and boot he can get his hands on, thinking if I don't have footwear, I won't be able to leave. "You stay here!" he shouts.

I will not be controlled.

I head out the door barefoot. But Jasper is at my heels and grabs onto my leg. His grip is tight.

"Get off me!" I yell. Then I try to get ahold of myself, and I use the softest tone I can muster to say, "I'll only be a few minutes. Ama will take care of you. Please go inside."

"No!" Jasper screams.

Red-hot anger burns through me, and I grab a handful of Jasper's hair. I feel a strong urge to pull it with all my strength, tear it from its roots, cause pain. I can already see it happening. But something stops me—my entire body freezes. I see stars for a moment, then collapse, falling to the ground. I begin to sob.

Maud has rushed over. "What happened?"

Jasper is bending over me, asking me for "nantos," his word for nursing.

The sight of his suddenly softened face, the pleading sweetness of his voice saying, "Nantos? Nantos?" and his urge to connect with me despite my anger make me cry even harder.

I tell myself I'm just like all those mothers of the emotionally disturbed kids I used to work with, the women who lashed out at their innocent children, leaving bruises and scratches the kids tried to hide.

I did not believe I had it in me to strike a child in a flash of rage, but now I know the truth. I'm failing my child. My perfect plan to become the perfect mother has come crashing down around me.

When I calm down a little, I tell Maud I know what I need: "Your therapist's phone number."

* * *

"So, why are you here?" the therapist asks as I settle into her soft couch.

"Well, mainly because I find motherhood crazy-making and I need to be told what I'm doing wrong on that front. That's pretty much it, other than finding out my true purpose, what I'm doing here on earth. I don't want to waste any more time on things that don't matter."

"You want answers."

"I want to cut to the chase, focus on the essential."

"And you want it now."

"Yes, that's why I'm here. I know I'm flawed, and I want you to tell me how to fix myself."

The therapist smiles.

I look at the small clock on the table next to her and notice that five minutes have passed. That's six dollars so far, plus the money the babysitter is costing me. I start to fiddle with my hair.

"You look uncomfortable. Why don't you sense in and see what's arising."

"What do you mean, 'sense in'?"

"I mean close your eyes, check in with your body, see what physical or emotional sensations you notice."

"I notice that I don't want to do that. I notice that I want you to do the talking, the noticing. Isn't that why you're getting paid in this transaction?" I smile nervously at my own irreverence, wringing my hands.

The therapist smiles again too. "You want the answers to come from outside of you, that's what I'm noticing."

Yes, she's right. I want a therapist, a doctor, a guru, a psychic, *anyone* who can tell me what to do. This is what my spiritual, open-minded, seeking mother has modeled to me all my life. Pay someone who knows better than you to fix your problems. Yet I'm driving with the brakes on, because inside me there's a streak of my father's skepticism. He is rational, agnostic, and loyal to what he calls his Scots blood, which makes him extremely frugal. My father has always had a strong work ethic and an equally strong aversion to extravagant spending, especially for intangibles like faith healers and energy workers. He even considers psychiatry self-indulgent, unnecessary except in extreme situations. He would have preferred that instead of studying psychology, I'd followed what he believes is my gift, writing. Meanwhile, my wealthy social-worker mother spends lavishly on dozens of such "indulgences," from massage to chiropractic to Polarity therapy to Filipino psychic surgery.

I am caught in the middle, as I have been since their divorce when I was fourteen. I go back and forth between the extremes my parents represent, one part of me always second-guessing the other, doubting myself and my decisions, rarely sticking with one plan for long because the cynic pulls the plug. Then I am more confused and self-critical than ever. I've seen therapists, but I've never fully trusted or opened up to any of them, pulling back and figuring my father is right: they're no help and just after my money and I should be able to get by on my own. But on my own, with the harsh inner critic at me almost constantly, I spiral lower and end up more convinced that salvation can only exist outside of me. So again I search for the cure, willing to pay well for it, at first. Thus, the cycle continues.

"Tell me why you think you need to be fixed."

"Well, I have everything anyone could want. A hardworking and loving husband. A beautiful son I adore. Enough money to build a dream house and not have to work while my son is small. I have friends, a great family, good health. And yet I'm feeling trapped and miserable a lot of the time."

"How old is your son?"

"Jasper's four," I say, my voice breaking as tears well in my eyes. "I have this one chance to enjoy having him as a four-year-old, and I'm constantly wishing I were somewhere else. What a waste. And it's probably my last chance with a four-year-old, because I can't imagine ever feeling confident enough in myself to have another child. And it can't be his fault, it must be mine, so I obviously need fixing."

I explain the shattering experience of seeing myself as a less-than-ideal mother. "If I'm not parenting effectively, if my child shows any sign of maladjustment, I am failing at my only purpose. I set aside everything to raise this child. All my expensive degrees, all my ambition, all my time. I have no excuse to not be doing this well."

"It sounds like your entire sense of self-worth and meaning is derived from this identity."

"Exactly. So when the slightest thing goes wrong, I lose my bearings. I panic."

"You've really set yourself up with impossible expectations," the therapist says. "Is there any room for you to just be human?"

"I don't understand what you mean."

"It just seems like you expect yourself to be beyond human."

"Oh, I know I'm human. I just think I should be doing a better job with all I've been given."

"Who's telling you that you need to be doing better?"

"I don't know, me, I guess. I just don't think I have any excuse to be struggling so much when I have nothing concrete to worry about. Most people in the world have real problems."

"You don't seem to have much patience for yourself."

"I don't want patience, I want results. I want to straighten myself out, raise my child well, and help the world. There's no time to lose. So can you please just tell me what I need to know? I can tell I'm missing something."

"Why do you think you're missing something?"

"Because it's not supposed to feel this way. I'm so close to the answer, yet so far, and what a waste if I'm this close to the truth yet never grasp it."

"Why don't you take a big breath and close your eyes for a moment."

I do what she says, then open my eyes suddenly. "I don't want to spend a long time on this. I've already done two years of therapy in grad school and I have my life to get back to."

I look out the window and notice a young man in a down jacket carrying pruning shears across the large landscaped garden. Leafless trees stand still in the fading afternoon light.

In time, I will see that landscape change from sleepy winter to blooming spring to arid summer to crisp, colorful autumn and through the cycles over and over. I will begrudgingly write out checks that increase by five dollars every year or two. I take breaks from therapy, pulling the plug now and then, but parenting crises blow up like landmines with enough frequency to bring me back, humbled. I will also see a handful of less conventional healers over the years, usually one-time visits that disappoint my hopes of getting "the answer" to my perceived problem.

It will be a few years before I begin to entertain the idea that maybe nothing in me needs to be fixed, and that the process of therapeutic inquiry is not only supportive but fascinating, even joyful at times. In the meantime, I begin separating out the parts of me that reflect my mother, the parts of me that reflect my father, and the mysterious essence that is me, stand-alone me.

A quote from my father-in-law's commonplace book: "Those who say, don't know. Those who know, don't say." My mother says a lot. She seems to have read nearly every self-help book and religious classic and sampled every spiritual tradition from East to West for at least a weekend. My father doesn't say much about spirituality, but what he does say is revealing. He has always written off religion with remarks like, "How can there be a God when there is so much suffering in the world?" End of discussion. In my mind, his approach is just as shallow as my mother's, only there is less room for curiosity.

I start to seek out religious writing and ideas. I want a path that keeps me on the straight-and-narrow, imposes discipline, gives me clear instructions I can follow. Something based on sound reasoning that no one, not even my dad, can question.

At the same time, I also crave a path that provides reassurance, peace, inspiration. Something to soothe me in the darkest nights. And on top of all that, I am just plain curious; I want to know why we are here, I want to be taken deeper, to brush up against the mystery by forces greater than I can imagine.

I begin to embrace spiritual practices like prayer, dance, and silent retreats led by my therapist. The path of Sufism calls me because I am introduced to it gradually, not directly. It finds me, not the reverse. My therapist imparts her teachings subtly, over years and by example, and somehow my inner critic isn't able to catch on fast enough to reject it outright. My teacher is like Sufism itself: consistent, yet paradoxically always changing. You can't pin her down, yet she is always there, and she can be counted on to be authentic in each moment. The form of her teaching evolves over time, building on itself but never remaining stagnant. She changes what she calls her practice from "psychotherapy" to "spiritual counseling."

The retreats begin as weekends, and evolve to be five days long. She focuses primarily on the enneagram, a system of personality types, for years, then moves on to themes like relationships and instincts. She develops a way of using movement as a teaching tool. Yet some things remain constant: Rumi's poetry, the Dances of Universal Peace, periods of silence, inquiry, and meditation. She doesn't broadcast these as Sufi practices, and she doesn't recruit students, but by the time I realize I'm on this path in a serious way, it's not an abstraction I have to think my way through: I've already experienced the power of its practices in my emotions and in my body. I feel at home and grateful to have my teacher as my guide.

As I become more willing to receive help, life gradually eases for me, and the joys of parenting begin to stand out, while the struggles seem more manageable. Soon I am seriously considering getting pregnant again.

CHAPTER 5

In the early hours of February 19, Maud gives birth to Sam Patrick in her wing of our house. I get to hold him minutes after he is born. Big and bald, he reminds me of Jasper as a newborn. I am filled with a giddy, warm joy.

The next morning, Tom comes to find me.

"Maud's having terrible after-birth pains when the baby breastfeeds. She's wondering if you can nurse him for a while so she can get a break."

I dash to their room and try not to act too eager as I take Sam into my arms and offer him my breast. He latches on easily and begins to gulp milk, which flows copiously because I still haven't completely weaned Jasper. I wonder if my milk might not be made up of the right nutrients for a newborn but decide not to say anything.

I'm happy as can be, nursing this sweet little boy, marveling at his tiny fingers and hairless head as if he were my own.

I find it hard to leave the house for the next couple of weeks because I want to be near the baby as much as possible. Whenever I hold him, I feel transformed, like I've entered a new realm, more peaceful and sacred than the outside world. "Baby energy," the midwife calls it when she stops by to check on things.

Dicken is moping a bit, probably because I'm not paying enough attention to him. He finds Jasper's baby album on the shelf, sits down at the table, and gazes at the photographs.

"What a beautiful baby he was, look."

I stand over him and look at the images of the three of us in postpartum heaven. I put my hands in Dicken's thick brown hair and it makes me think of Sam's bald head.

"I'll be back in a bit," I say, heading for Maud's room.

While in one way having Sam around fires up my longing for another baby of my own, it also puts things on hold because I have access to as much baby energy as I want, right in my own house. I can even nurse him and get the bonding-hormone high. And I'm not losing sleep or having to change diapers.

Summer 2003

Maud and I decide to take Jasper, Grace, and baby Sam to Costa Rica for six weeks. We are in the mood for adventure and figure Costa Rica will be affordable and give us all a chance to learn some Spanish. We stay in a rustic house our mother bought a few years before in Cocles, a small village on the Caribbean coast.

Costa Rica is a world away from the dry, hot Southern Oregon summer: Technicolor green, balmy with sea-scented air, almost always between eighty and eighty-two degrees Fahrenheit, with brief dramatic downpours two or three times a day. Jasper spends most of his time running around the village, playing with a pack of local children. A natural leader at five, he has almost everyone at his service, shouting out orders in English. He doesn't learn more than four words of Spanish the entire time we are there, but he makes many friends. At the beach, I watch Jasper chase screaming girls, play soccer with passionate intensity, and let waves topple over him as he hangs onto the hands of his closest chums, Burlington, Jakel, and Kevin. I'm impressed by how Jasper fully embraces these friends, how he curls up in their laps, covers them with kisses, and says whatever he wants to these older boys with backgrounds and looks about as opposite from his as you can get. *Hermanos sin sangre*, the boys say of their bond with Jasper, *brothers without blood*.

I am struck by Kevin. Seven years old, he has a thick mass of dark, curly hair and a broad grin. Instead of stealing mangoes from our open kitchen as some of the other kids have done, Kevin climbs trees and brings back offerings: coconuts, limes, and something new to me called *fruta gorda*, a delicious fleshy fruit with a flavor that reminds me of bubble gum. When I prepare dinner each night, Kevin eagerly helps me peel garlic and cut stalks of fresh lemon grass from the garden. I know he is staying with his aunt, our neighbor and friend Liliana, who with her husband Bobby takes care of our mother's house. But I don't learn Kevin's story until I'm helping Liliana hang out laundry one morning toward the end of our trip.

Kevin has just skipped by on his way down the road, and I mention to Liliana that he seems like an especially bright and thoughtful little boy.

"Ah, yes," she says in her thick Caribbean accent. "But I don't know what to do with him."

"What do you mean?" I ask as I hang a boy's button-down school shirt on the line.

"His mother can't take him back," she says, shaking her head slowly. "She gone crazy, hit him and his brother really hard and all."

"What about his father?"

"My brother?" she says, then raises her eyebrows and shakes her head again. "Him have no job. Drinks, you know."

"Kevin's a sweet kid," I say.

"I know. I love him. But, ooh, we have so many children!"

"I'd take Kevin in a second," I hear myself say.

"Yes," Liliana says in her lilting voice. "Wouldn't it be good."

We hang the rest of the laundry in silence. I'm aware of a heaviness in my chest. I've just received an e-mail from a childhood friend with the sad news that he and his wife have lost their first (and what will turn out to be only) baby, stillborn at nine months along. I wonder why the child lottery works the way it does, with eager parents who can't have children or lose them, and others with healthy, beautiful kids they don't want or can't take care of.

* * *

I try to put the idea of adopting Kevin away, considering it crazy and impossible, but on my return home I find myself thinking about him quite a bit. I imagine his soft brown curls, his big grin, the way he dances in the waves of the ocean. I don't want him to live in a family where there isn't room for him, where the resources are stretched too thin. I want to take him in my arms, spoil him, let him know he belongs somewhere, is not just cared for but wanted.

I've raised the idea of adoption with Dicken several times over the years, but he's always said he wasn't interested: "If we have another, I'd like it to be our own." So I'm not even planning to tell him about Kevin, but one day, as we drive back from an Ultimate Frisbee game at a friend's place, I blurt it out: "There's this kid in Costa Rica, his name is Kevin," I begin. "He's very cute, and he and Jasper get along really well. And he needs a home. His parents have abandoned him."

Dicken is quiet, and I think, *Oh well, I tried. I knew he'd say no.* I look out the window, turning my head so he won't notice the coldness I feel.

Then Dicken slows the car down and says, "Wow, I just got a really strong positive feeling."

"Really?"

"Tell me more about him."

A few weeks later, after some exploratory calls to Liliana and her family, including the news that Kevin says he wants us to adopt him, Dicken flies down to Costa Rica. His first few days, he remains in San Jose to undergo Lasix eye surgery and see a dentist to have several crowns replaced, saving us thousands because medical care is so much cheaper there. Then he takes a bus to the Caribbean side and with my written directions makes his way to Liliana's house. I check e-mail every hour or so that day and light up when I finally see a message from him in my inbox. His e-mail says his eyes are improving—he'd been unable to e-mail earlier because of his blurry postsurgery vision—his mouth is sore, his laptop was stolen on the bus, and he can't get over what a stunningly beautiful child Kevin is.

The next day Kevin's uncles, Bobby and Walter, take Dicken by car, dugout canoe, and on foot into the jungle reservation near the Panama border to find Kevin's mother, Flor. She has two little boys underfoot in her simple wooden house. Flor gives Dicken her blessing for the adoption. "She loves Kevin and recognizes his intelligence and wants to give him a chance for a good education," the uncles translate. "She is only in agreement with this because it's what Kevin wants, and because Bobby and Liliana admire your family and assure her you are good people."

Dicken e-mails the news from the Internet café just across the road from Liliana's house. He says he sees Kevin as a special child with great potential.

He'll be very suited to getting an advanced education, learning English, getting out of provincial Cocles. I think Kevin might end up doing something great, maybe going back to Costa Rica as an adult and making a difference on a big scale.

I have been looking at this potential adoption on an interpersonal, intimate scale—thinking of how Kevin needs a home and loves attention, seeing the ways it will affect all of us as individuals. I love hearing Dicken's broader, more global view.

As I sit with all of this, I am filled with a strange, subtle peace, a profound sense of expanding space within me. I am so grateful to Dicken that I vow to give him another baby of our own. In my mind, it's the only reward worthy of the heroic journey he's undertaken for something I initiated, something I didn't expect to get.

This begins what will turn out to be a lengthy and complicated adoption process. The agency we hire takes our $4,000 deposit, sends us a few forms, and then mysteriously stops returning my phone calls. Then the number goes out of service. A Google search reveals a newspaper headline reporting that the agency has been closed by authorities in Florida—its owner was arrested on child-smuggling charges. We almost give up. But a lawyer we know in San Jose offers his direct services, so we hire him, paying him a lot less than we would have an agency. This means we have a representative in Costa Rica, but none in the US. We have to track down just about every family document on both sides, ours and Kevin's, and have each one certified, authenticated, recertified, and stamped by the US Secretary of State's office. It is a long, laborious, frustrating process, especially as the laws in Costa Rica seem to change every few months, including one period of time where the government outlaws foreign adoption altogether. But we persist.

My brother is supportive, but comments, "You've always been the good child. You're gonna get even more points from Mom now that you're adopting a needy kid."

I think of all the ways I haven't been good, the mistakes of my youth, the dark judgments and self-recrimination. Ben's image of me seems almost absurd. But I know what he means. The self I present to the family is the one I have always so badly wanted to be, the good girl, a deserving, lovable person.

"I'm not trying to get points with Mom," I tell Ben, a little defensively. "This is really a selfish move. He's a super cute, bright child. It's not like we went through the usual adoption route, which is such a crapshoot. We're doing this because we really want him, and because it all seems to be lining up so perfectly, like it was meant to be."

This is all true—and at the same time my brother is right. We were raised with the message that we should make up for all we were given by doing good works for the less fortunate. And this plays into my deepest parenthood angst. I feel painfully responsible for anything negative Jasper experiences because, I reason, if it weren't for me and my choices, he wouldn't be in the world having to go through all the trials of being human. In my twisted logic, I don't take credit for any of the joy Jasper feels, only the pain. Having another baby would only compound this conflict, I'm sure.

But adopting a child is different. I will not feel completely responsible for Kevin's pain. I will not rake myself over the coals for every mistake, for every time I fail to protect him from a negative emotion. However painful his life may be with us, I'll tell myself it will never be as painful as it would have been if he had stayed in Costa Rica. And even if he ends up in jail or rehab, I can blame it on his early childhood, not on myself. I will be sad for him but I won't feel at fault, I won't hate myself for failing him. In my more rational moments, I know this is all ridiculous, that there is no way to measure pain, compare childhoods, or know what Kevin's life would have been like if we hadn't met him. But mostly I see myself being Kevin's mother in all the outward, glorified ways, without having to bear the weight of mother-guilt.

I don't discuss this deep-seated motivation for adopting Kevin with Dicken, and I don't know what his own inner process is. I only know he supports me in my desires and is a generous, loving person, especially when it comes to children. He felt utterly abandoned when his family sent him to a strict all-boys boarding school at the age of eight, so I figure he deeply empathizes with the pain Kevin must have experienced when he was sent away to live with an unknown aunt and uncle at six.

Sometimes I envy Dicken's ability to trust in his intuition as a parent. He doesn't try to puzzle out what adopting Kevin means; he's eager to get Kevin here, but doesn't feel the sense of urgency I do. He's simply ready to welcome him whenever he arrives.

Fall 2003–Summer 2004
I will fly down to Costa Rica four times in the next eighteen months, Dicken joining me on two of those trips, to meet with lawyers, judges, and social workers. When obstacles pop up, or unexpected financial demands present themselves, I look at Dicken and say, "Are we crazy? Should we give up?"

Dicken peers at me with steady, reassuring eyes. "Don't worry. This is going to work out."

I believe him, and feel the strength of our partnership, which gives me the courage to keep moving forward.

Each time I fly down for meetings in San Jose, I take a bus to the Caribbean coast and visit Kevin for a day or two before going home. One time he is at least an inch taller, and his hair is cut so short I don't recognize him at first. But he runs to me and reaches up to kiss me on each cheek. *Oh my gosh, I've never had a Costa Rican greet me this way!* Costa Ricans tend to be more physically reserved, friendly but not demonstrative. The double kiss on the cheeks is more European; it was how Dicken said goodnight to me the first time we met. Kevin so clearly fits in our family.

Kevin takes me to his cousin Cristina's sixteenth birthday celebration, an informal gathering in the alley with a few strings of cheerful streamers hung between palm trees. Kevin reaches past the bowls of candy and plantain chips and stuffs tuna-covered crackers in his mouth. He tells me his favorite foods are chicken, rice, and beans. *No sign of a sweet addiction. A dream kid.* He offers me a cracker, calling me "Mami." An older boy cousin hears him and asks Kevin in a mocking, challenging tone I can easily discern even in Spanish, "Who is your mother?" Kevin looks worried, falters. I quickly coach him to say he has three mothers: Flor, Liliana, and me. His cousin smiles broadly. "Tres mamas, que suerte!" *Three mothers, what luck!*

I hear Kevin telling everyone at the party, "Tengo tres mamas y tres papas." *I have three mothers and three fathers.*

I fly back home from that trip more sure than ever that we are on the right course.

CHAPTER 6

August 2004

I'm rereading *Awareness* by Anthony de Mello, an Indian Catholic priest and teacher. I've found this book comforting since I first came across it in my early twenties. Each time I read it, I discover something new.

This time, one passage in particular strikes me:

> *Generally, we seek to cure our loneliness through emotional dependence on people, through gregariousness and noise. That is no cure. Get back to things, get back to nature, go up in the mountains. Then you will know that your heart has brought you to the vast desert of solitude, there is no one at your side, absolutely no one. At first this will seem unbearable. But it is only because you are unaccustomed to aloneness. If you manage to stay there for a while, the desert will suddenly blossom into love. Your heart will burst into song. And it will be springtime forever.*

For me, this describes an inner experience, not an outer one; I don't need to be in some remote mountain range to get this. But I wonder: will I ever learn to be alone, to slow down and be with the vastness inside me?

September 2004

Dicken now works from home, writing and consulting, no longer running a day-to-day practice. He teaches seminars to health professionals about once or twice a month around the US and occasionally abroad. I spend most of my time with Jasper, who we've decided to homeschool. With the spare hours I get from sharing childcare with Maud and a group of families nearby, I help Dicken with writing, editing, and odd jobs like trips to the post office.

At last we've struck a balance, a way of sharing roles that works for all of us. Dicken gets to be even more involved as a parent, and that makes the daily work of childrearing easier for me. Jasper and I are both reassured by Dicken's presence; and I feel like I'm contributing to the business. This arrangement is closer to how I originally pictured life on the farm: everyone interconnected, working toward the same goals.

Right now I don't want to explore the vast desert of solitude. This feels like the beginning of idyllic times.

I'm lying in bed one afternoon holding Chippers, one of our two new baby guinea pigs, against my chest. He's making sweet, chirrupy noises as I stroke his soft fur and thin, veined ears.

Dicken walks in and says, "You look happy."

"I am. I'm a proud new mother."

"Shouldn't that be *grand*mother? Doesn't he belong to Jasper?"

"Technically, yes. But who do you think is going to end up doing all the work?"

"Well, you are the expert," Dicken says. "And look how happy the little guy is with you."

We adopted Chippers and Patch from a local rescue organization. I've always had a thing for guinea pigs; I raised eight of them when I was little. I especially love Chippers, who is small and brown and named after one of my childhood favorites.

"Won't he pee on you eventually?" Dicken asks.

"No, he's much too polite for that." I lift him to my face, kissing his furry cheeks and smelling his sweet cedar-chip scent. I can feel his hot breath on my skin.

"You really love him, don't you?"

"It almost hurts, I love him so much. You know, I think I won't need another baby. This is just as good."

At breakfast the next morning, Jasper and Grace, ages six and five, are hatching a plan.

"Let's build the guinea pigs a huge fort by the chicken coop," Jasper says.

Grace's eyes grow wide. "But what if the mean rooster gets them?"

"He can't get out of the coop, Grace."

"Oh. Okay."

"We can make them tunnels and a loft," Jasper continues.

"And a kitchen and a hot tub and a trampoline," Grace adds.

Jasper rolls his eyes as he stuffs a big mouthful of pancake into his mouth. "Papa made these pancakes," he says. "I only eat Papa's pancakes."

"Me too," Grace says. "Papa Dicken's pancakes are the best."

The kids talk about supplies they can get from the barn for their project. I'm pretty sure the idea will be dropped before it's actually started, but then I catch Dicken, who has been quietly reading the *New Yorker*, peering at the kids from behind the magazine. I can tell by his expression that he's getting ideas.

Sure enough, by the end of breakfast, Dicken has sketched an elaborate design on a scrap of paper.

"Papa, you need to make this part much, much bigger," Jasper says, pointing to a section of the blueprint.

"Yes sir," Dicken replies, obediently erasing and redrawing the section.

The kids are excited and run out the door, headed for the barn.

I pick up half-eaten plates of pancakes and head for the sink.

"I'll be at my desk in a little while," Dicken says. "Let me know if I get any important calls."

I spend the morning editing a book Dicken has written on blood chemistry analysis. I can hear occasional hammering outside.

In the early afternoon, Jasper bursts in the office door. "Mom, you have to come see the guinea pigs' new house!"

I walk down to the bushes by the chicken coop. Dicken, bent over adjusting wire mesh, straightens up and smiles a little sheepishly.

"I got a little carried away."

"Wow!" I say, genuinely impressed. "This is amazing."

The guinea pigs' new home is a large, elaborate dwelling made of wood and wire mesh, with multiple levels, sheltered areas, and access to fresh grass. The kids are squealing like little guinea pigs themselves.

"Let's try it out!" they shout, running to get Chippers and Patch from inside, where they've been in a large plastic storage container full of cedar chips.

We leave the guinea pigs in their big outdoor dwelling all day and night. They look content, munching fresh grass and exploring the tunnels.

One night later that week, I get up from bed and shiver in my T-shirt on the way to the bathroom. The hot summer is giving way to cooler nights. As I climb back into bed, Dicken asks me if I'm okay.

"Yup, just had to pee. Hey, do you think the guinea pigs are too cold?"

"No, I'm sure they're fine," he says. "They're covered in fur."

I think of their coats, guessing they've shed a lot in the summer heat. I consider going outside to get them, but the bed is warm and inviting, and I'm sleepy.

In the morning I wake to Jasper's alarmed voice: "Chippers is shaking! I think he's sick."

Dicken and I bolt out of bed and fly downstairs, where we run into Grace, on her way inside with Chippers cupped in her hands. He is shivering and has green stains on his chin. His coat looks shabby, the fur sparse and stiff in places.

"Oh, Chippers, are you okay?" Jasper asks, touching the guinea pig gently. "We'll help you. You'll be okay."

"We'll help you, Chippers," Grace says, then looks up at Dicken. "What's the matter with him?"

Dicken takes him and inspects him.

"What's wrong?" I demand, my voice shrill.

"I don't know."

"Well, do something!" I urge.

"I don't know what's wrong with him," Dicken says. "You're the one who's had guinea pigs before, not me. Anyway, he's still alive and moving. Don't be so dramatic." He looks at me then, and I can see him register my worried expression. His voice softens. "Listen, I'll call a vet."

He hands Chippers to Jasper, and the two kids bend their heads close to him, talking in soothing tones.

After the phone call, I ask Dicken to tell me everything.

"The vet thinks he ate too much grass; it's something guinea pigs do occasionally. That's why he has the green stains. He probably threw up."

"Is he going to be okay?"

"We'll see. I'm going to take him in now. The vet wants to look at him."

"I want to go to the vet with you!" Jasper wails.

"Me too!" Grace shouts.

"Okay, okay, everybody get dressed and we'll go."

I don't go. I feel frozen. I can't bear watching Chippers shake that way. I wait, my stomach in knots, too distressed to eat or concentrate on anything. I try to picture Chippers healthy and happy, with a perfect shiny coat.

Has it been hours, minutes? I can't tell. The phone rings. It's Dicken.

"How is he?"

"Honey, Chippers died."

I am stunned. I hear ringing in my ears.

"I was holding him," Dicken says. "He died in my hands. The kids were right there too."

"Okay," I say quietly, and hang up.

I'm in a fog. I sit silent, staring blankly ahead. Inside I am furiously pushing away a vortex of emotions, a whirlpool threatening to pull me under.

I don't break down until the kids get back, running up to me in tears, talking fast, wanting to tell me everything. I kneel down and they wrap themselves around me, soft hands holding onto me tightly. I begin to sob. The kids cry with me. They are completely in this, and their raw grief, which matches mine more than Dicken's, comforts me.

"Do you want to see him?" Dicken asks, his voice gentle. He is holding a small cardboard box.

I shake my head.

Dicken and the kids take the box out to the garden and bury it.

Jasper makes a huge, ornate collage with cut-out magazine photos of animals, painted hearts, misspelled words.

"This is for you, Mama."

"It's beautiful," I say through tears.

"It's to cheer you up," he tells me.

"I made this," Grace says, showing me a small collage. "But it's not for you, it's for Chippers." She takes it down to the garden and sets it carefully in the grass by the grave.

I sleep fitfully that night, my head throbbing, with a pain in my chest as if someone has literally pummeled my heart. I wake up at one point hot with anger. Angry that Chippers has died, angry at Dicken for building the outdoor cage, angry at myself for being too lazy to go and check on the guinea pigs that night. I beg God to let me go back to that night and do it differently.

I also feel self-indulgent for taking this so hard, comparing it to the profound suffering in the world. I tell myself I'm a wimp for letting the death of a six-month-old guinea pig sink me into such a dark place. I feel guilty for feeling guilty.

I don't consider myself an especially fearful person. I like challenges; I like to turn over stones, not step around them. But

I've always had a deep fear of death. The idea of my own dying doesn't trouble me much—it's the knowledge that I'll inevitably lose people I love. If I'm this upset by Chippers's death, how will I ever handle a greater loss? If something should happen to Dicken or Jasper, I'm afraid I'll scream until my throat is bloody and shredded. I'll tear my hair out. I'll have to be restrained, taken to a psych ward, put in a straitjacket, and sedated. I will wail until I can't wail anymore, and then I'll shut down entirely, go into permanent shock. I won't be able to move, talk, eat, or breathe, and soon after that I'll die, which will be a great relief.

At one point, I wake up and can't get back to sleep. I get out my journal and a flashlight and pen. I write: *I want to face death. I'd like to be with grieving people, do hospice work, or go to Africa to work with people who have AIDS or families who've lost loved ones. I want to talk with someone who's lost a child. Maybe one day I'll write about death.*

The following weekend, I'm on a silent retreat facilitated by my therapist. As the group enters into silence the first evening, I feel scared. I don't want to leave the avenue of verbal connection with others behind. I'm resistant, telling myself, *Don't worry, I can whisper with my friends, or I can sneak a call or two to Dicken.* For a few hours, I struggle. I feel dark, lonely, agitated. I want to distract myself somehow, and wish I had a book, but we've been encouraged not to read on this retreat.

Then I recall the Tony de Mello passage, about the vast desert of solitude: if you manage to stay there for a while, the desert will suddenly blossom into love.

And something shifts as the hours pass. I'm beginning to unwind into the quieter realms. My attention sinks deep within me, and it is soothing, relaxing, not the terrifying void I'd imagined would be there. I begin to feel like I'm safe and sheltered inside a wondrous garden. I dream deeply that night, in vivid colorscapes. I dream of my grandmother, and my childhood dog, Moose. I wake feeling connected to something sweet and familiar I'd forgotten from long ago.

Near the end of the retreat, we gather in a circle and sing a Sufi chant, *Hu Allah*, taking turns whispering the words into our neighbor's ear. We are told *Hu* means divine presence, beyond definition; and *Allah* means God. The woman to my left cups her hand around my ear and leans in, a gesture that is almost uncomfortably intimate. In a beautiful soprano voice, she sings Hu Allah. The words touch me so deeply that tears form in my eyes. Then the woman on my right sings it into my other ear. I'm in an altered state: the voices sound like angels serenading me, and I think, *Wouldn't this be an amazing way to die, with someone singing like this as I slip away?*

The whole group joins in a chorus, "Ahhhhhhh-la!" Then we switch so that those of us who have been serenaded have the chance to sing. Coming back to my body, I find my voice and breathe the words from deep within, into the ears of the women on either side.

We always close with a final sharing circle. Normally, I am reluctant to say much in the big group, feeling too self-conscious to be able to articulate anything. But today, I give it a try:

"I had a lot of fear come up this weekend—fear of silence, of being alone, of the void inside me. But when I got through that layer of fear, I got a glimpse of how much there is in that rich darkness, and I'm actually kind of excited to explore it. And the main thing I want to face is death. It scares me the most, but I can sense the treasure it holds. I think I'll look into doing some kind of hospice work. That would be a way to expose myself to death and dying and get more comfortable with it." Then I describe the experience during the last chant, and my vision of slipping away peacefully to the sound of an angelic voice singing.

My friend Courtney is nodding her head vigorously at me as I speak, looking like she's about to burst, and then she blurts out, "I know I've already shared twice, but I have to tell you something, Cinda! There's a woman I know who's starting a local chapter of this group called the Threshold Choir. They sing at the bedsides of people who are dying. It's just like you described in the Hu Allah chant. It's perfect!"

I smile at her. It does seem perfect.

When I get back home, Jasper and Grace come running up to me with shouts of glee and arms held open. Their beauty is almost blinding.

The next morning, I go through all my pockets and find the scrap of paper Courtney gave me, with the name and number of the woman who runs the local chapter of the Threshold Choir. Just the thought of calling makes me nervous. Will I really be able to do this?

I know I have to try. Chipper's dying has made me aware of the depth of my resistance to death and the passing of time. I must face that resistance. I can't clap my hands over my ears when the song of death approaches. I have to listen. I have to sing it, not in whispers but loud and strong.

CHAPTER 7

December 2004

One evening, Dicken is home from a business trip, and we're sitting in the living room, holding hands and watching Jasper and Grace dance to a George Harrison album. Jasper keeps coming over to touch Dicken briefly, as if he needs to make sure his beloved Papa is really here, in the flesh. It's already dark outside at not quite five o'clock. I feel warm snuggled up next to Dicken. Harrison's beautiful, stirring voice sings, "*Beware the darkness . . . beware of sadness . . . All things must pass, all things must pass away . . .*"

"Do you realize that if I die when I'm seventy, my life is half over?" I say to Dicken.

He smiles dumbly and nods in rhythm to the music.

"When I look back on all my years so far and think that I only have that many again to get to seventy, it doesn't seem like much time. Not that I want to live in this world forever. I guess I'm just not sure I'm ever going to be able to let go and face the great mystery of death all on my own."

"The things you think about, wow," Dicken says, shaking his head. I can't tell if he's admiring or disapproving or a little of both.

"Why, what were you thinking about just now?"

"Nothing."

"Nothing? You're listening to George Harrison's stunningly soulful poetry and you can only think of nothing?"

"Okay, okay, maybe I was thinking of something."

"Like what?"

"Well, I have been considering a new hard drive."

I laugh, but within seconds I'm back to thoughts of death and being separated from my loved ones. Maybe this is just my annual winter gloom, compounded by the recent reelection of George W. Bush, which hit me hard. Everyone knows I get extremely internal in the winter, and that I turn into a dreadful Grinch at Thanksgiving and Christmas. Only this seems more extreme than my usual holiday funk. For weeks I haven't wanted to see anyone other than my family. I haven't felt like going anywhere. When I look in the mirror, I see spots and wrinkles on my face and a patch of gray in my hair. I have cellulite on my thighs. My teeth ache. My gums bleed. My appetite is off. Coffee doesn't sit right. My knees throb. I have pain during intercourse—nothing feels right. *What strange watershed am I crossing? Youth into middle age? How dreadful.*

"Are you sure you love me?" I ask Dicken, moving as close to him as I can. He smiles and puckers his lips. As I look at him, I wonder how I can ever be gloomy when I'm convinced I am one of the most comfortable, sheltered, loved humans on earth. I watch Jasper and Grace dancing and giggling, smell the lasagna Maud has in the oven. *We're almost able to bring Kevin home; Dicken is flying along in every way, our relationship is better than ever. So why this darkness? This death rattle?*

Like most things in life, the Threshold Choir is not the perfect experience I hoped it would be.

For three months, I've been attending biweekly meetings and singing for people approaching death. I get to sing the hymns I loved when I was little, the familiar words and tunes fortifying me as I stand in the face of the mystery. Standing at the bedsides of the dying, I can't deny old age, illness, decay. I search for my courage, and I find it. I don't look away. I stand and sing, feeling strong. I know it is a privilege to be a witness.

The singing shakes all scary thoughts from my head and brings me into my heart. Mostly it makes me feel sad, humble, insignificant. I tell myself, *Enjoy your life while you're young and healthy. Enjoy your loved ones while they're still here. Stop whining or wait-ing for people and circumstances to change. Keep looking at death and get friendly with it. Wake up to death, and to life!*

What I can't understand is why I'm so afraid of my own aging when I'm just thirty-five. I can't understand why I still have this terrible sense of foreboding. I thought the choir would make me stronger in the face of death, and it has. But it does not mitigate my terror of personal loss. Rather, it seems to have in-tensified that terror. The choir brings me close to the terminally ill, but it seems that it's only *their* dying I can handle. It's as if I'm able to face death only when it promises to end the deep, irreversible suffering of strangers: the erosion of self brought on by dementia, the strength-sapping pain of inoperable cancer. Dicken's in robust health, Jasper positively radiates energy—and I can't bring myself to imagine them ill or injured. I feel immense gratitude for my life as I sing for these unknown, unknowable people entering the mystery, but then I go home to count the years I have left, to cling to those I love as if my hanging on will keep them here forever.

While we wait for Kevin, I keep wondering if we'll have another baby. I know this isn't the time to consider such a momentous decision, but I find myself obsessed. It is a question I have been struggling with for a few years; Kevin's impending arrival and my awareness of encroaching middle age have now brought this issue to the fore. Will he be the last child we welcome into our family? Or is there room for a brand-new life, a counter to my musings on death?

I love babies. The year Jasper arrived was the happiest of my life. The joy and laughter he's brought us are immeasurable, so why would we say no to another baby? Yet I feel hesitant—afraid another child will upset the fragile balance of our lives. I worry about morning sickness and debilitation, and the heavy burden that will shift to Dicken as a result. I already feel overwhelmed by the number of children in the house. There are compelling ecological reasons not to have another baby: overpopulation, the gigantic resource footprint each North American represents. And there are those dark moments when I question the wisdom of incarnating at all, when I see earth as a hell-realm, a place where even the most fortunate among us suffer and struggle, where all of our desires and pleasures are either denied outright or rudely taken away from us.

Like the joys, the demands of parenting can't be adequately comprehended by the human mind. Mothering brings me some of the most frustrating, humiliating, exasperating, heartbreaking, exhausting, marriage-challenging, dream-killing moments imaginable. At its worst, I could argue that it is relentless, tedious, unglorified, and unpaid work, something that denies me the freedom to pursue fun, relaxation, peace, and my own goals in life. And yet there is an odd, math-defying reckoning that happens, where one glorious moment—like watching my son run to hug my own mother, or hearing him use a word in some humorously misunderstood way, or seeing him rescue a wounded bird and keep watch by the shoe box for hours, even after the bird has died—and all at once the entire weight of parenting evaporates. It's like the sun suddenly comes out, warming me from the core in a way nothing else could.

There is a gift in the humiliation parenting brings me. I was arrogant enough to believe that I could avoid all the challenges and pitfalls of parenting. I thought I was smart enough and in control enough to figure it out, to be a perfect mother. I've come to see that all my best intentions, my master's degree in child psychology, my giving up everything to focus single-mindedly on my child, haven't kept Jasper from experiencing the pain of being human. I've been profoundly humbled, again and again. Motherhood deepens me, helping me as I try to make peace with myself, and life.

If one child has done this for me, will another mean twice the blessing? I can't seem to turn off the noisy mental process of reasons for and against. I just want to know. I am tired of waiting for Kevin, waiting to see what happens, waiting for a direction to make itself clear. I want to be able to plan my life one way or the other. I keep hoping Dicken will have a strong opinion and take the burden off me, but whenever I raise the subject, he either dodges it or says something like, "Whatever you want, dear."

One night I demand a serious answer.

He thinks for a moment, his expression sober, so I know I'm not going to get a brush-off response.

"Well, I can think of plenty of reasons not to have any more. I can see us filling our lives with other things as we move out of the childrearing stage. But I think that's on a rational, surface level, and when I feel into it a little deeper, I have a sense we're not quite done. I think we might have one more, a girl."

"I don't really want to have another baby," I say, surprised and a little skeptical of my sudden clarity as I hear the words come out of my mouth. "But I'd do it for you."

"That's a terrible reason!"

"True," I admit.

We're silent for a few seconds.

"I don't know why I said that," I say. "I think I might want to have another one. I resonated with what you said about our not being quite done. I guess I just wish we didn't have to decide so soon. I can't imagine having another baby now. I feel so pressured."

"There's no big rush, is there?"

"Oh yes, there is. At my age, it's now or never. This is it. The longer we wait, the more out of the realm of possibility it becomes."

"So why don't we think about trying?"

Typical of me and my oppositional streak, as soon as I get a green light from the outside, my internal brakes slam on. I think of Maud, exhausted with her two small children. I think of how I don't feel all that healthy: coffee addict again, gray hair invading. I'm yearning to write, travel, romance my husband—

not change diapers, organize playgroups, go through the pain of separating. How I hated leaving Jasper when he was little. His crying broke my heart, even though I felt I couldn't survive without breaks. But I love babies. Seeing the joy Jasper gives so many people, mostly us two, and the laughs and the magic and the wonder and the lessons, the growth, the sweetness—how could anything keep us from the amazing gifts we get all the time?

"I'm so confused. This is driving me crazy."

"Listen," Dicken says firmly. "Stop thinking about this. We don't have to decide anything tonight, or even this month."

"Okay, but I'm not getting pregnant after I turn thirty-six."

"Fine. That gives us ten months, plenty of time."

He takes me into his arms and I close my eyes.

The baby is on his way, he's eight years old, he's in Costa Rica waiting for us to come get him. He's ours, he's beautiful, he's miraculous, and we'll go from there.

I fall asleep with an ache in my chest, like a great unknown abyss.

The next morning our lawyer in San Jose calls with instructions on getting Kevin and his birth mother blood tests, one of the last requirements in the adoption process. They both live a long way from the only clinic in the country that performs the test. It takes me numerous phone calls to line everything up. Kevin's uncle Bobby promises to arrange to get Kevin's mother and put them on the bus and buy them round-trip tickets which I will later reimburse him for. I think about them all that day, seeing them on the bus together, arriving at the station and then making their way to the clinic in downtown San Jose, wondering what it is like for Kevin to be with his mother again, to have all those hours alone with her. Does he realize this trip is one of the final steps in severing any chance he might have of being raised by her? And how is it for her? Does she feel any shame in giving up her child? Is she sad? Hopeful? Relieved? Conflicted?

I call the clinic the next morning to make sure they've

taken the tests. I have butterflies in my belly. We are getting so close to bringing him home! In my basic Spanish, I ask if the Brown-Gallardos made it to their appointment.

Expecting a yes, I hear the opposite: "No, they never showed up. No show, no phone call, no nothing."

I call Kevin's uncle a dozen times that day, finally getting through in the evening.

"What's going on, Bobby? I talked to the clinic, they said Kevin and his mom never showed up!"

"No, we had a big flood, lot a rain. All the roads washed out."

January–February 2005

It takes six weeks to get the Brown-Gallardos another appointment. Christmas comes and goes, without Kevin. I call Kevin's uncle and aunt every day for a week leading up to the next test date to remind them. This time they make it. The clinic faxes me the results of the report a week after that: the chances that Kevin is Flor Gallardo's biological child are 99.5 percent. The government of Costa Rica approves the adoption. He is clear to go now, just about.

I book myself a round-trip ticket to Costa Rica and a one-way ticket to the US for Kevin. Our lawyer says four days will be enough time to wrap everything up. We give it two weeks just in case. I end up staying four weeks, spending most of my days in line at visa and passport and embassy offices. One day I stand in line to get Kevin's Costa Rican passport, finally making it to the window after four hours, only to be told I've been in the wrong room the whole time. Another day I'm told by a harried official that I have all the wrong documents. I break down crying. He opens the file to show me my mistakes, only to discover he's got another family's file. He doesn't apologize. When my file is located, I'm told it is complete. I am hugely relieved.

Then they ask me where my husband is. I tell them he's back home in America. They say he needs to sign the final document before they can approve it. I try to remain calm as I explain what my lawyer said, that only one of us needed to come down to complete this process. They are firm: Dicken needs to sign this last form.

I break down again. I call our lawyer from a pay phone. He doesn't sound surprised. He says he'll look into it. I go back to the hostel and watch cartoons with Kevin. When I speak to the lawyer again, he says the newest regulation does require both parents' signatures on the final decree.

"Can your husband fly down as soon as possible?"

Are you kidding? A last-minute flight would cost thousands. Does he think we're made of money?

"Are there any other options here?"

"Well, yes. Your husband could go to the Costa Rican Embassy, or a consulate, and sign in front of an official."

The next day, Dicken flies to the consulate in Los Angeles and signs the document. A copy is faxed to the officials in San Jose. We are done with Costa Rican bureaucracy and sail through the US immigration and passport process. After the weeks of struggle and frustration and waiting in long lines in sweltering rooms, I can't get over the customer service at the US Embassy. They are so friendly and helpful and organized that for the first time in a very long time, I feel grateful to be an American.

The US Embassy gives us Kevin's passport entry stamps, meaning he can come home now. I can't believe we are cleared to go—it seems too good to be true. Then I start to think we'll never get home, because for days I've been trying unsuccessfully to get through to the airline to change our tickets, which have been on hold for weeks now. Every number I try is either out of service or for the wrong department, or I run out of time on the cheap local phone cards I'm using while I'm on hold.

Standing in the hostel in San Jose two nights after our approval, I finally get through to Dicken on a pay phone, techno music blaring in the courtyard behind me.

"Dix?"

"Is that you, Cinda? I can hardly hear you."

"Yes, it's me."

"Did you get my e-mail?"

"No, a storm blew out the Internet connection."

"I've been worried about you. What's the story with your flight home?"

"I still haven't been able to reach United to get seats tomorrow. The phone system down here is terrible."

Kevin is next to me, looking up at me with big, inquisitive eyes. I smile, trying to reassure him.

"Listen, give me the pay phone number and I'll look into it right now and call you back," Dicken says.

I give him the number.

"Now, stay by the phone and don't let anyone use it. I'll call you back as soon as I know something."

I cross my fingers and wait, reminding myself that Dicken and his British accent seem to have a way with airline agents.

Five minutes later, after fending off a number of young backpackers desperately wanting the phone, it rings.

"Honey, United has no seats available until late March, because it's tourist season right now. They're booked solid."

I feel like I might break down. We're still in February.

Dicken continues, "But I managed to get you tickets on American for Tuesday."

I start to cry. I can feel how badly I want to get home.

"I explained the story to the agent," he goes on, "and she was so moved she got you seats in first class, no extra cost."

"Wow, Kevin's first time on a plane, and he's in first class."

"Tell him not to get used to it!"

Kevin has a million questions as we ride in the taxi to the airport in the early morning. He wants to know how many days the flight will take, and if there will be food and a bathroom on the plane. He wants to know why I'm giving my bag away when I check it in at the desk. He has no suitcase to check; all his belongings fit in the small backpack he's carrying. On the plane, I give him the window seat. As we take off, I watch his face, pressed up against the plexiglas. He pulls my arm and gets me to look out the window over and over, sharing his amazement at all the miniature things he can see below. Whenever the flight attendant brings us a drink or food, which is frequent in first class, Kevin looks at me with wide eyes and exclaims, "Free?! It's free?" After we land and the flight attendant holds up people's coats for them to claim, Kevin's refrain rings out again: "It's free?!"

I am pinching myself as we make a smooth transit through immigration at LAX. Then, after two more flights, we finally arrive in Medford at midnight. Dicken and a wide-awake, super-excited Jasper are waiting at the gate. Jasper takes a big step forward to hug Kevin, but Kevin steps back, and the hug looks awkward.

Dicken kneels down and looks into Kevin's face. "How are you doing? Are you hungry? Thirsty? You must be tired."

Kevin smiles a little shyly, maybe not understanding Dicken's words, but clearly feeling his warmth. Then he reaches into his backpack and gives Jasper the chocolate bar he bought him at the airport in Costa Rica with his last *colones*.

"I'll carry your packback," Jasper tells Kevin. "I been to Costa Rica seven times and one time I threw up on the plane so I know it's a looong way."

Kevin holds onto Dicken's hand as we walk to baggage claim.

CHAPTER 8

After Kevin's arrival and our fairly smooth integration into a four-person unit, I feel a new sense of fullness. And still, the question that keeps nagging me in a never-ending cadence is, "Are we complete as a family?" Is domestic life too complicated now to think of adding in another factor?

One morning, I wake up and see that it's light out, but there is no sign of Jasper, who very rarely gets through the night without ending up in our bed. Dicken, already dressed and carrying two mugs of hot coffee, comes into our bedroom. "You've got to see something," he says, handing me one of the mugs. He leads me downstairs and opens the door to Jasper's room. Jasper and Kevin are sitting in Jasper's bed, looking at a Tintin book together, both in their blue all-in-one footed pajamas.

"Salt and Pepper," Dicken says. I smile, remembering how on the beach one day in Costa Rica, that first summer we met Kevin, someone said the boys looked like salt and pepper shakers, with their exact same height, Kevin's dark skin and bushy black hair contrasting with Jasper's pale skin and fine blond hair. The description fit so well that the names Salt and Pepper stuck for a while, which made Jasper ask one day, "Mom, which one am I, the salt or the pepper?" Now here they are, the happy pair bundled up in their northern-climate attire, Kevin reading aloud to Jasper, and my heart floods with a sense of well-being. I remember what my youngest sister Cecily said to me on the phone the other day: "You guys have done an amazing thing, adopting Kevin. I just know good fortune will follow you from now on."

April 2005

Dicken returns from a business trip in England, where we'll be spending the summer. The long stay over there makes sense to us because one of Dicken's new business ventures involves bringing a line of American nutritional supplements to the United Kingdom. He's also been invited to teach several seminars in London. Plus, I've always loved England, especially in the summer, and it will give us the chance to spend time with Dicken's family, as well as my own English cousins and uncles.

"I can't wait to show you the guest room at Mum's house," Dicken says as he unpacks his garment bag. "It's so romantic! I have a feeling I'm going to get you pregnant there."

Hearing him say that gives me a thrill. Not because of the reference to sex, although I like that, but because of his clear declaration that he wants another baby. In some ways I see having another child of our own as a way to thank Dicken for going along with the adoption. He'd always said that if we had a second child, he wanted it to be ours biologically. Yet once he felt the instant yes for Kevin, he never wavered. So I want to show him my deep gratitude, and honor the part of him that wants another baby of our own. Dicken adores babies and is an unusually hands-on father, happy to wake up in the night to change diapers, happy to have Jasper still sleeping in our bed half the time at the age of seven. I write in my journal that night, April 27:

Positive Intention: I'm inviting a soul to come through, to be our baby. I'm only receptive to a girl, one who is easy to gestate, give birth to, and raise. A soul sister, a seeker of enlightenment, one with a great sense of humor, a huge heart—loving, forgiving, generous, wise, calm, calming, beautiful, radiant, free, positive, with a huge yes to life. A sparkly diamond soul—perfect, awake, alive, a celebrator, a teacher, a friend to all people and creatures of the earth, one who is supported and supports a wide web of beings. Healthy. Smart. A cozy joy. A great sleeper and eater. Cheerful, outgoing, eyes the color of Dix's. Bringer of unsurpassed joy. Enlarger of all hearts, especially ours (Dix, me, Jasper, and Kevin).

That night, when Dicken comes to bed, I initiate lovemaking. He asks, "Where are you in your cycle?"

"I'm not exactly sure. How about taking a chance?"

We take the chance, and afterward Dicken says something lighthearted about throwing caution to the wind.

Dicken falls asleep, but I can't. I lie in the dark wondering if we're about to conceive a baby, my mind racing with thoughts of what that would mean for us. I worry about Dicken's new business, which is demanding and might require a lot of travel in the next year or two. But I secretly hope I will get pregnant.

I calculate that I'll probably ovulate sometime in the next five days. I fall asleep with images of an egg about to burst from my ovary and make its way down the fallopian tube to meet a swarm of eager sperm, a whole school of perfect miniature replicas of Dicken.

The next morning, I check my fertility status by licking the slide on my mini-microscope. I've been using this device as a way to avoid getting pregnant ever since Jasper was born. It works by using saliva patterns to predict ovulation. During a woman's menstrual cycle, estrogen surges around the time of ovulation and can be detected by changes in how saliva dries on the microscope. High estrogen makes it dry in snowflake-like patterns, a signal that ovulation is about to occur. Just before estrogen levels peak, little stick-like shapes begin to emerge. If I see those, it means I'm approaching my most fertile days. These simple sticks are normally followed a day or so later by large, complex fern structures—the big kahuna.

This April morning, after the saliva on the slide dries, I take a deep breath, click the light on the tiny instrument, then peer inside. At first, nothing but indistinct round blots. I adjust the focus, which can sometimes change a blurry landscape into one with identifiable objects. Still nothing. I shrug. Without a sign of even slightly increased estrogen, chances are I'm not about to ovulate.

A few hours later, I check again. Nothing. *Oh well, I guess it's not meant to be right now.* The next morning, I give it another try. This time, I find something that looks shape-like, adjust the focus, and there on the screen is a giant, beautiful fern. Not a pre-ovulation stick, but a big, complex design, as stunning as an Andy Goldsworthy sculpture.

I calculate that I might have timed things right—they say sperm can live for forty-eight hours or more inside a warm body. I smile to myself, excited by the possibility that a secret process is unfolding within me, and even more excited at the prospect of surprising Dicken with the news once I know for sure.

May 2005

Over the next couple of weeks, I'm preoccupied with lots of other things, including a visit from our brother-in-law, Giles, who's been battling metastasized colon cancer for more than two years. Giles, married to Dicken's sister Becca, has been having phone consultations with an Ashland-based herbalist and cancer specialist, and has decided to come all the way from England to see him in person. Dicken is also helping Giles, doing research on his case and taking suitcases full of herbs and supplements over to England. Dicken has known Giles since high school and considers him a brother and close friend. He's also one of my favorite people, so we happily drop everything to be with him during his short stay.

Before we know it, it's time to prepare for our summer in England. The day before we fly to London, I feel decidedly hormonal: tender breasts, volatile moods, slightly bloated abdomen. I even detect a tiny spot of blood and figure my period is on the way. I make sure to pack tampons in my carry-on luggage.

So it looks like I'm not pregnant—not a big surprise or letdown, since I ovulated at least a day or more after lovemaking; and I didn't expect to get pregnant after a single unprotected encounter. According to most medical experts, the chances of someone my age getting pregnant each attempted cycle is somewhere around one-in-ten. And that's for couples who are actively trying—the scenario people joke about when the calendar-obsessed woman is demanding sex five times a week and the exhausted man starts to complain that he feels like nothing more than a sperm donor. In our case we've taken just that one uncalculated chance.

The flight to London is one of the most uncomfortable I've ever experienced. My ankles swell up for days, which has never happened before.

We base ourselves at the home of Caroline, Dicken's mother, in Suffolk. Caroline owns holiday rentals and a health clinic, all part of an old thatched barn and outbuildings she and her sister have restored. The property overlooks the sea and borders a lovely forest and fern-covered heath.

Normally, I would be quick to settle into the lovely existence we have over here, but this time I have uncharacteristically miserable jet lag. I'm up for hours during the night, with a maddening mixture of extreme tiredness and boiling agitation that makes reading or any other relaxing activity impossible. Once I finally drift off, usually as the sun is coming up, I sleep so heavily it feels like a Herculean effort to rouse myself before the afternoon. Soon I feel exhausted and irritable, trapped in a cycle that leaves me unable to function. I write distressed e-mails to my friends back home, blaming PMS for my state.

On our second day, we're out in the back garden, about to eat lunch. I've just dragged myself out of bed. I squint in the sun.

"What a lovely lunch," I say, trying to sound convincing. "Thank you, Caroline."

My stomach feels sour; I'm not hungry at all. The boys, who seem entirely unaffected by jet lag, are famished after a morning of running around on the lawn. They're watching the food with eager eyes.

"Can I say grace?" Kevin asks.

This is surprising, especially considering how hungry Kevin looks and how grace will delay eating a few moments more. He's never asked this before. We rarely say grace, but have nothing against it, so we tell him to go ahead.

"Dear God," he begins in his heavily accented English, "please bring me a baby brother."

I am stunned. He's never mentioned babies or wanting more siblings, and we certainly haven't discussed any such possibility with or in front of the kids. I know I might be pregnant, but no one else has a clue, not even Dicken. I glance at Dicken to see if he's as struck by Kevin's words as I am, but he's looking at the potatoes. I smile to myself and don't say anything.

Dicken heads to London for a series of meetings and seminars. My jet lag eases, and I begin to feel more human. My period doesn't come; I get excited as the days tick by with no sign of blood. I also get nervous, wondering what months of morning sickness and starting all over again with a new baby will mean to our recently expanded family. Life feels a bit too full, with Jasper's larger-than-life personality, Kevin getting adjusted to everything, and Dicken's exciting but ever-growing and fast-paced businesses. Maybe a newborn will tip the scales into major overload.

The boys and I spend a night at Becca and Giles's house just before Dicken returns from his business trip. The next afternoon, Becca and I have an hour of free time in town while the boys join their cousins Olivia and Fergus, Becca and Giles's daughter and son, at after-school soccer, and she suggests having coffee.

"You do drink coffee, don't you?" Becca asks.

"Well, normally I love it, but these days I shouldn't . . ." I falter a little, not wanting to tell her. But she's a sharp cookie.

"Why not? Are you pregnant?"

"Well, I think—I mean, yes, I might be."

"I knew you'd changed shape! Was it a mistake?"

"No," I say, feeling prickly and defensive.

She has coffee, I have strawberry-flavored herbal tea. I explain about wanting to give Dicken another baby.

"Yes, he's such a superb dad. You're incredibly lucky."

She goes on to say that she mentioned to Giles the night before that I'd put on weight. I tell her it's too early to see pregnancy weight gain; it's just middle-aged fat she's noticing. My face must show my dismay, because she gives me a disapproving look and says, "Oh no, don't get anorexic on me. Anyway, the extra weight suits you. I always did think you were too scrawny."

As often happens, I am not sure how to respond to Becca's directness. It doesn't help that she's hit a nerve. Though I'm built a little more like my tall, slim father, I had periods of chubbiness in childhood and adolescence, which I seized on to emulate my frequently dieting mother, and boy, did I enjoy the masochistic struggle of controlling and guarding my weight. In my pregnancy with Jasper, I only gained twenty pounds, mainly because of morning sickness, but also because I was careful. Lately, I've gained a little, as Becca has noticed. I'm worried that another pregnancy will be the breaking point, when I transition out of my slender youth for good. I can feel the vigilant weight-obsessed part of me mobilizing.

"Hey, there's a chemist round the corner," Becca says, smiling broadly. "Let's go get you a test so we can find out for certain."

Like sisters, we head out arm in arm, and soon we're looking at rows of pregnancy tests. One brand comes in either blue or pink boxes, which I find strange. Are you expected to have a preference this early on? And even if you do have a preference, like I secretly do, isn't it tempting fate to pick that color, to openly declare your position?

I buy a pregnancy test in a beige box and plan to save it until Dicken returns from his trip and joins us at Becca and Giles's home. When we get back to the house, I keep an eye out for Becca, wary that she'll corner me and convince me to take the test right away, but she quickly gets caught up with the demands of her busy family life. I steal a quick lie-down and try to concentrate on a novel, keeping an ear out for Dicken's arrival. At this point I'm more than a week late and convinced I'm pregnant.

I hear a car on the gravel driveway and head outside. Dicken gets out of the car and grins broadly at me, opening his arms as I run toward him.

"You two are pathetic!" Becca calls from the garden, where she's weeding a flowerbed. "You've only been separated for three days!"

That night, after the boys are asleep, I tell Dicken to check under his pillow.

"A present for me?" he says, moving the pillow aside and picking up the package. He looks inside and pulls out the unopened pregnancy test.

"Wow! You mean you haven't had your period?"

We head to the bathroom together, trying to be quiet, and I pee on the stick. Less than thirty seconds later, the jury is in.

"Oh my," Dicken says. "Here we go!"

CHAPTER 9

Inside my uterus, the embryo has implanted successfully in the endometrium, or uterine lining, and is beginning to produce a hormone called human chorionic gonadotropin (hCG), which is what makes over-the-counter pregnancy tests turn out positive. The placenta is beginning to form, along with early versions of the heart and brain and spinal cord. Every cell, and therefore every organ, including the placenta, is being influenced by the faulty thirteenth chromosome. Chances are, one or more systems will be affected enough to prevent a viable embryo from developing, or my body will recognize that something is wrong. In either of these scenarios, a miscarriage will result.

In the guest room at Becca and Giles's house, where we stay through the weekend, there are twin beds. Dicken and I hug goodnight, then get under the covers across the room from one another.

Lying in the dark, with the confirmed pregnancy presenting an unknown road ahead, I can't sleep. I'm on the edge of panic, like the bottom of the world has dropped out and everything around me is spinning. I almost wake Dicken a couple of times but decide he needs a good night's sleep, especially after the news I've sprung on him. The last thing I want is for both of us to be tired and grouchy and looking at the future through bleak lenses. I wish we were in the same bed so I could at least feel the reassurance of his warm body next to mine.

We wake early and take Becca and Giles's dogs for a walk around the nearby fields. I feel much better out in the fresh air, the sunbeams beginning to spread across the quiet, green landscape. We don't say much, but hold hands, a sense of new adventure upon us.

Back at the house, I go online, find a pregnancy information site, and type the date of my last menstrual period, April 17, into the due-date calculator. I've never stopped to think about what month or even what season we'll be looking at for the baby's arrival.

"Dicken!" I whisper, since no one else is awake yet. "You're not going to believe this. The baby is due on Jasper's birthday!"

We confirm the news with Becca, and tell Giles at breakfast. The whole scene seems surreal, with no one expressing the jubilation that usually follows the announcement of a planned pregnancy. Somehow, it all feels muted. There we are in the kitchen, with me trying to eat healthy food and Giles making his nasty-tasting cancer-fighting concoctions with the herbs Dicken has carted over with him in his suitcase.

"Maybe you won't feel so sick this time," Dicken says to me, as we watch Giles gag on one of his herbal shakes. My first trimester of pregnancy with Jasper was miserable. I actually lost a few pounds and ended up on an intravenous drip to boost my fluid and mineral levels. But by the second trimester, I felt much better, my only complaints from then on being occasional heartburn and backaches. My mother reported feeling dreadful during her first trimester with my brother, her first baby, but not with me or my two sisters, so I hypothesize that in our line, either firstborns or males cause morning sickness. Maybe this time I'll get a reprieve.

But within a week, the unmistakable sensation returns after an eight-year hiatus. I begin to feel queasy most of the time, especially on an empty stomach. When I do manage to find something I can eat without gagging, my belly burns for hours afterward, until the burning gives way to nausea again.

Though many parents we know wait until the second trimester to tell siblings about a pregnancy, we decide to tell the boys now, knowing they're both smart enough to figure it out soon enough anyway.

"We're going to have a baby," I say.

Kevin beams, his eyes full of wonder. I think about but don't mention his prophesy the week before.

Jasper makes a sour face and says, "What if it's a girl?"

"A girl probably won't break your toys as much as a boy," I say.

"Good point, Mom."

After lunch, Dicken loads the dishwasher and then disappears into the study to do some work. I settle the boys into a game of Monopoly before heading to the forest for a walk. I can only go about a mile before tiring, but I know a little exercise will do me good, and being in the fresh air and greenery is soothing. The bluebells are out, blanketing the forest floor in dazzling electric indigo. It's so beautiful I want to cry.

That night, Dicken puts the boys down to sleep while I sit in bed, writing in my journal.

"It's good to see you writing," Dicken says, coming in and starting to undress. "Seems like it's been awhile."

"I've been dried up lately," I say.

"Well, no wonder, you're tired and sick."

"Anne Lindbergh only ever missed her journal entries during the first trimesters of her pregnancies."

Dicken blows his nose and sighs. "I can't stand these allergies. I always forget that I get them so badly in England. I'm wondering if coming here for so long wasn't such a great idea."

"Oh, honey," I say, "if I weren't so sick I could keep up with the boys and everything would be better. Maybe it's this pregnancy that wasn't such a good idea."

"It isn't the greatest timing, is it?"

This is crushing. I was fishing for reassurance, not confirmation of my doubt. Tears sting my eyes.

Dicken sees my expression. "Oh, Cinda," he says, sharp disapproval in his voice. "Don't take me so seriously! I'm just tired."

Instead of engaging with him, talking it out, I follow my usual pattern of turning inward when I sense conflict. I avoid his eyes and look at the white walls of the guest room. I focus on how the bed annoys me; it's lumpy and lopsided, not supporting my weight evenly. Everything feels wrong right now. I try not to get swept into the swarm of negative thoughts clamoring for air space in my head, but the tide is relentless. *Why did I do this? I'm way too old.*

I fight this downward spiral by breathing in deeply and recalling Eckhart Tolle's *The Power of Now*, which I've been reading bits of lately. It's the sort of New Age book my mother reads avidly, accepting its teachings at face value. I read it as a kind of spiritual self-help, taking from it only what resonates. Tolle asserts that expecting anything other than the present moment to make us happy is pointless, even insane. *Stay in this moment: that's your only job, Cinda, just take care of now. There is no problem in the now. There is no better place to get to, no greater happiness than this very moment.*

I look around at the white walls again, feel the horrid sensation of nausea in my mouth and stomach and the accompanying panic, and wonder how this could possibly be the best there is.

June 2005

"What do you feel like for breakfast?" Dicken asks.

"The usual."

Minutes later, he carries in a tray of scrambled eggs and toast.

"When did I start feeling better with Jasper?" I ask, swallowing the first bite without chewing so I taste as little as possible.

"I can't remember. It was second trimester, I think."

"I know it was second trimester," I snap. "I want to know *exactly* when."

"I'm sorry, it seems so long ago."

"If I had my old journals here, I could look it up. I'm afraid it wasn't until thirteen or fourteen weeks, which would mean seven more weeks of misery."

Dicken looks at me with sad, earnest eyes. "Thank you for going through this."

My eyes tear up. "I hate being a whiner, but this is hellish."

"Is there anything I can do?"

"You could be pregnant instead of me. You'd sail through this."

"I would if I could," he says, and I know he means it.

"You're already doing more than your share," I say, thinking of how he's been taking the boys so I can rest, and cooking for me, and very rarely complaining.

Unlike me, Dicken is generally cheerful and upbeat, and only occasionally gets sucked into one of my moods. He kisses me on the cheek and leaves the room. I'm left with my dark thoughts. *This pregnancy was a terrible idea. Maybe I'll get lucky and miscarry.*

I get through another night and another plate of scrambled eggs and am on the sofa in front of the TV by noon the next day. I've been watching hours and hours of tennis lately. It takes my mind off my waking nausea better than anything. So far this month we've had the Queen's tournament followed by Wimbledon, and to my great fortune the matches are aired pretty much all day long, with no commercials. When the boys aren't outside jumping on the trampoline or building forts or kicking a ball around, they join me.

"Mom," Jasper says, "who are we voting for?"

Like me, he needs to pick a player to root for; otherwise the match is less exciting. I often choose the underdog, players who aren't seeded or who have faced some adversity in their lives. This year it's seventeen-year-old Scottish newcomer Andy Murray and the raised-on-public-court prodigies, the Williams sisters.

I watch the spectators with a mixture of intrigue and envy. They look relaxed and yet wholly engaged in what's happening around them, in a way I can't relate to at all right now. It's impossible for me to imagine feeling well enough to sit in a crowd and watch a sporting event, though attending Wimbledon in person has always been a dream of mine. It seems far-fetched in my state of exhausted sickness, but I tell myself maybe one day I'll feel well enough to enjoy life's pleasures again. In the meantime, I'm only using tennis as a weak but appreciated distraction.

"Mom," Jasper says, "when I grow up, I'm either going to be a tennis player or a ball boy."

This comment pierces my malaise. I smile broadly for the first time in a while, warmed by this example of the entirely original, off-the-cuff things kids say. The simple wisdom of his words—that being a ball boy is just as acceptable as being a star player—is exactly what I need to hear right now.

That night I write in my journal, *Today I had this strong sense that I have no idea the gift this will be to me—that under all my worries and second-guessing myself there's such a perfection to this.*

The next afternoon, I feel a gush between my legs and dash to the bathroom. When I wipe, there is a glob of brownish red discharge. It suprises but doesn't scare me. Mostly, I'm curious.

I find Dicken at his computer and tell him about my discovery. He looks pensive, but like me, not upset. "Is there any more bleeding?" he asks.

"No, just that one gush so far."

"Maybe you should lie down for a while."

"Okay."

As I leave the room, Dicken calls out after me, "Hey, I'm curious. If you are miscarrying, do you think you'll want to keep trying?"

"Gosh, I don't know. What about you?"

"I'm not sure. It's hard to think of you having to go through all this again."

Lying in bed, I think more about this. *In all honesty, I'd probably want to close this chapter of childbearing for good. I feel too old and delicate to go through this much longer.*

Experts say that somewhere between 30 and 50 percent of all pregnancies end in miscarriage, many of them so early they go undetected. While there are many reasons for miscarriages, the vast majority (up to 75 percent) result from chromosomal abnormalities in the embryo. Error in the process of cell division can add or take away chromosomes, creating a gamete with faulty genes. When genetic instructions contain errors, building a healthy human being is often impossible. In most cases, the embryo will stop developing, and hCG will stop being released, shutting off the hormonal signal to continue building and retaining the endometrial lining that would have nourished a growing fetus. In most such cases, without the hormones to sustain the lining, blood begins to flow from the uterus, by far the most common way a mother learns she is miscarrying.

I decide to ring my mom. She's been calling every other day or so, highly attentive to me and this pregnancy. When I told her the news on the phone a couple of weeks before, she cried with joy, displaying by far the happiest reaction of anyone. Today, I tell her about the discharge.

"Oh my gosh," she says, clearly alarmed. "Do you think you should see a doctor?"

"No, I don't think that would help. If I'm miscarrying, we'll know soon enough."

"Oh, I hope everything's okay, sweetie. I'll send prayers to you and the baby."

She wants this badly for me, I can feel that. I hope she's right, that this pregnancy and second birth child are nothing but good news.

The nausea persists, and over the next twenty-four hours I don't have any more discharge.

"Looks like we have a keeper," Dicken says.

But the next night, I have the first of what will be a series of nightmares, something very rare for me. In this one I find myself in the middle of an apocalyptic war. In the next weeks, I will dream of vampire attacks, creatures in a primordial swamp, being on a team of people who pick up dead bodies, my grandparents coming back from the dead. The line between life and death, people I know who have died, communicating with those in the other world—these themes pervade my psyche throughout this pregnancy, in a way that I'll look back on months from now and find uncanny.

I'm sitting in the study dialing my good friend's number. Vanessa and I went to high school and college together.

"Oh, it's thrilling to hear from you!" she beams down the line.

I tell her I'm pregnant, and she is full of enthusiastic congratulations. Then I tell her how sick I'm feeling.

"Yes, you don't sound like yourself."

"I don't feel like myself at all. I don't even recognize myself. It's the strangest thing. I've lost all my familiar desires, all interest in life. I suddenly find myself questioning everything, but from a different perspective. It's like I'm just visiting my body, this life, and it's not where we belong."

"My gracious," she says, her voice animated. "This is changing the very way you see reality. How incredible!"

It feels good to tell her about my odd insights and experiences so far in this pregnancy. She has her own ideas about it, many from her years of religious study.

"You're experiencing the way of the Buddha, nonattachment. You're so fortunate! People seek such a change in perspective with years of meditation and practice, yet rarely have such success."

"Well, if this is nonattachment, just tell all those wannabe Buddhists to get pregnant. It must be the shortcut."

"Too bad monks take a vow of celibacy," Vanessa says, laughing.

"Celibacy sounds pretty wise to me right now. But wait a minute, you're a Sufi, aren't you, not a Buddhist?"

"Oh, it's all the same thing when you boil it down," she says. "And I would guess that you're having a very blessed experience, in any spiritual tradition's cosmology. A dark night of the soul, a vision quest, an initiation."

"If I'm being initiated, who is it that's initiating me?"

"Well, the little one, of course. Maybe your baby's a mystic!"

This excites me, and I want to believe it, just as every mother wants to think her child is somehow special.

She ends our conversation with, "Blessings on your little miracle!"

I let that sink in for an exhilarating moment, then start the usual minimizing: *It's not really a miracle, it's just a result of unprotected sex in a moment of abandon. The real miracle will be whether I can actually survive this hell.* I am too sick and discouraged to see my situation as anything more than an ordinary burden that many mothers before, with, and after me have suffered or will suffer through.

CHAPTER 10

These June weeks are a nightmare of constant seasickness, a relentless hangover that makes every waking moment seem unbearable. Dicken continues to take up the slack, letting me sleep in and bringing me whatever I think I can stomach. He comes into the small bedroom and pretends to be a crowing rooster as he opens the curtains, or he puts on one of his hilarious accents to amuse me. I eat scrambled eggs and toast day after day until they begin to disgust me. Then, for a number of weeks, all I want are crêpes. Dicken throws himself into the art of crêpe-making with his usual aplomb, bringing a plate of eight paper-thin delicacies to my bedside every morning.

"I used a tiny bit more vanilla this time, what do you think?"

"You're an angel," I say with my mouth full.

Dicken flies back to the States for ten days to teach a seminar at the end of June. With help from Caroline, I grit my teeth and will myself to make it through the long days.

Pouring out all my thoughts and feelings into my journal helps:

When this sickness passes, I look forward to returning to a more active and joyful existence. Although now, I can see that life is all a dream, that my love for most things—nature, eating, exercise—is based on biochemistry. Only with this physical balance is the earth made bearable. Our souls aren't specific to this realm, that much I'm sure of. I've lost my body for the time being. My desires seem pretty expendable.

Sometimes, knowing that the earth is not our home and that our bodies will die makes me feel extremely vulnerable, and at other times it makes me feel free.

Dicken comes back from his trip with a suitcase full of my requests—about a dozen bags of Barbara's Cheese Puffs, both the plain kind and the jalapeño ones, papaya enzymes, and some prenatal vitamins. The cheese puffs taste like heaven, and I ration myself carefully so they'll last through the trimester, or at least until the next fortifications arrive. I count down the days, willing myself to make it to the bearable land of non-nausea second trimester.

I find the boys a trial sometimes, and occasionally a welcome distraction from my physical state. One afternoon Jasper runs into my room with a very stern look on his reddened face.

"Mom," he begins, his eyes narrowing, "someone stole a piece of my gum, and I have a grudge it was you!"

I try as hard as I can to look serious and concerned, but I can't suppress a slight smile.

His cheeks get even redder as he points at my face. "Now I know it was you!"

July 2005

By this time, I'm finally entering the second trimester of pregnancy. The developing fetus is somewhere around three inches long, beginning to take practice inhalations, perhaps even starting to suck its thumb. The placenta will now begin to supply all of the fetus's nutrition. In most pregnancies, reaching this stage would greatly decrease the chances of a miscarriage, and the hormonal shifts would probably reduce the nausea. In our case, we don't know we are facing a high-risk situation. With the chromosomal abnormality, development is not going according to plan.

The idea of prenatal testing does occur to me, but I don't feel concerned about the baby, nor do I want to get caught up in the medical system. We know a handful of parents who've had false positive results for various tests, which they agonized over for weeks or months—needlessly, because all ended up with normal babies. Dicken's brother and his wife were told their sixteen-week-old fetus would almost certainly have problems and were offered an abortion on the spot. Their son, my godson Dominic, now six, is healthy and brighter than average.

Maybe it's a blessing I'm not worried about the baby's well-being; I'm struggling enough as it is. Much of the unpleasantness of the first trimester stays with me. The morning sickness isn't getting worse, but it's still there. Everything around me smells revolting, time crawls by, I'm exhausted. I force myself to do some activity with the boys almost every day. I continue with my walk each afternoon, finding that the once heartbreakingly beautiful bluebell-covered woods now look so unfamiliar and bizarre, I might be walking on the moon. *The world is not our home . . .* After the exertion, I give myself permission to collapse in front of the TV to watch tennis or a video or anything else to get my mind off the nausea.

My mother comes for a week and I am very glad to see her. She entertains the boys and sweetly attends to me. One morning, after I've asked her to tell Dicken to make me my usual breakfast, she returns carrying a plate of food.

"I made the crêpes myself," she says, and, seeing the look of alarm on my face, quickly adds, "Don't worry, Dicken gave me the recipe and I followed it exactly."

I take the plate from her hand and gaze down at the crêpes. Instead of the usual eight or nine thin crêpes, there are two thick, greasy, rubbery-looking discs.

"You made a full batch of batter?" I ask.

"Yes, it's not much, is it, only enough for a couple of crêpes."

I saw off a bite with my fork and put it to my mouth. I nearly gag, and tears well in my eyes. I feel terribly ungrateful, yet I can't stomach this offering of Mom's. I'm reminded of years of childhood disappointment, a deep, burning ache that despite all her efforts, I'm somehow never able to take in her nurturing.

"I'm sorry, Mom. I guess I'm worse today than usual."

"Don't be sorry," she replies in a cheerful tone. "I'd be happy to get you anything else. How about some fruit?"

I lie down on the bed, upsetting the plate and spilling greasy crêpes onto the white comforter cover. I grab the food, drop the plate to the floor, and weep into the pillow.

"It's hard, isn't it," Mom says, coming to sit by me and stroke my head. "I wish there was something I could do."

The way she's touching me doesn't feel good. I move away from her slightly, hoping not to hurt her feelings. I've always craved attention from my mom, yet whenever I get it I seem to find flaws in her delivery.

"I'm glad you're here," I cry. "I just feel so useless. Such a waste of space and no good for anyone."

"You're doing the most important work there is," she says. "In the long run you'll see that."

Every day as I walk in the woods, the thought that keeps me going is, *This is the last time I'll ever be pregnant, thank God.*

Mom flies back home. I'm sad to see her go. Dicken is away in London for a seminar and I'm lying in bed that night, feeling a little lonesome. *I should have encouraged Jasper to sleep with me.* I feel an ache for Jasper, a familiar feeling of yearning that's been absent for several long weeks. *Oh no, I'm becoming human again.* My attachments are back and I can feel how vulnerable, how fearful they make me. *What if I lost Jasper?*

Just then, the door creaks open and I hear a sweet voice say, "Mom?" We snuggle.

"Mom, where's the baby going to sleep? There's not enough room for all of us."

I smile in the dark. "We'll just have to get a bigger bed."

Dicken gets home late the next night and makes me crêpes. I sit at the kitchen table, wanting to be near him. Caroline shakes her head and says, "If I had asked your father to make me crêpes, he would have said no."

"I don't understand that at all," Dicken says. "If you love someone, why wouldn't you do anything you could to make them feel better?"

I sleep well with Dicken beside me and in the morning am back on the couch watching TV while he makes the boys breakfast. Watching a show on African heroes, I am astounded to hear that Nelson Mandela spent seventeen years of his prison time almost exclusively in solitary confinement. The annual G-8 Summit is about to happen, with the main agenda being the top industrialized nations' discussion of debt relief to African nations. The UK is hosting this year's meeting, and the British news is full of stories about Africa's political and economic woes, as well as reports on global warming and other environmental urgencies. I hear about boy soldiers in Africa, see images of villages devastated by war, drought, and famine.

In my debilitated state, the chaos in the world seems all the more overwhelming and insurmountable. I write in my journal:

> It really does seem like this existence is pretty much hell for most of humanity (and just about all of the animal kingdom), and I'm not sure how to go forward in a way that's justifiable. Too much reality to digest. The oddest part is trying to hold the excitement of this new life when everything seems to be collapsing.

The next afternoon, Caroline comes in from the garden to report that the boys have taken some valuable tools from the barn and broken them. I drag myself upstairs to their room and find them listening to loud music. Jasper is hurriedly stuffing something into his pillowcase and eyeing me carefully.

"What do you have there?"

"Nothing, Mom. Just go away!"

I walk toward him and try to see into the pillowcase, glimpsing what I'm fairly sure are candy wrappers. He pushes me. Hot anger rushes through my body, and at the same time, from a detached place, I'm thinking, *Wow, when did he get so strong?* Kevin laughs, egging Jasper on.

"You shouldn't push a pregnant woman!" I shout. "And you shouldn't have broken the tools in the barn, you didn't even ask permission to use them!"

"Liar!" Jasper shouts back. "We didn't use those tools!"

"Then how do you know what I'm talking about?"

"What tools?" Jasper says. Kevin giggles like a schoolgirl.

"I'm ashamed of you boys!" I run from the room, angry tears forming in my eyes. *I've lost control of them.*

I slam our bedroom door behind me, throw myself onto the bed, and start sobbing. I feel done.

Jasper opens my door and shouts, "I hate you, Mom!"

"Get out of here, you can't come in without knocking!" I yell.

By bedtime, Jasper is still angry at me, curling up in Dicken's lap, giving me the evil eye from his safe haven. I apologize to him and offer a hug, a story, but he makes a face and says, "You're the worst mom in the family."

The next day, Dicken reads me Walt Whitman's poetry to buoy my spirits. He plays me a Beatles album that belonged to his father, looks in my eyes, and says, "I love you, you're the only one I want. I love you so much it hurts sometimes." I feel emotional in a sweet way, and I'm abruptly back to feeling happy about the pregnancy, excited to give birth and meet the baby and have Dicken share that.

August 2005

I am still very tired, but not as sick, as we get ready to fly to Northern Ireland for a large family gathering on my dad's side. I dread the travel, even though it's a short trip, but I also can't wait to get a change of scene. A stab of sadness comes over me as Caroline kisses us goodbye at the departures curb.

After the hour-long flight to Belfast, we head to Limavady,

the town where both my and Dicken's families have lived for generations. Ardmore, the house that now belongs to my father, was once part of the grand estate Caroline grew up on. My father and Caroline grew up knowing each other because their fathers were lifelong friends. My dad remembers attending dances and beach picnics organized by Caroline's mother. My dad and Caroline reconnected when Dicken and I were in our late teens, which is how we ended up meeting and falling in love.

I feel the lovely old house embrace me as we step inside, and I can hardly believe the almost instantaneous change. I sense energy literally seeping back into my system. I begin to do yoga again, take longer walks, drink very weak tea, and eat a wider range of food. I still have constant low-grade nausea, but the contrast with how I was in England makes this a different existence. I actually feel like part of the world again.

I have always loved Ardmore. There is something magical about it, something indescribable. Even with stories of violence in the ongoing conflict between the IRA and the British Loyalists, as well as fairly vicious Limavady gossip—including the terrible rifts between families we know—I walk around feeling I'm in heaven. The rooks that nest in the trees and darken the sky as they fly around at dawn and dusk, with their distinctive caws. The huge leafy trees bordering the land and sky, the soft grass, the hundreds of shades of green, the shabby yet elegant house humming with generational memories, the soft beds, the warm radiators, the cozy kitchen. The dusty old books, hardbacks from past ages. Poppy, the young daughter of Ardmore's tenant-caretaker, Faye, galloping around the house with her chirruping so accented it sounds like a foreign language. The quaint courtyard, soft rain alternating with bright sunshine, clouds moving through constantly. I putter around all day and feel open and at home. Picking wildflowers and a rose or two from the few surviving bushes of long-ago gardens. Playing family football and dodgeball on the lawn.

It is a joy to see everyone again. My beloved uncles, our

cousins; my sister Cecily and her husband Michal; Maud, who's brought me maternity clothes and the dried pineapples I've been craving; our brother Ben and his wife Paula. Dad arrives a day later than planned because of a much-delayed flight from Washington, DC, where he lives, looking tired but happy to be in his favorite place in the world.

"You're very brave to have another," he tells me. *Thanks a lot*, I think, wishing he'd say something a little more encouraging or enthusiastic.

I get pampered, especially by my sisters. Foot rubs, food prepared for me, and extra attention that feels like sunshine after a long winter.

The week goes by quickly, with games, day trips to the beach, and evening gatherings with the whole family. I have the energy to take part in most of it, though I'm always tuckered out by the end of the day and fall asleep putting the boys to bed while the rest of my siblings and cousins stay up late. I'm also up earlier, along with my father, who usually sleeps only a few hours a night. Sometimes he and I wash the dishes left from the night before or sip hot tea together. Our conversations are predictably one-sided, with him dominating. He loves to talk, and I generally enjoy his stories and jokes, up to a point.

"Dad, I've heard this one three times already. You have to keep better track of your audience or we feel insignificant. I mean, weren't you impressed by how hard I laughed the first time you told me? Or didn't you even notice?"

"You know me, darling, I can't keep track of which of my three daughters I've told. And at my age, you have to allow for a little memory loss. Oh, that reminds me," he says with breathless glee, and proceeds to tell me about the time his aunt forgot her son somewhere. I know this one too, but I don't interrupt, because I happen to like it, and besides, I can't quite remember how it ends.

I laugh at the punch line, then quickly excuse myself to go do a little yoga before he can start the next story.

"Oh, can I join you?" Dad asks.

This is a first.

"Sure, why not?" I say. "Funny, I didn't think you believed in anything so New Age."

"It's not that I believe in anything, I just need to stretch more. My doctor said it would be good for my blood pressure. So you see, it's purely self-interest that motivates me."

I skip the prayers and breathing exercises in my routine, bashful about acknowledging that side of myself in front of my father. Dad is a willing, if somewhat comical, student.

All that week, I don't mind missing the late-night revelry with the siblings and cousins, realizing that even if I weren't pregnant I'd almost always prefer an early bed with book and husband to a party.

One night, I get up from bed to pee, and as I stand in the chilly bathroom I'm suddenly seized by violent chills. They run up and down my spine in painful spasms for about a minute. I flash to childbirth—the closest experience to this I can recall, a feeling of being out of control, at the mercy of a strong sensation originating in my body and taking over for seconds that seem endless. I almost cry out, but don't want to wake any of the sleeping people nearby, so I grimace through the pains. They stop, and I dash back into bed. I don't think any more about them until a month or so later.

The next day, we catch an early flight back to England, then fly home to Oregon. After the long journey, I flop into our big, soft bed for the first time in four months. *You're halfway through this pregnancy, done with traveling for a long, long time.*

CHAPTER 11

September 2005

I f we'd chosen to go with an OB/GYN for our prenatal care, as do the vast majority of American women with access to health care, this is about the time I would have an ultrasound. The technician would look for a number of things, including the thickness of the skin behind the baby's neck. This marker, known as the nuchal fold, is often thicker in fetuses with chromosomal abnormalities. If this had been found in our case, which is likely, a more detailed ultrasound and other prenatal testing, such as amniocentesis and chorionic villus sampling (CVS), would be recommmended. Both amnio and CVS involve penetrating the uterus with a sharp tool such as a needle and removing either amniotic fluid or a tiny piece of the placenta, which is then tested for DNA abnormalities. Both are associated with a risk of miscarriage.

We would have waited about two weeks for the results of an amnio or CVS. These would have come back with the news that our fetus had trisomy 13, and we would have been faced with two choices: abort the pregnancy or carry on, knowing the chances of the fetus surviving to birth were limited, and beyond birth, almost nil. Of the 2 to 5 percent of trisomy 13 cases not miscarried before the twentieth week of gestation, the vast majority are aborted after testing reveals the grim diagnosis. Of the few who make it past the twentieth week, 60 percent are stillborn. Of those born alive, 50 percent die within the first month, and most of the rest die before their first birthday.

Looking back at how sick I felt, I am fairly certain I would have opted for an abortion. But you never know how you will react to such an intense situation until you're in it, as I will learn nearly five months later at the birth.

Four and a half months along, I'm certainly more functional than I was during the first trimester, but I'm still nauseous, very finicky about food, and discouraged. I feel like a complete wreck:

irritable, easily tired, my sacrum and pelvic bones creaky and sore, my head aching much of the time. When the scale reads 154 pounds, a record for me, I go back to skimpy eating, hoping to avoid gaining more weight than is necessary.

October 2005

By the sixth month, with no new improvement in the nausea and irritability, I give up trying to make myself feel better. Supplements, tinctures, and food scheduling don't help at all.

I tell Dicken, "I think I'm just meant to be sick for the duration."

"Maybe you're right. I just hate to see you suffer. It's heart-wrenching."

"If one more person asks me a question about the state of my health or how I feel with a certain supplement, remedy, food, whatever, I'll punch them. I'm fed up with it. I've accepted that I feel like shit and will until the birth. Now why the hell can't they?"

"So what should I tell people who offer an idea?"

"Tell them to leave me alone and stop trying to rescue me. Rub my back, rub my feet, tell me a joke, take my kids, but don't suggest ginger tea or ask me how I felt when I started or stopped the last thing you suggested."

A few days later, I spend the night at Mom's house because I have an early appointment the next morning with my therapist in town. Before heading to Mom's, I stop by the co-op to pick up a few items I've been craving: a cinnamon raisin bagel, some seaweed salad. I run into one of Dicken's men's group members, a family friend.

"You still look small," he tells me. "How far along are you?"

"I'm six months," I say, pulling up my bulky fleece jacket so he can see my shape a little better. I only mean to pull back one layer, but all three come up, and here I am in the dairy section with my midriff exposed.

Our friend gasps and says, "Your belly is so beautiful!"

I feel a little bashful, and also touched. "Thanks," I say. "I should get back to shopping. I need to keep this baby fed, even though I hate eating."

He frowns and says, "Yeah, I hear you're still feeling pretty sick. Have you tried ginger tea?"

I take in a big breath to stem the tide of irritation rising in my chest, hoping to muster a polite response, but then I see that he's laughing.

"Dicken told you, didn't he?" I ask, a smile forming on my face.

"Yeah, he said, *Whatever you do, do not mention ginger tea.*"

That night, in the guest room at my mom's house, I wake from an intense dream and find my whole body shivering violently. I get up to go to the bathroom and can barely walk because of the forceful spasms. I manage to grab another blanket from the closet on my way back to bed and bundle myself up tightly, but I can't stop the shaking for quite some time. I wonder if I'm coming down with something.

The next morning I see my therapist. We meditate for a few minutes together, then I settle into the couch and she asks how I'm doing.

"I had a bad night," I begin. "My head has been aching, my stomach sick as always. I've been feeling negative through and through. I wonder if my state will ever shift. Will the sun come out after all this darkness, will I have energy and enthusiasm for life again?"

"It's hard to stay with what's happening."

"Yeah, it's hard to be so blah for so long. I mean, I can see that there are plenty of positive things happening in my life, but I can't feel them. They bring me solace at best, but not joy. I can't remember the last time I felt joy. Even the sweet moments like the kids trying to make me feel better after a crying spell or Maud rubbing my back don't really reach me."

"What comes up for you as you talk about this?"

"I can feel how much I hate my body. Even Dicken hates it right now, for making me feel this sick. And he's not interested in sex at all."

"That must be really hard."

"Yeah, it makes me mad. Frustrated with my body."

"What happens when you sense in?"

I close my eyes. "Well, I feel burning in my stomach."

"Can you let that be there?"

"No. I can feel myself tensing up all around it, willing it to go away."

"Huh, that's curious. Why would you want it to go away so badly?"

"Gosh, it seems obvious. Who wants to feel sick?"

"I know, but you see, you're tensing up in the face of a sensation, making it into a much bigger thing than just a burning stomach, and you're not giving yourself any space to be with what's happening, because you're fighting it so hard. It would be interesting to find out why you're so eager to avoid this feeling."

"Hmm," I say, thinking about this. "I just find this constant nausea and burning pain unbearable. Well, not unbearable, but super irritating. And I'm afraid it's going to get worse, and be here forever, and ruin my life."

"Wow, that's a lot of scary stories you're telling yourself. Is what's going on in you right now really that hard to bear? Is it really that overwhelming?"

"Well, no, I guess it's not. It just makes me mad because it keeps me from being able to concentrate on anything, to escape into one of my imaginary worlds."

"So it keeps you very much in the physical here and now."

"Yes, and I would rather be anywhere else. I'd rather be thinking about some lovely memory, or composing a story in my imagination, or planning an exciting future event, or exercising, or accomplishing something that needs accomplishing. But I can't do any of that with this physical discomfort."

"So what's happening in your body doesn't count."

"No, I guess I don't really consider that life. Anything that's physically distracting is keeping me from my real life." I can feel how badly I want this pregnancy to be over, how much I want my life to start again.

"Interesting," she says. "This reminds me of how you describe your mother in your childhood."

"Really?" I say, not seeing her point at all.

"Well, you've talked about how busy your mom was, how you always wished she would slow down and join you in the quiet things you did."

"Uh-huh."

"And it seems like your body, and maybe this baby, are asking you to slow down and just be, the way you longed for your mom to just slow down and be with you."

Wow. I never would have connected that. She's good.

"What would it be like," she asks, "to let everything else go and just experience what's happening for you this very moment?"

For the rest of the session I stay with myself quietly, closing my eyes and occasionally commenting on what I'm feeling and noticing. The slowed moments are calmer, always shifting and changing subtly. When I inhale deeply, I can feel expansion throughout my body, and this lessens the intensity of the nausea, creating some room to explore. I feel like a deep-sea diver, plunging down inside my cells, atmosphere by atmosphere, until I can almost sense being on the cellular level. I run my consciousness over the contours of my abdomen and up through my esophagus, into my mouth, over my tongue, and the pain no longer feels solid and homogenous. I find places that feel bitter, others that feel sour, some that feel numb and tingly, and even places where the pain is close to pleasure, almost exquisite.

I leave taking bigger breaths, feeling less panicked about making my physical symptoms go away, and with a distinct tenderness for the little one calling me home to this moment.

* * *

After my appointment, I meet a couple of other women from the Threshold Choir, which I've been part of for over a year and have recently become active in again. We will sing at the bedside of a dying woman in her eighties. We debrief outside the house and hear that this woman has hours, maybe a few days at the most.

We walk quietly into the house, which is her son's home, and are shown into a room off the hallway. The woman is lying prone in a hospital bed, her face partially covered by the mouthpiece of a respirator, a loud, thrumming machine that helps move air in and out of her lungs with a dramatic shudder every ten seconds or so. Her eyes are closed; she looks unconscious. Her son, who is probably around fifty, is lying next to her on the edge of the bed, leaning his whole body as close to her as he can get. He's holding her limp hands in his, looking into her face almost eagerly, talking to her constantly, his eyes concerned, loving. He does not acknowledge us or the nurse and hospice volunteer standing by. His entire attention is on his mother.

We get out our song folders. The Threshold Choir has a large repertory derived from almost every spiritual and religious tradition. Songs are selected by talking with family members beforehand. We try to find out which music will be soothing, asking about favorites and especially songs that might evoke the person's childhood.

I begin to sing the hymn "Abide with Me," but choke up almost immediately. The sight of the man trying hard to connect to his mother as she slips away from him is almost unbearably poignant. I try singing again, "*Abide with me . . . swift to its close ebbs out life's little day . . .*" I can feel my throat closing as tears well up in my eyes. I look away from the woman and her son, but the words and melody of the hymn convey the emotion of the scene as powerfully as the images in the room. Fortunately, my singing partners have strong voices and carry along fine without me. I'm actually not a very good singer at all; I just like meaningful songs and the challenge of being with dying people. I sometimes feel extremely emotional at bedsides, but this is the first time I haven't been able to force myself to sober up and get back to at least mouthing the words and looking somewhat composed. *It must be my hormones.*

I put a hand on my belly, wondering what mother-child scenes will play out between me and this baby in our distant future. Will this child, or Jasper, or both, whisper to me as I prepare to leave the world, and them? It breaks my heart to think of saying a final goodbye to my children, or to my own mother, only fifteen years shy of eighty herself. Yet what a beautiful way to go, on the wings of the children we once welcomed over the threshold into life.

On my drive home from town, I'm still emotional and don't feel quite ready to face the noise and needs of the kids. I stop at Sterlingville Cemetery, a historic site not far from where we live, home to over a hundred graves from the pioneer gold-rush days. It's set in a lovely wooded spot. No one else is here today, and I savor the solitude. It's cold and overcast. I can see my breath, but my progesterone-fueled body is warm. I wander around reading markers and monuments, noticing how peaceful I feel here, not scared or disturbed by the irrefutable evidence of death all around me. I calculate people's ages by the dates on their markers, finding few over fifty. Ah, here is a woman of eighty-two, like the woman I just saw in town who will soon leave her body and life and have a marker like this in a graveyard.

I'm always fascinated and horrified by the number of deaths in infancy and early childhood. I see that one family, the Saltmarshes, has two grave markers, both white marble columns that look like mini Washington Monuments. One is simply marked, *Joseph B. Saltmarsh,* with his birth and death dates, 1825 to 1906. The other is marked, *The wife and children of Joseph B. Saltmarsh.* Under that, the script carving reads, *Mary, wife of Joseph Saltmarsh, died 1878, forty-three years.* Another side of the same marker lists four children, *Ann, Charles, Birt,* and *Lyman,* with death dates and exact ages noted: *Ann, 9 years, 10 mo 2 days, March 29, 1864, Charles M., 7 mo 11 days, November 19, 1856*, and so on. The opposite side of the same marker reads, *Infants, born and died*, and lists the years: *1870, 1872, 1874, 1876*, and *1878*. Under that is another child's name, *Sornoria, 3 years, 4 mo 1 day, 1868*. I note that the last infant's death year is the same as their mother's and wonder if she died in childbirth. I also calculate that her first listed child was born when she was twenty-one. From then on, and possibly before, this woman had at least one pregnancy about every other year, or probably more than that, assuming there were surviving children not listed on this marker. And ten of her babies and young children died, in the years 1856, '58, '64, '64, '68, '70, '72, '74, '76, and '78.

Standing there, I cannot imagine what this woman went through, so many pregnancies and losses. It is dreadful to think of losing a baby after the months of sickness, the pain of labor. And then to start all over with another pregnancy, knowing it very well might happen again. I tell myself to be grateful I live in these modern times.

Late that night, I rise to go to the bathroom, but before I get there, I am again seized by intense, painful shivers rhythmically shooting up my spine. I can't stand by myself. I feel completely out of control as the spasms take over, making me tremble uncontrollably. I'm freezing. I call over to Dicken for help. He leaps out of bed and holds me up as the next wave rushes through—it reminds me of labor. Even Dicken's warm body doesn't help. I can't make it to the bathroom; I crawl back into bed. Dicken wraps the duvet around me and fetches a heating pad. By this point I'm screaming when the spasms overtake me, my teeth chattering. Thoughts of various diseases flash through my mind: cancer, shingles, Lou Gehrig's, MS, epilepsy.

"I have some terrible disease, I know it," I say between bouts of shivers.

"Don't let your mind make this into anything more than it is," Dicken says.

I still have to pee, but moving the slightest bit starts a tremor—it's like a force standing behind me waiting to pounce. I imagine the Grim Reaper and think I might be dying. Finally, I make myself get up and go to the bathroom. Dicken brings me warm pajamas. I get back under the covers, feeling bewildered and shaky. This has happened twice before during this pregnancy, once in Ireland the night before we left, and last night at Mom's. But never as powerful as tonight, which makes me fear that whatever I have is getting worse. At some point in the night, I wonder if this pregnancy will cripple me or even kill me. I seriously consider getting an OB, having tests on me and the baby, and planning a hospital birth.

From a web investigation the next morning, I come up with two hypotheses. The first is vague, an inadequate explanation for the force of the sensations: lying on my back does something either to the nerves or the blood flow (related to the venae cavae). The second, while certainly more out there, resonates the most: I'm having what are known as Kundalini experiences, which are considered a sort of spiritual awakening that affects the body as well as the mind and soul. The material on the web describes the two sides of Kundalini energy as fire, which can be so strong it kills, or ice, which is powerful but less dangerous. I certainly felt like I'd been iced, out of the blue. Strange, because my normal pregnant state is to be on the overheated side.

The websites I find consistently describe an energy that begins in the base of the spine and shoots upward. They say the symptoms of Kundalini include sweating, trembling, sensations of heat and cold, rushes of energy through the body or up and down the spine, fear, and anxiety—the list exactly mirrors my own. I follow different links, finding many divergent views on the subject. Some say Kundalini energy is a sought-after experience leading to awakening and bliss, while others warn it is not to be toyed with. I decide I was lucky to get the icy version. I am not surprised to read warnings. Apparently many yogic seekers try to cultivate Kundalini experiences and often end up with physical or emotional troubles. I have no doubt about this possibility if what I felt was indeed Kundalini energy, and I certainly am not planning to go looking for any more.

Reading all this alarms me but also reassures me somehow. For whatever reason, maybe because pregnancy makes me more open, I'm experiencing something real and powerful. I now know I'm not making this up; I'm not being histrionic or melodramatic, as I so often tell myself. I am sensitive, I always have been, and I might as well accept that and go gently with myself in this strange world. Fortunately, I've been blessed with a companion who is there for me, who shows up when things like this happen. I can accept this grace and let in all the seen and unseen support that holds me.

Feeling stronger and less fearful, I'm actually fascinated by what I find on the web and copy quotes in my journal. One sentence will stand out to me: *These experiences are often triggered by meditation, prayer, psychedelic drugs, or being in the presence of an illumined being or spiritual master.*

Months later, I will reread this and feel an intense electric charge at the words "illumined being." I will also note the timing, that my first Kundalini-like encounter was in August, four months into the pregnancy. According to Sufism and other spiritual traditions, this is right around the time the soul enters a fetus.

CHAPTER 12

Nine weeks to due date

At the next prenatal, Rhione, our senior midwife, measures my fundal height as usual, but this time she frowns, and repeats the measurement.

"You're a little low this time," she says. She checks my chart to make sure and nods, saying this is the first time I've come in under normal.

I immediately assume it's my cautious eating. I've been watching the scale hit record highs, and I'm dreading the post-pregnancy weight battle. I figure I can preempt it by starting the steady decline now, or at least prevent any further gain. Since I'm fairly nauseous anyway, this hasn't been difficult. But now I feel subversive, because the midwives have been urging me to eat well, and I've been feigning utter compliance.

"Is this a problem?" I ask Rhione.

She explains the possible implications, but I'm so convinced I know what's causing this, I don't listen very carefully. I'm trying to decide if I should continue avoiding weight gain, if there's any danger to the baby. But nothing Rhione says alarms me. She offers me the option of an ultrasound to check on things, but I am sure I don't want one. And Rhione seems relieved when I say so. She palpates my belly and smiles as she finds the baby with her experienced hands. "I just love this little one," she says.

As I undress for bed that night, Dicken gazes at my naked body for longer than usual and says, "You are so beautiful." I can tell he means it. He hasn't said this often during the pregnancy and hasn't been initiating sex.

"It's funny," I tell him, "for some reason I'm no longer scared of having another shivering episode, or going through labor."

"You seem really different. You're in your pregnant power now."

He's right. Everything is shifting. I'm happy to be in my body. I look down at my swollen belly and feel tender toward myself and the baby, proud of how far we've come in this long pregnancy. After all these months of struggling, my body is finally an ally. Having to slow down has been a gift, preventing me from escaping into my usual distractions. My belly keeps bringing me back, forcing me to practice being with myself.

One evening just before Thanksgiving, Dicken and I attend a chocolate-making class in Ashland. Our instructor, the owner of a local organic chocolate company, begins the class by writing the word *theobromine* on a white board.

"This is the scientific name for the principle chemical in chocolate," he says. "*Theo* means god, *bromine* means food. So chocolate really is the food of the gods." He hands out samples from his company's line. I eat so many I feel my heart begin to beat like a rabbit's.

"Dicken," I whisper, "how 'bout the name Theobromine for the baby?"

Dicken smiles, licks melted chocolate from his lower lip, and gives me a thumbs-up.

Silently, I note the name Theodore, which means "gift from God." And it's close in sound to the magic substance in my favorite food. I stick it in the back of my mind.

December 2005
Five weeks to due date

I can only eat small meals as the baby fills up more and more of my abdomen. Heartburn is unavoidable when I eat. I always have a snack just before bed, hoping it will carry me through the night, but it rarely works. I wake to pee, then can't get back to sleep because of growling hunger pains. I fight it for a few minutes, urging myself to overcome the sensation and sleep, but at some point I realize I've lost the battle. I roll out of bed sideways, shivering a little in the chilly air, and lumber down to the kitchen. I rummage through every shelf and corner of the refrigerator until I find something acceptable. Toast, a grapefruit, an apple, some nuts. I sit in the dimly lit kitchen, the big room's corners swallowed up in darkness, chewing my food and counting the days until our due date.

In hypnobirthing class with Rhione, Dicken is a surprisingly disappointing partner.

"Your voice sounds insincere," I say after a relaxation exercise. "You don't want to be here, do you?"

"Ugh!" he groans. "I'm just tired, okay?"

"Well, you better not be tired at the birth if this is the best you can do."

"Maybe you should have Maud be your hypnobirthing coach," he says.

"I hate you," I hiss at him quietly, so none of the other blissed-out couples will hear.

"Boy, your hormones are out of control today."

"This is me talking, not hormones," I seethe. "And right now me *and* my hormones hate you."

"Then I quit," Dicken says, lying down and burying his face in a pillow.

The baby kicks. Rhione is talking about being extremely calm and quiet during labor.

"Well, it might just be you and me at this birth," I tell the baby, looking at Dicken still collapsed in a heap.

Back at home, I have a phone conversation with Paul, our friend who teaches energetic seeing. Mom has been studying with him for a number of years, and Dicken and I take a class or get a reading from him once in a while. He is always full of fascinating insights from his unusual view of people and events. I ask him what he sees about the baby and the birth.

"You know, if I were you, I'd consider not having the boys there—it might be too distracting for you."

He says this baby is Dicken's and mine, so the presence of other family members would somehow dilute the experience for us. This is the direction I've been going in anyway, seeing the birth as very quiet and dark, occurring at night. Paul says the baby seems creative, feminine, speaks my language; is very well-suited to the family, unselfish, forward-thinking. He sees a happy couple of years for us, not a hard adjustment. The one challenge he sees is getting my strength back: this pregnancy has taken a lot out of me. He suggests no more kids. I laugh.

Four weeks to due date

Christmas is hectic and exhausting. My Grinchiness seems as magnified as my midsection. The boys tear open present after present and sulk when they run out. I expect this from Jasper but am surprised and disappointed that Kevin is behaving this way on his first American Christmas. According to him, he never received any presents in Costa Rica, other than a pair of shoes one year.

A large family group gathers at our house. Ben and Paula come from New York and announce their first pregnancy. They look anxious and excited and stay close to each other all day.

"This is the only time we'll overlap pregnancies," I tell them, looking from my protruding belly to Paula's flat one.

Dicken cooks a feast; Maud and I debrief and gossip while we do mounds of dishes. Afterward, I lie on the couch and Maud asks if she can feel the baby.

"Sure," I say.

She kneels down next to me and begins to press gently on my belly. "You're so lucky you have a baby inside you," she gushes.

I roll my eyes.

"You *are*," she insists. "I miss being pregnant so much, and Tom is firm that we're not having any more kids."

"I can't wait for this pregnancy to end. I'm so over it."

A few days after Christmas, as I'm lying in bed reading birth stories, I have a few crampy contractions. At first I'm just curious about them, but when they start to come fairly regularly, I get alarmed, afraid I'll end up in the hospital because I'm not quite far enough along to have a home birth.

I call Dicken upstairs and let him know what's happening. He looks wide-eyed with concern and immediately says, "I'll get Maud."

Maud, who trained as a midwife for a year or so, feels my belly, times the surges, and checks in her midwifery manual. Dicken calls Rhione, who shows up within half an hour and checks me—all seems fine. Just Post-Traumatic Christmas Syndrome, we joke. Rhione prescribes bed rest until the contractions stop.

It seems that everything keeps telling me to slow down and go inward. It's hard not to be able to get up and feed myself, tidy up, do a little writing. But at this point I'm willing to do whatever it takes to last five more days, when I'll be thirty-seven weeks along, technically full-term and able to have a home birth.

January 1, 2006

With three weeks to go, things are calm until this afternoon, when I notice brown-stained watery discharge on the toilet paper after I pee. I immediately think, *Meconium*, the thick tarlike excrement a baby poops during the first few days of life. When it shows up prenatally, it can be a sign that the baby is in distress.

I start to feel agitated and call Dicken, who gets the midwives on the phone. They come over and check me and the baby.

"You seem fine," Rhione says, her voice soothing. "But the

discharge looks suspicious, especially considering your fundal height has been low the last few weeks. I think we need to carefully monitor the situation."

When I see her concerned expression, I begin to shake and cry, stroking my belly and saying, "Baby, I hope you're okay. You're okay, aren't you? Please, please be okay."

"We should think about getting an ultrasound, and maybe having you closer to a hospital, just in case," Rhione says. "But it's up to you, Lucinda. Why don't you check in with your deepest self and see what you want to do."

I cry some more. I want my baby to be okay, and I'm now very nervous that something is wrong. I don't want to ignore warning signs. I also don't want to be fear-based and end up in the hospital with a high-intervention situation that turns out to be unnecessary. I want a straightforward, uncomplicated home birth. I want all the faith I have in the process of birth to shine through for me and this baby. But I am spooked now, and afraid I won't be able to relax and trust what's happening. I can't see a good option right now.

"I feel so trapped," I say.

I look to Dicken, but he just looks right back at me, his expression uncertain.

I take a deep breath, close my eyes, and search inside for guidance, for a hunch, for anything. There is nothing but blankness, fear, confusion.

Just pick a direction and go with it, see how it feels. I can take a little step one way, backtrack if it seems necessary. I decide to go to Mom's, which is closer to a hospital, for the time being, and have an ultrasound the next day. Rhione will come with us for the test.

We drop Kevin off at a friend's house, then drive to Mom's, where our midwife friend Jennifer comes to take my blood, do a culture, and feel the baby. She seems very positive, which is hugely reassuring. I'm also glad to be close to my mom, who is always a trooper in a crisis.

January 2

I sleep okay, and we get ready to head to the hospital for the ultrasound.

On the way to the hospital in Grants Pass, I tell Dicken, "In an hour or so we'll be driving home, thinking there was no real point in doing the ultrasound, that it was an expensive and unnecessary procedure, but at least we'll be relieved. Then we can go home and wait for the birth."

"Exactly," he says.

Dicken, Rhione, and I wait awhile at the hospital before a technician comes to get us. We make our way through a maze-like hallway to the exam room. I lie on the metal table, have the cold gel applied to my belly, and get hooked up to the machine. The screen comes on, and there is the baby, its head very low down and in the right position for birth. I look at Dicken and smile, but his eyes are on the screen, staring hard at every detail.

Debbie, our ultrasonographer, is upbeat and talkative. We've told her we don't want to know the baby's gender, and she's careful not to reveal it.

"Look, there's a foot! I'll take a picture of it, it's cute." She clicks something on the controls she's holding. "Here are the four chambers of the heart," she says, pointing to the screen. "Those all look in order."

Phew, I think, normal heart.

"And there's the baby's head. You can see the face, there. I think it has its thumb in its mouth. I'll take a picture of that too."

I gasp, seeing an image of my child's face for the first time. I look over at Dicken, whose eyes are wide.

"Look at that," he says. "I think it's a real baby."

I smile, recalling how Dicken didn't fully comprehend that Jasper was an actual human being until he held him the first time.

The head looks like it's turned to the side, as if it's purposely looking our way, greeting us. *Sucking its thumb, head turned toward us as if posing for the camera. All must be well.*

"You see those dark shadows coming and going on the screen? Those are practice breaths."

"Wow, it's really getting ready, huh?" The idea that this baby will be outside my body within days is still hard for me to fathom.

"Hmm, your fluid level looks a little low," Debbie says, her eyes narrowing in concentration. She clicks on a few coordinates, then peers at the computer screen. "Yes, you're on the low side of normal, but I can't see any tear or leakage in the amniotic sac."

I turn to Rhione, whose eyes are on the screen. "Is that a problem?" I ask.

"I see it quite a lot as women get close to term," Debbie says.

"You naturally lose fluid near the end," Rhione adds. "It's nothing to worry about."

Only twice does Debbie become inexplicably quiet: while she is examining the kidneys, and later the umbilical cord.

"I'll be looking at the umbilical cord to see the three vessels," she says. "In babies with things like Down syndrome, you only see two."

She finds the umbilical cord, stays on it for quite a long time.

"Is it okay?" I ask.

"Um, well, I'm not supposed to say anything," she stumbles.

I strain to see if I can detect anything about the cord myself, but it all looks like a strange Cubist painting to me, with indiscernible shapes.

I find it odd that she doesn't say anything more after all the previous talk, her expression suddenly serious. But I'm not too nervous, considering how the heart and brain look normal, with the baby sucking away at its thumb and taking practice breaths.

As we get ready to leave the room, Debbie pulls Rhione aside and says, "I'd like you to stay here, I need to talk with you."

I go to the bathroom and relieve my very full bladder, then walk with Dicken to the waiting room. We sit in silence. Rhione comes out after about ten minutes.

"It's so strange that the regulations allow Debbie to tell me immediate results, but not you," she says, shaking her head. Then she tells us there were a couple of abnormalities in the ultrasound. "The right kidney seems to have some extra fluid in it, and the umbilical cord has only one artery, not the usual two. Meaning it's a two-vessel cord, with one vein and one artery, not the usual three-vesseled. That's all. Everything else seems perfectly normal."

Rhione's attitude is relaxed. She implies that these kinds of anomalies are usually nothing to be alarmed about, but I feel the beginnings of panic. I tell her about Dicken's father's kidney failure. "Could that be a genetic issue?" I ask.

"There's no hard sign of any problem. I've seen that extra fluid on a kidney before, and it turned out to be nothing. And nowadays, with so many of these minor issues, there are incredible technological advances to deal with them." She tells us about a friend's daughter who was born with a cleft lip and how the surgery was so good you can't tell at all now.

I can hardly hear her. I am in my own dark mind, praying furiously there is nothing wrong, that we aren't heading for life with a disabled child and surgeries and a future I can't even begin to face.

Rhione says she thinks it's fine for us to go back to the farm and wait for the birth. That's reassuring, but I still feel upset. Dicken is on the quiet side but insists that I relax. "There's nothing to worry about. You know these medical types. They find minutiae to scare you with, and then it turns out to be nothing."

"I just want to go home and get this labor started," I say. "I can't stand the waiting, the not knowing."

As we leave for the parking lot, Rhione stops me, pulling something from her purse. "Debbie wanted me to give these to you." She hands me three black-and-white printouts from the ultrasound. One is of the baby's foot, the other two of the face. I hold them close to my chest the whole way back to the farm.

I'm relieved to get home and climb into our big, soft haven

of a bed. But I'm too worried to relax, so I go downstairs to our office and do some research on the single-artery umbilical cord and the kidney fluid. I scour every book we own on pregnancy, and I go online. I come out of that thinking we have a much greater chance of a baby with Down syndrome, maybe one-in-five odds. But I focus on the information that gives us the best chance of a normal baby, the research that says Down's is almost always associated with a visible heart problem. I keep reminding myself that the major organ systems in our baby looked fine, and that this puts us in the lowest risk category. I also underline to myself the research that insists the kidney-fluid issue is a separate thing, entirely unrelated to the cord issue. But deep inside I worry that the presence of these two factors together indicates a significantly higher chance of a problem.

Dicken keeps looking up from his computer, staring at my face with concern. "Stop reading all that stuff. It'll just upset you more," he says.

"At least it's something to do."

I feel very much alone right now. Instead of being reassuring, Dicken seems dismissive, critical of how I'm handling this. At the same time, I'm glad he's not as worried as I am about the ultrasound. He's highly intuitive, and I hope his lack of concern is a sign that as usual, he's right and I'm being overly dramatic.

January 3

I'm up a lot that night, going over the ultrasound, the research, the statistics. I keep imagining I'm pulling a coin out of a jar filled with eighty normal pennies and twenty marked ones, or ninety normal and ten marked, or whatever statistic I recall from the reading I've done. I can never see what coin I've pulled out. I'm always too scared to look.

People who know what's happening pour in stories of their own or from someone they know about prenatal scares that ended up being nothing. I can count at least ten of them among my own friends and relatives. I think of all of them with their beautiful, healthy children, recalling weeks or months of worrying about test results, and I can't wait to join the club. Just a week or two more and I'll be there, I keep telling myself.

I'm trying to reassure myself with what I read on the web about ultrasounds and their ability to detect major abnormalities. *Many babies with chromosomal abnormalities will have ultrasound markers that may be seen during the mid-pregnancy ultrasound*, the website babycenter.ca says, *but most will also have structural abnormalities. So if a marker is seen, the sonographer will carry out a careful examination of the baby to look for other problems.* This is extremely reassuring, given that so many of our baby's organs look fine: *If the baby looks normal in every other way, it most probably is normal.*

Rhione calls me and says she's been talking our case over with other midwives. She thinks we should consider seeing a specialist in prenatal genetic screening. "I really believe the chances are very much in your favor, from everything I've heard and read. But why not be on the safe side and get a second opinion?"

I agree with her, and she says she'll call the one midwife-friendly specialist in the state and see if we can get a last-minute appointment. Maud overhears me on the phone and bursts into tears when I explain Rhione's take on the situation. I steel myself to stay positive.

Rhione calls back to say Dr. Vernon Katz in Eugene has very sweetly agreed to see us the next day during his lunch hour. In the meantime, I do some more research on the Internet. Again, the single umbilical artery (SUA) seems to be the factor most likely to indicate a problem. Statistics I read vary, saying that somewhere in the range of 5 to 20 percent of babies with an SUA also have serious complications, including chromosomal abnormalities. The risk for Down's is higher. But much of what I read tells me that if the heart looks okay, the chances of anything major like that are much lower.

All that long afternoon, I try to stay calm and take extra care of myself and the baby. I cry a lot. Dicken still refuses to admit out loud that anything could be wrong with the baby, and I'm finding him somewhat remote. Jennifer and Rhione will come with us to Eugene tomorrow. I pray all is well, that we'll return entirely reassured and ready to settle in for a home birth. I feel incredibly grateful for our baby's health and well-being, something I promise myself I'll never take for granted, ever.

In bed that night, Jasper is so sweet, telling me, "Mom, everything is going to be okay with the baby," and he sleeps next to me. I reach over every now and then to stroke his face or his arm as he sleeps and marvel at his health, his beauty, his perfection.

Unable to sleep, negative thoughts play through my mind unceasingly: *I told you that you were too old to have a baby. Your eggs are defective. Now you've done it, you idiot. What were you thinking? You're not strong enough; you're not healthy. How are you going to cope with the baby, especially if it has problems? It's your fault for not eating well enough, for not wanting to gain weight, for eating too much protein and stressing the baby's little kidneys.* I think of Simon, Dicken's father, and his kidney failure and how Dicken couldn't pee as a newborn. It is a night filled with fear.

January 4

In the morning, Dicken, Rhione, Jennifer, and I drive the three hours to Eugene. The ultrasonographer spends over an hour looking at the baby and taking measurements, focusing on every major organ, the umbilical insertion, the mouth (looking for a cleft lip or palate, Jennifer later explains). Nothing seems to alarm the technician or the midwives. I gaze at the images and silently talk to the sweet-looking baby: "Please be okay." It has its mouth pressed up against what the technician thinks is the placenta.

"They like to nuzzle things," she explains. I imagine my newborn nuzzling up against me very soon.

After what seems like a long wait, the geneticist enters. He is a tall, thin man in his fifties who looks a lot like Sydney Pollack. He is carrying a folder and has a grave look on his face. Seeing his expression, I feel the ground beneath me recede.

But his words aren't as terrible as I imagine. He tells us the baby is smaller than the size he'd expect but still in normal range, about the twentieth percentile for gestational age. This could indicate growth retardation, but he says the small size might be due to any number of factors, including smaller build (I imagine my dad's slim frame), my eating patterns in pregnancy (terrible), or a virus (*Didn't I have a touch of stomach bug at the beginning of my third trimester, just when the fundal height started stalling?*). He describes the kidney as having what looks like a reflux issue, not related to anything genetic, he guesses, and one that might correct itself on its own. He says the low amniotic level could be explained by the approaching birth, when levels decrease naturally.

"Just make sure to get the baby a checkup at three months to see if anything is still going on with those kidneys."

Relief sweeps through me. If this expert doctor is already jumping ahead to the three-month checkup, what could be seriously wrong?

He adds that in his opinion, the kidney issue has nothing to do with anything else, such as the low fluid, but that if we go online we'll probably find contradictory information about it. I feel very reassured by his confidence on that one.

He then discusses the amniotic fluid level, which is still in normal range but near the low end of the spectrum. He restates that this is not unusual to see as the birth approaches, but that if it drops any farther, intervention might be called for.

"Drink a lot of fluid and stay resting most of the time," he advises. "And you'll want to monitor the fluid levels with another ultrasound in five days, and keep track of kick counts."

"What about the two-vessel cord?" I ask.

Dr. Katz looks puzzled and says, "I saw a normal cord." A moment of massive relief almost knocks me over, but then the doctor looks down at his notes and corrects himself. "I'm so sorry," he says. "The cord is indeed two-vesseled. Which, along with the size being smaller, and your age, puts you at a higher risk for Down's. But I see single-umbilical arteries half a dozen times a week, and more often than not, they don't turn out to be a problem."

He takes out a pen and draws a bell curve, two large humps overlapping slightly, showing us that we are in the small middle area between Down's and normal babies, the "gray area," the unknown.

"The good news is there are no hard markers for genetic abnormality," he says. "But no one can guarantee your baby doesn't have an abnormality."

I ask if we can do an amnio, and he says no, the fluid levels are too low.

He says many reassuring things, including that it's fine to go ahead with our plans for a home birth. "Even if the baby does have Down's, there's no increased risk based on environment."

That is thrilling to hear, and I burst into tears. I leave elated about being approved for the home birth, and mostly relieved by what the doctor has said, though slightly anxious at the idea of having a baby with Down's. But given the overly cautious tendencies of mainstream medicine these days, the fact that we are okayed for the home birth makes me think the situation can't be dangerous.

As we walk to our car, Dicken says, "Wow, I never thought of the possibility of having a baby with Down syndrome."

"I don't think we have a Down's baby," I say.

Once we get a signal on our cell phone, I call Mom to tell her the report. When I mention the possibility of a Down's baby, she immediately says in her cheerful voice, "Oh, they're such lovely people! We'd be happy to have one in our family."

Maud cries with relief when I call to tell her we can have a home birth. "I was so worried," she says in a confessional tone. "I didn't want to let you know, but I've been doing research on the web and it's been freaking me out. Oh, this is such fantastic news! I have to go tell the kids. We've been waiting to hear from you all afternoon."

On the drive home, Rhione talks about her son Jared, who was killed in an accident three years ago. Typical of a road trip, I learn more about her in those few hours than I have in all the years I've known her. I never knew that she raised her four boys almost entirely on her own, and that she doesn't even know where Jared's father is. I can't imagine going through such a loss alone, to have the other parent on the planet but not connected to the terrible reality of the situation. We talk about the challenges parenting brings, and she repeats several times, shaking her head with sweet conviction, "The little ones bring the gifts." I've been trying not to think of our baby too much during this conversation, because it just makes me worried, but I feel more confident when Rhione with all her wisdom says, "These babies bring us things we don't even know we need."

At home again, the worry reasserts itself. I search the web for more data—some is scary as hell, some is reassuring. It's very hard not to know, to trust the unfoldment. I hang onto Paul's saying he sees the baby as fine. But I keep hearing the doctor mention Down's.

I cry a lot. When I think of how precious the baby is, remembering how its little face was pressed up against the placenta like an older child with a blanket or a teddy bear, I feel enormous compassion for its tender fragility. I long to hold and comfort this baby.

Maud and Grace come to visit me in bed that afternoon.

"Oh, are these the ultrasound pictures?" Maud asks, seeing the printouts sitting on my bedside table.

"Yeah, take a peek," I say.

"Oh, look, Grace!" Maud gushes.

Grace peers at the prints and makes a sour face. "It kind of looks like a monster," she says, and half smiles.

"Don't say that, Grace," Maud admonishes.

I try to smile, wave it off. But I feel dark. *This is not what I need to hear right now.*

January 5

I spend the next day wandering the house aimlessly or sitting at my computer looking for information on Down syndrome. I feel agitated and can't sit still for long. Dicken is at his desk, working on some web project. He hardly looks up when I come in and out of the office. Once in a while I tell him something I've found.

"This website says we have a fifty-fifty chance of a problem."

"Oh," he responds.

"Is that all you can say?"

"Sorry, but I don't think any of this is worth worrying about. Everything is just fine. You'll see."

I feel unsupported, wishing he understood my need to look for answers. I also envy his ability to not think about it. I would love to be in that state myself, but it's impossible. Every waking moment, I am with this baby, a mystery tucked under my ribs, so all-consuming and close I can't see anything else.

With so much time and restlessness, and without reassurance from Dicken, I decide I might as well go to Rhione's dance class. She has women come and dance for each other, sharing what we see in each one's movements, offering support. Dicken seems pleased to see me go. I'm sure he's sick of my worried face.

I hardly feel the cold as I step out of the house. It is dark out already. I drive in silence, still thinking of the baby, wondering, yearning to know.

Rhione greets me with a long, belly-to-belly embrace.

"I just love you guys so much," she says. "How are you doing?"

"Oh, you know."

In the opening circle, Rhione dedicates the class to me and the baby. I begin to cry, and imagine my dance will be vulnerable and weepy. I sit and feel sorry for myself, thinking of Dicken practically pushing me out the door, his face hard, remote.

Then I begin my dance, and everything shifts: I feel the power of the earth come through me, especially in my feet and legs, filling me with enormous strength and energy. There is so much space within me I can't feel any boundaries. It seems I'm floating into the stars, yet I can feel that my feet are solidly grounded. I don't recognize this part of myself. I wonder if the baby is asking me to be strong, to protect it. I feel powerful and capable for the first time in a while, completely willing to do whatever it takes to take care of this baby. I know with certainty I can do it on my own—I don't need to rely on Dicken, or anyone. I have it in me.

I open my eyes and see the faces of the other women peering up at me in reverence.

"I saw you as a warrior," one of them tells me. "You were awesome."

Rhione nods her head slowly. "You're ready, honey."

The next day we watch a football game on TV at Mom's house. My lifelong favorite team, the Washington Redskins, manage to eke out a win in the wildcard playoff game, which is exciting, something positive and hopeful in this uncertain time. Maud stays by my side almost constantly, monitoring the baby's heartbeat, checking its position with her hands. Dicken takes me in his arms when I ask, his great big bear hold comforting.

But still, I feel alone in what seems like an interminable waiting period.

It occurs to me that the ends of both my pregnancies, along with the final stage of adopting Kevin, have been challenging to the core. They initiate me, call me to levels of presence and strength I'm not aware of in any other situation. Jasper's three-day birth awoke my power in this way, and my trip last year to get Kevin was incredibly intense; Mom called it my "hero's journey." In both cases I felt supported, but I had to do the final battle on my own, without the possibility of rescue.

This is shaping up to be another of those battles. I have to face it, to endure these long, hard moments without any guarantees. Character-building, I hope! If we do have a baby with physical challenges, we'll get by. I know that. Meanwhile, I'm being called to stay in the moment and not listen to the scary stories my mind is conjuring. I'm being called to trust.

CHAPTER 13

January 7
Two weeks and one day to due date

Mom comes to spend the day with me. I love our quiet time together; we've had more of it these past weeks than I can ever remember. She plays me a CD of my sister Cecily and her husband Michal's new recording, "Mere Gurudev," a song they arranged for cello, voice, and piano and performed live for the yoga guru B.K.S. Iyengar at a celebration in Boston last month. The lyrics are about devotion, the music hauntingly beautiful. As we listen, I pick up my journal and out fall the three printouts from the ultrasound. As I gaze at the black-and-white images, I feel such a searing tenderness for the baby, and the music is so moving, I burst into tears and weep quietly while Mom rubs my back.

I mostly stay in bed and drink as much water as I can to keep the fluid levels up. In two days I'll go in for a follow-up ultrasound to check my levels—fingers crossed that they haven't dropped. If they have, we may not be able to do a home birth. I'm still confused about the meconium scare, praying it was just a fluke and not a warning sign.

I love this baby so much, I write in my journal, *more than I imagined possible, such a gift, and the details fall away from the enormity of the love that moves my heart—who cares if it has Down's or a cleft palate or kidney issues. We'll take the best care of it we possibly can, and what a huge privilege it is to be this one's mother. I'll savor every diaper change, every feeding, every single time I can touch its skin, kiss its cheeks, hold it close.*

At around nine that evening, I have a bit of a bloody show, a sign that things are moving along toward labor. There is no other activity yet, besides Dix cleaning out closets and preparing birth supplies. I go to bed, hoping to sleep a lot. We may be looking at a day or two or possibly several before labor starts, but probably no more than a week. I'm excited; I'm nervous. I don't feel quite ready somehow, but maybe this really will happen soon.

January 8

Dix is busy organizing our whole house. I'm not too scared about labor; I'm mainly nervous about the baby. The suspense is what's hard. We've only told Maud and the midwives about the bloody show. We don't want to feel that everyone is on edge, expectant.

Grace comes to me in bed with her wool and knitting needles, determined to teach me how to knit. She spends a lot of time these days making the baby little gifts and writing love notes.

Two-and-a-half-year-old Sam, Grace's brother, calls my belly "Buddy" and loves to snuggle and climb all over me. He talks to the baby through my bellybutton and asks me to open my mouth so he can look down my throat and try to see the baby.

January 9

In the morning, we go to have my fluid levels checked at the hospital in Grants Pass. Same ultrasonographer, Debbie. She is very alarmed, first saying, "I can't find any pockets of fluid," and then asking if we've done a fetal stress test. Then she tries to get the baby to move, and when it doesn't, she becomes more distressed—"I need to see some movement!" Then she leaves the room to consult the radiologist.

While Debbie's gone, my terror grows. I imagine an emergency C-section on the spot. My lip starts to quiver, but I don't want to cry. I feel small and vulnerable, like a young child, not a powerful woman getting ready to give birth.

Rhione and Dicken are looking fairly calm, both of them

muttering about the ultrasonographer "trying to play doctor." Debbie comes back, grim-faced and not saying much. She examines the baby for ten more minutes, finding a little fluid here and there, visibly relieved when the baby moves and takes a practice breath. The fluid reading is slightly higher than Dr. Katz's the week before, which according to him was okay, as long as it didn't drop.

On our way out, Debbie runs down the hall after us. She stops me and asks, "Are you really having a home birth? Where do you live, close to town?"

I feel insulted. Dicken looks at me sternly and says, "Please don't take that on."

We go to Rhione's office nearby. She feels the baby and measures my belly. My fundal height has grown, and she thinks I have as much fluid as before, if not more—she's not too worried. She also thinks the baby feels bigger. I am reassured, trusting her hands and experience, almost wishing I'd never had an ultrasound to begin with. It's created so much fear in me. But I have to admit, it has probably made me drink and rest more than I would have. And I've fallen more deeply in love with this baby than I imagined possible. It looked so adorable on the screen, its little nose and mouth.

I don't have any more mucus secretions; I seem to have dried up at the hospital. I wonder if I stalled the labor process by going into flight-or-fight mode. The medical world is very scary; I'm astounded at how disempowered I felt on that table, immersed in fear and completely cut off from any sense of intuition or wisdom.

January 12
Ten days to due date

At a home visit with the midwife team, including Karen, the homeopath we've asked to be at the birth, Rhione admits some concern. "To be perfectly honest, if it were any other client, I would suggest being closer to town. I just know how much a home birth means to you and have been holding back."

I look out the window at the gray drizzle and wish I could stay here in the warm house for a very long time. But deep inside, I know Rhione is right. I nod, and Dicken reaches for my hand.

"Let's go," I say.

So even though it feels like an upheaval, we repack all the birth supplies and take Jasper with us to town, leaving Maud to pick up Kevin after school.

Maud calls about an hour after we arrive at Mom's house. "I'm worried about Kevin," she says. "I picked him up from school and when I told him you were in town, he burst out crying and said he felt strange." She goes on to say that he went to his room to lie down, and she later convinced him to come to the main house so she could keep a close eye on him. She asked if he wanted to hear some music, and he said he'd like to listen to Bob Marley sing, "*Every little thing is gonna be alright.*" Maud said he seemed calmer but still not himself.

"Can I talk to him?" I ask.

Kevin comes on the phone and says, "I feel kind of weird. I've been hearing voices."

I start reeling and sit down, trying to stay present. Mom sees my distressed face and takes over.

"Oh, I see," I hear her say, "the voices have been telling you things about the baby." I feel a deep sense of shock. I remember how, back in the early days of the pregnancy, Kevin knew I was having a baby before I took the test. Now these voices are telling him I'm going to have the baby this weekend. According to Kevin, they say his name and he doesn't like the way they say it. They speak English to him. It started in England but hasn't happened again until now.

Mom goes to pick him up and bring him here. I feel completely overwhelmed, wondering how I will ever be able to relax and have this baby. *We're going to end up with a Down's baby and a schizophrenic child. My life is fucked up.*

I meditate awhile, telling myself, *Remember what the mystics say, life is all an illusion anyway, a temporary dream.* But my life feels more like a nightmare than a dream right now.

I go to Mom's computer and look online under *children hearing voices*. I feel reassured as I read that it's quite common and usually passes, especially if adults don't make it a big deal. It often happens because of stress around major life changes.

Mom arrives and says she's been telling Kevin about Paul, who had his first "seeing" experience at the same age. She told him that Paul says many of the most amazing people can see or hear things others don't; that the universe is filled with mysteries, things that would love to get our attention.

"I told him he's safe and can ask the voices to go away," Mom tells me. "He said he wasn't sure he wanted them to go away because it was kind of neat to know things before they happen."

Kevin comes into the room, looking a little shell-shocked, vulnerable. I try to act nonchalant. Then he says to me, "Mom, I hope the baby doesn't die. Sometimes babies die, and if ours does, I'm going to cry a lot."

I freeze up. Kevin does not know about the ultrasounds, or my web searches, unless he has overheard something. I will myself to forget what he has just said about the baby dying. It's too much for me to take in right now. I eject it from my mind. The main thing that concerns me is the possibility that Kevin is psychologically disturbed in some way, that this might progress into something that needs treatment.

January 13
Nine days to due date

The next morning, my friend Mary comes over. I immediately tell her about Kevin hearing the voices.

"Wow, that's interesting." She seems genuinely curious, for which I am very grateful. "You know, if he does have some kind of strange energy preying on him, we should send him to this healer I know in town. I sent my grandson to have an entity re-moved and it worked great. I'd be happy to take Kevin for you. You have enough on your plate right now."

I love Mary's unfazed, helpful approach to what seemed so heavy and unmanageable a few minutes ago. I think about Paul and other energy workers we know and realize how fortunate we are to be here in Ashland, where people don't immediately assume kids hearing voices necessitates psychiatric care.

Courtney comes over and I tell her about Kevin's voices. She looks intrigued, and says, "I have a hunch Kevin has a strong psychic connection to this baby, especially since the voices came around the time of the conception, and now the birth."

"It is pretty striking," I say.

"I wonder if Kevin and the baby are karmically linked, that maybe they agreed to be adopted siblings and lined everything up."

I love that my Harvard-educated friend talks about these things as if they were as widely accepted as the law of gravity.

Another of my closest friends, Gabriella, calls to tell me she's been dreaming about the baby every night. "In a dream last night," she says, "the totem animal of the baby became clear to me—the black panther."

"That's funny," I say. "That's the animal Kevin is obsessed with. He talked to me all about it a few months ago, how he saw one once, in the jungle in Costa Rica."

"Well, I'm convinced that's the baby's totem. I even knew I was dreaming, and I asked myself in the dream, *Is this real or is this just a projection of my own stuff?* I was told to go see a shaman in the dream, and he confirmed that yes, this is the baby's totem."

"Wow," I reply, grateful for the attention she's paying to my baby, though not interested enough in totems to think about this much right now.

Meanwhile, it rains again, as it has for weeks now. It seems that all my labors to bring forth children happen in inclement weather—driving rain the night Jasper arrived; the flooding last year in Costa Rica that washed out the roads and kept Kevin and his mom from getting their blood tests. Even Grace was born in a fluke of an early-December snowstorm, and Dicken in a March snowstorm. I'm getting ready for whatever the skies might deliver.

CHAPTER 14

Eight days to due date

Saturday, January 14, brings more rain and dark-gray skies. I spend the morning taking a hot bath and resting. At lunchtime I eat a piece of toast in the kitchen. Dicken sits with me, reading a magazine.

"Look at this," he says, showing me one of the magazine's glossy pages. It's a photograph of a boy with a badly deformed mouth.

"It's an ad for a charity that does cleft surgeries in third world countries. They do each operation for two hundred and fifty dollars."

I don't want to hear about birth defects; it's too close to home right now. But I am reluctant to admit that, afraid Dicken will think I'm being melodramatic. I look down at my plate, hoping he'll change the subject.

"Isn't it crazy?" he goes on. "The surgery is that cheap and a boy his age hasn't had it. He must be, what, eight or nine years old?"

I grunt.

"Hey, what's the name of that actor in the movie we rented the other night, the one who has a scar on his lip?"

"I don't know," I say quickly. "Can we talk about something else?"

We watch the Redskins lose their playoff game in the afternoon. During the game, I notice less movement in the baby and try to ignore it. But by nightfall I am worried and mention it to Dicken.

"Eat something," he suggests. "The baby's probably just low on energy."

I eat a bunch of carob chips, hoping the sugar will have an effect, but nothing changes. My mouth tastes sour and metallic.

At around nine o'clock, I ask Dicken to listen to the baby's heartbeat. The fetoscope feels cold on my belly.

"It's a little bit higher than it's been."

I start to get panicky. Dicken calls Rhione, who suggests we think about going to the hospital to have a tracing. *They'll induce me, I'm sure,* I think, feeling my fear of getting caught in the medical system. But my anxiety about the baby is stronger.

We decide to go in.

We tell Mom our plan, and she jumps into action. "Don't worry, I'll put the boys to bed. Call us when you know something."

I say goodbye to the boys, wondering if the next time I see them will be their introduction to the baby. As we buckle our seatbelts, Dicken tells me Rhione and the other midwives are on their way and will meet us at the hospital.

"I'd hate to be a midwife," Dicken says.

I nod, noticing the cold, dark evening, feeling guilty that the midwives have to drive an hour for what might turn out to be a false alarm.

The rest of the short drive to Ashland Hospital, Dicken and I are quiet. I think about the surly ultrasound technician from the hospital in Grants Pass and pray for a gentle, friendly practitioner.

We park and head into the emergency room, where a man on duty interviews us, then sends us to the birthing ward, a short walk down the hall. We see hardly anyone. The hospital corridors are bright with fluorescent lights but feel deserted.

The birth center is empty except for Sage, the young nurse at the desk. She gives us a warm smile, telling us, "You're the only ones here so far tonight. It's unusually quiet." She looks nervous when I explain that the baby has slowed down, and quickly settles me into a bed and hooks me up to a fetal monitor.

"Ah, a steady heartbeat," she says, smiling. "That's a relief. I'll go get in touch with the doctor who's on call."

Meanwhile, the three midwives arrive. Karen tells me a song came to her while she was driving to the hospital, and she begins to sing quietly, *"Don't worry about a thing, 'cause every little thing is gonna be alright."* It's the Bob Marley song Kevin asked Maud to play for him the day before, when he reported hearing voices talking to him about the baby.

Dr. Moreno, the on-call obstetrician, arrives and looks at the tracing. She frowns and asks Sage, "Is that the baby's heartbeat or hers?"

There is an anxious discussion about the slow heartbeat the machine is reporting, but no one can tell if it's mine or the baby's. Dr. Moreno decides to do an ultrasound. After a few minutes of looking at the screen, she tells us the baby appears to be in distress. She also mentions the small size, her expression grim as she says, "Looks like fetal growth retardation."

She recommends a C-section, then leaves the room so we can decide.

Rhione expresses some puzzlement at the doctor's urgency, wondering why she wouldn't suggest trying to induce labor first. I am shaking hard, and know what I want to do.

"Let's go with the C-section. I can't take any more of this not knowing." I look at the clock. It is eleven thirty. I figure the baby will be born after midnight, making its birthday January 15. *Martin Luther King's birthday.*

The doctor nods when we tell her our decision, and one of the nurses describes what will happen in the rush to get me to surgery. The next ten minutes are spent in a flurry of activity—a nurse hooking me up to an IV, beginning to administer antibiotics and fluids. Someone asking me about my last meal. "I ate about two hours ago. A whole bunch of carob chips. I was trying to get the baby to be more active."

A very pregnant woman comes in. "I'm Jennifer Theone, the family doctor. I'll be in charge of the baby when it's born." She looks at the chart, then says to me, "I've seen lots of small babies, and there's never been a problem. So don't worry too much."

Relief floods me for a moment. *Everything's going to be fine. Let's just get this baby out.* Meanwhile, my whole body is shaking.

Someone explains that I will get a low, horizontal incision, "so you can wear a bikini." I can hardly comprehend the words, they seem so irrelevant. I nod automatically, thinking, *Why in the world would anyone mention a bathing suit at a time like this? How could it ever matter what I look like again?*

The anesthesiologist enters, wearing street clothes. She smiles at me. "I wanted to introduce myself before the surgery," she says. "I'm Kathy." I notice her chic coat, her New York accent. She describes the process I will go through shortly. She calls me "honey," and I like her warmth.

"How many people can go into the OR with her?" Dicken asks.

"Just one."

I look at Dicken and he nods. "Don't worry, I'll be right there with you."

My clothes are removed and I'm put in a papery gown and cap. The nurse tells me to take off my jewelry, so Dicken unclasps my necklace and then struggles to wrest my engagement and wedding bands from my swollen ring finger.

"I can't get these off," he says, a little breathless.

"Don't worry about the rings," the nurse says.

Somehow I am lifted onto a gurney and wheeled into the hall. Dicken tells me he'll get his scrubs on and meet me in the operating room. "I'm going to give your mum a call and let her know what's happening," he adds.

"You're going to be holding your baby soon," someone says to me as I am being wheeled down to the operating room.

"Remember to use your hypnobirthing!" one of the midwives calls after me.

I keep taking long, deep breaths as best I can.

"I'm Jani, the assisting physician," a young woman says, smiling warmly. "You look familiar to me."

I don't recognize her but I nod my head.

"Do you have a child at Willow Wind?"

"Yes," I say. "My son Jasper goes there."

"So does my son," she says.

I smile. I like that so far, the growing team of four doctors and at least as many nurses are all women.

The anesthesiologist, now in her scrubs, greets me again and tells me how to sit on the edge of the table with my back hunched over so she can get a big needle in my spine.

I try to hold myself steady yet I'm still shaking all over. I feel the needle go in but don't flinch or make a sound. I just want this over.

"You're doing so great, sweetheart! I hope it's not hurting you."

"I don't care about any pain," I struggle to say through my chattering teeth. "I just want the baby to be okay."

They have me lie back on the table as my legs and abdomen go numb. Dr. Moreno keeps testing me by poking different places with a sharp tool. One or two of the nurses are constructing a paper tent around me to keep me from seeing the surgery. Dicken is by me with his blue cap on. He takes one of my hands in his. I can hear the doctors getting ready to open me up.

"Well, we've brought children into our lives in three different ways," Dicken tells me. "A home birth, an adoption, and now a C-section."

For some reason this makes me smile, and I relax a little. "Keep talking to me," I tell him.

He does, but then a minute later I feel the pulling sensation as the baby is delivered, and we are both quiet, listening for news, waiting for the outcome.

There is no sound for a while. No baby's cry. Then someone calls out, "We need to get a pediatrician here, right away!"

My heart falls. My upper body begins to shake more violently.

The next hour or so is a blur: "Your baby has an extra finger." "She's pink."

"You mean it's a girl?" I ask, seeing a future with a daughter.

"Oh, I don't know why I said 'she.' It just came out. I didn't look to see what gender it is."

I'm hearing someone say "he." Dicken telling me it's a boy. Me telling Dicken to go over and find out what's happening. "Does he look normal? Is he Down's?"

"He's really small."

Mom appears in a blue surgical cap and coverall. Lots of activity. Faces look serious. No one congratulating me, no one telling me what's happening. Being wheeled into the recovery room. As I leave the operating room, I don't want to look but I do. There's my baby, on the table with an oxygen mask over his face and lots of people leaning over him. The sight of him washes over me, a tug of tenderness, a relaxing, *Oh, he's adorable.* A yearning to hold him, to get this awful period of separation over.

In the recovery room with Mom, I have no concern for my own physical well-being. I hardly notice the nurse taking my vitals, checking my monitors. The fact that I've just undergone the first major surgery of my life couldn't matter less. My attention is on the state of the baby, the vast gulf between me and him, and my not knowing what is going on. I am shaking again, my teeth chattering as if I'm freezing cold, but I don't feel a thing physically.

Dicken comes in, his face serious. "Some of his intestines are in his umbilical cord. And he has a cleft palate."

I imagine a deformed baby. Suddenly I don't want him anymore. I tell myself I don't have it in me to mother a less-than-perfect baby. I'd rather have him die. I wish with all my heart I could go back to April and undo the pregnancy. I kick myself for taking this path. It feels like a complete nightmare. One I can't cope with. One that will ruin my life, Dicken's life. Why can't I ever be happy with what I have? I feel like the dog that goes for the extra bone in the water's reflection and loses the only one he has.

"Can they fix his problems?" I ask.

"Yes, they can do surgery for the palate and the intestines. They're talking about transferring him to Rogue Valley—there's a neonatal unit there."

I think of the magazine ad Dicken showed me earlier today, with the boy and his deformed mouth. *My baby will have the surgery, he'll be fixed.* Then I imagine the parents of children who don't have the security I do, and I feel overwhelmed with sorrow so intense I'm not sure I can withstand it. It is grief for mothers everywhere, and grief for me and my own child, for what is happening in this hospital right now.

Dicken leaves again. My mother is trying to reassure me. I hardly hear her. I'm drowning in thoughts of surgery, separation, drugs pumping into my baby's pristine body, tender newborn skin scarred by scalpels, untold psychological trauma. I wonder if he'll ever be able to breast-feed.

My mother leaves and comes back. She mentions something about the baby's skull, possible brain damage. I feel another layer of reality drop away. I'm spinning in a terrifying vortex.

Dicken returns and tells us of a plan to helicopter the baby to Portland for surgery.

"Can you go with him?" I ask.

"I think so. Yes, of course I will."

He leaves again.

I feel desperate and helpless. I ask my mother, "What's going to happen next?"

"We don't know. We're in the *mysterium tremendum.*"

I'm wheeled into the hospital room. I see the three midwives' faces, their massive concern. Karen puts her hands together in a prayerful gesture and bows at my feet. Rhione says, "Cinda, I honor you." Everything feels so fast, I can't catch my breath. I'm still shaking.

I see Maud's face near me.

"The baby has a lot of problems," I tell her. I'm ashamed: I want to tell people about my perfect baby, not this terrible mess I've created.

Maud looks worried, tells me she knows. She goes into the hall at some point.

I won't remember the next period of time. Only the moment Dicken and Maud come into the room, their faces grim, eyes downcast. I know the news is horrendous. I am afraid of what Dicken will say, and I'm distressed for him, knowing he doesn't want to have to tell me.

He kneels down by me. "Did he die?" I ask. He shakes his head. I envision the worst kind of handicap, a long life of disfiguration, surgeries, drugs, mental retardation, adult foster care, and on and on. I see an endless tunnel, an existence dark and meaningless and against everything we believe in. I see ruin. Human ruin, family ruin.

"The baby has some serious challenges," he begins. He tells me the team suspects trisomy 13. I flash back to a piece I read on the Internet about trisomy 13, the list of problems, how I skipped over it without resting on the possibility because it was too dreadful. "These babies don't live long," Dicken says, breaking into choked sobs. I reach for him, reassuring him with my hands as best I can given my limited strength and mobility.

"We have a decision to make," Dicken says, when he can speak again. He manages to tell me about the option of sending the baby to Portland for testing, then possible surgery; the poor odds. "They may not be able to stabilize him—they can't get a breathing tube in his mouth because of the cleft palate. If he does have trisomy 13, which they will do a blood test for, they won't operate because the chances of survival are so slim."

I know right away we are not going to put our baby through all that.

"We have to let him go," I hear myself say. Dicken nods, begins to sob again. I reach for him, and everything in me wants him to know there is nothing wrong. We are facing a terrible loss, but at the same time I am filled with a strange certainty that all is unfolding in some sort of natural perfection. Compared to the terror my mind has been putting me through, this eventuality is so simple, so clear. To me, that clarity is a gift, even though what we are dealing with is the most difficult news I've ever had to confront.

Something in me relaxes—the part of me that was clenched in the face of the unknown. Now that there is a definite out-come, an end in sight, I am flooded with relief. I hope that it happens quickly, that we get to the end once and for all. "How long will he last?" I ask.

"They don't know. Could be minutes, could be days."

When I see that Dicken has regained his composure, my re-lief vanishes, and I go cold with fear. It's as if we are switching places, one gathering strength as the other wavers.

"I don't want to see the baby," I tell Dicken. I am scared of what he will look like and how that will affect me. I don't believe I can love him. I want this loving husband and father to carry his son through life and death. *Dicken is strong, he can do it. It's better if I never see him.*

"Take him and hold him until he dies," I tell Dicken. I am worried that I'll reject him. I don't yet know the difference between a cleft palate and a cleft lip and imagine a deformed, grotesque-looking baby. I'm afraid that if I do see him and feel a connection, letting him die will be beyond my ability to endure. I just want the whole thing to go away. I think that if I don't see him, I can forget the pregnancy and birth and go on as if none of it ever happened.

Dicken looks at me with a serious face. I tell myself that he will do whatever I ask, that he will stick to his birth philosophy of always honoring the mother's requests, without question. "Honey," he says very gently but firmly. When I see that he isn't just going to turn around and do what I've asked, I steel my-self to make him comply. "You're his mother. He knows you. He needs you now. I think you should hold him."

In that instant I know he is right, and I nod.

Dicken goes to see the doctors. I am overwhelmed and agitated. This has brought an end to the terror, but the sudden change in direction is making the world spin.

Mom comes in, still in her scrubs. She's been with the baby ever since I was wheeled out of recovery. When I was eight months along, I dreamed I had a beautiful baby boy, and just after the birth he looked up at Mom and said, *That my Nana, again?* It makes me think now that he knew her, and I imagine he recognized her when she came to him during the hour after he was born, when she was the only family member with him. Knowing that she has been with him, touching him, talking to him, welcoming him, giving him her unconditional love, is a great solace. I'll always be grateful to her for following her instinct to get to the hospital right away, talking her way into the operating room, and managing to get herself on the resuscitation team for that period of time just before they diagnosed him.

"He's so adorable!" Mom tells me. "And he's a real fighter. He keeps trying to pull off the oxygen mask. He looks just like Jabu. Oh, his chest, it's so beautiful!"

This message and my mother's softness and love melt me, and I feel a tiny surge of confidence. *I can love this baby.* Hope stirs in me. Then heartrending dread. A bittersweet burst of emotion. *He's cute, what a relief. But oh, what a waste.*

A hush comes over the room as a nurse brings my newborn son to me. I reach out for him. The nurse places him in the crook of my left arm. I look at him, and time stops.

There is no fear, no horror, no sense that anything is wrong. I am in a state of complete bliss, marveling at the wonder of this being. Thoughts stop. I'm no longer shaking. I look into his eyes, and he sees me and gives me a look of recognition, almost a smile. He is swaddled in a white blanket and wearing a soft white cap on his head. My beautiful, beautiful son, my baby, my love. His mouth is perfect-looking, everything is, and he has stunning dark blue eyes. A little like Jasper, a little like Dicken. I would never guess from seeing his face that he has any physical problems. Yet in the instant I meet him I know I'd love him even if his face were deformed.

I'm amazed at him. My sister will tell me later that I speak to him with loving words, reminding her of how I spoke to Jasper when he was first placed in my arms.

"The doctor says you can try to nurse him."

I position his face next to my nipple. He tries to mouth it, makes a distressed face and a small cry like a wounded baby bird. He seems to be struggling for breath. I feel desperate to help him in that moment, a searing stab of anguish I can't contain. Then he turns his head away from my nipple and puts his tiny fist in his mouth instead. He seems to have soothed himself. He doesn't show another sign of pain or distress for the rest of his life.

"We need to name him quickly, don't you think?" I say to Dicken.

He nods.

"Theodore," I say, the name coming out of my mouth without thought.

Dicken nods. "That's his name."

"Theodore Simon," I say.

"Yes. Theodore Simon."

Theodore came up during the pregnancy but was never high on the list. I know it means "gift from God." Simon is Dicken's father's name, and Jasper's middle name. Jasper has asked us if he and the baby can share middle names.

My stepfather Ralph arrives with Jasper and Kevin. Ralph hangs in the background, but the boys come over quickly, looking at their brother with wide eyes.

"Do you know he's not well?" I ask Jasper. He nods gravely.

As Jasper stands near us, the baby stretches his arm out, as if he's reaching for his brother. Jasper moves closer and strokes Theo's hand. His eyes grow wide as he discovers the extra finger, a tiny appendage next to his pinky. At first he seems a little taken aback, and I wonder if he's frightened.

"Look, Mom! He has six fingers." He touches the baby's hand with a look of awe and says, "It's his lucky finger!"

Jasper and Kevin kiss the baby, stroke his face gently.

Then Theo closes his eyes and stops breathing for what seems like a long time. He begins to turn pale.

"I think this is it," I tell Dicken.

Dicken comes over and touches Theo, beginning to sob.

"It's okay to let go," I tell the baby. "We'll always love you."

Theo suddenly takes a big breath and opens his eyes again.

Gabriella arrives, camera equipment in hand. We had asked her to film the home birth, so she had her gear ready to go. I introduce her to the baby and ask her to be his godmother. She smiles, tears falling down her face. A few minutes later, Tom, Grace, and Sam arrive. I'm happy Theo has made it long enough to meet his cousins. Tom hands Sam to Dicken, who holds him up to the bed so he can see the baby. Sam kisses me. Grace smiles at Theo, gently touches his face.

I ask Dicken if he wants to hold Theo, and he nods, then takes him from me, cradling him carefully in his large hands. They gaze at each other with a sense of awe and ease, like old friends meeting after a long, long time. It reminds me of watching Dicken hold Jasper for the first time, only Theo seems more awake than Jasper was. I ask Gabriella to film it. She gets out her camera.

When the baby comes back to me, I look at him and wonder how long he will be with us. I will stay awake as many hours and days as he's here. I have no sense of physical limitations, no tiredness. I don't know what time it is, whether it's day or night, winter or summer, whether we are on earth or on the moon. Nothing matters but loving this baby.

I know that all I have to do is love him and let him go. That is crystal clear. Everything else falls away. Loving like this is the purest, most powerful experience I've ever had. Overwhelmingly beautiful. I have to love him but I can't hold onto him. I can't cling, can't go into stories about what I would do if I ever lost him—I've already lost him. I can see the inevitable and relax into cherishing him while he is here. The intensity of this birth and death brings me into a presence I have never known. No fear, no doubt, no suffering. Maybe part of me is going through some of that, but my attention is elsewhere, on the pure love blasting through everything. The light is so bright that my personality, my physical self, and the drama of what is happening won't show up on Gabriella's film.

Theo closes his eyes, makes a fist, and stops breathing. I watch him get pale. I focus myself on him fully, telling him I love him and that it's okay for him to go. I don't grasp, don't want it any other way. I am so caught up in the unfoldment, I am almost willing it to happen. I hear Dicken say, "Godspeed on your journey," as he gently touches Theo's forehead. The baby is quiet, doesn't take another breath. A nurse comes in and listens to his heart with her small stethoscope. She says she can hear a heartbeat but it is faint. "I don't think it will be long now." A few minutes later she listens again and nods. "He's gone." She looks at her watch to note the time—5:14 a.m., almost five hours after his birth.

Dicken sobs. Grace wails. The room fills with raw expressions of grief. I hold onto Dicken, trying to comfort him with my limited physical mobility, trying not to tangle the tubes in my arm. His cries go straight through me: they are almost unbearable. At the same time, I am overcome with a feeling of peace. I hold Theo, touch his face, continue to bask in love for him.

I wait for the nurse to tell us what they will do with his body, expecting that soon we'll have to turn it over for whatever they need to do. Someone, maybe me, maybe Dicken, asks the nurse about the protocol. I steel myself to have to say goodbye and hand him over. I know I won't resist. There is nothing hard in me. I am completely soft, pounded into full surrender.

The nurse says, "You can keep him for as long as you like."

Relief floods me. I can hardly believe it. I gather the bundle of him and his blankets as close to me as I can, breathing in his baby smell, wishing I could press him through the boundary of my own skin and into my cells forever.

Dicken sobs and I hold him. I sob and he holds me. Again there seems to be a natural rhythm, one of us in despair, the other one there to support. We cling to each other after everyone has gone, looking at our baby son together.

At some point, all the ways I've resisted what was happening, all the rejection I've felt, it all fills me and I begin to shake. Then I am crying hysterically.

"What is it?" Dicken asks. "Are you in pain?"

I shake my head. "I have some terrible things to confess," I say, when I can speak. I take a big breath. "I didn't want to see him. I didn't want a baby with problems. I was happy when you told me he was going to die. Part of me was hoping he would."

The horror of it fills me as I look at my beautiful baby and hold him and wish I could take back all the hurtful things I'd thought. The guilt is crushing. I sob so hard I can't breathe.

"Of course you felt all that," Dicken says, gathering me into his arms. "It was all so intense. But you loved him, you loved him so much, and he knew that."

"But I was relieved when I heard he would die! What kind of a mother am I?"

"You just wanted to know it would all be over soon. You went through so much. And you were there for him when he needed you. That's what counts, not the brief moments of fear and doubt."

I cry even harder now, from the release, the relief, the comfort of being held in Dicken's loving arms, and the sadness bound up in all I've been keeping in. I weep for a long time.

Overlaying all the feelings of heartbreak and pain and shock and amazement, there is a palpable state of grace we both marvel at. It is similar to the way we felt the night Jasper was born. An exhausted relief mingled with a joy so profound it's indescribable. Yet the sadness is so intense, I wonder if I will actually survive it.

I cry on and off through the night. Much of the time tears just slide out continuously, and I get so used to them I hardly notice. It is not always painful, not always attached to sadness. It's a gentle and continual release, like someone is washing my face. Sometimes a violent surge comes over me like a strange, uncontrollable force outside myself, and I have to let it take over. Then the sounds that come out of me are nothing I recognize. They are animal-like, emerging from deep within. At times I'm feel like I'm falling, and I desperately cling to Dicken. Neither of us sleeps.

Between bouts of tears, we rest in the silence together and watch the sky gradually grow light. It becomes a gorgeous sunny morning after a night of light snow, the first day the sun has truly come out in ages. It has been raining, snowing, flooding for weeks and weeks. I remember how a few days earlier, in honor of all the precipitation, we'd considered the name Noah, which I will later learn, like Theodore, means "gift from God."

In the early morning, Dicken calls his mother, who is at a conference in Arizona. She knows nothing of what has happened, and is planning to fly to us later that day, expecting to be with us for the birth. When Dicken reaches her at her hotel, she is awake, getting packed and ready for her flight. Dicken tells her the news, breaking down between words. "Mum, I held him for a long time and we looked into each other's eyes that whole time. He was so beautiful."

Later, she will tell us that as soon as she heard, she noticed an enormous light filling the room she was in. She couldn't get over it, and still describes the light as huge and undeniably real. When she saw that light, she says, she knew the baby was an astonishing being. She will also tell us that she'd been crying on and off for the past couple of days without knowing why. At the exact time of Theo's death, she'd gone into the bathroom of her shared hotel room (not wanting to wake her roommate) and cried her eyes out. She wondered if it was some unresolved grief but couldn't identify anything specific. "I just howled and howled," she will tell us. "It was very odd."

The nurse says they will need to take the baby for a short time to measure him and photograph his body for their records. They ask us if it's okay to bathe him, and we say yes. I miss him dreadfully while he is gone and hold tightly to Dicken.

The nurses bring him back dressed in a shiny white outfit with lace trim and a tiny lavender flower. They tell us he weighs five pounds, fourteen ounces. They give us a pretty white box with a stuffed bear, a necklace set with a small ceramic heart that fits into a larger one, a birth certificate and a death certificate, both with Theo's footprints in ink, and materials on grief and on trisomy 13, which they suggest we read later, when we feel stronger. They tell us there are Polaroid photographs of Theo's unwrapped body in the box. One of the nurses has run home to borrow her husband's digital camera so we can take our own pictures of Theo. Later, she will print them up for us at home and bring us copies.

Maud comes back early in the morning, her eyes red, her face puffy and tired-looking. She brings me a brush, and she and Grace help get the tangles out of my hair.

Visitors stream in and out all day, bringing flowers and cards. Almost all of them, especially the children, want to hold Theo. His body is cool but still soft. Several people comment that he looks just like a sleeping baby.

The phone in our room rings. Dicken answers it, listens, whispers for a moment, then puts his hand over the receiver and tells me it's my brother, Ben. I nod and he hands me the phone.

At first all I can hear is Ben sobbing, then choking out, "I'm so sorry, Cinda." More sobbing. Then, "When Cec called me, she was crying so hard she couldn't tell me what happened. All she said was, *It's Cinda.*" He breaks down again. "I thought it was you, that you had . . ." He cries some more, and I cry too. Then he composes himself and asks if they're giving me any drugs.

"I think there's a painkiller in my drip," I tell him. "And they're offering me something strong, morphine maybe, but I'm too numb to need anything."

"Well, save some of the good stuff for me," he says, and I find myself laughing.

Ralph visits. "Theo was so lucky," he says. "He had the ideal life, held in his mother's arms the whole time. What more could anyone ask for?"

Ralph sits by our bed and reads us the words of his guru, Paramahansa Yogananda: *"Though the ordinary man looks upon death with dread and sadness, those who have gone before know it as a wondrous experience of peace and freedom."* This washes through me without starting any analysis or evaluation in my mind. I've read and heard Yogananda for years, and for the first time in my life, I know these words as truth, rather than just hearing the ideas and hoping they're true.

Time seems to stop and expand into a huge white space. I have very little mental activity. It is like sitting in a vast nothingness. I can't even begin to consider reading, listening to music, or thinking of anything past or future. For days this will be the case. I can only be with people, talking and listening, even laughing occasionally, or sit blankly, or cry. I have very little interest in food, and it takes severe hunger pains to remind me to eat.

I've found myself in a state that is weightless, as if I've dropped every ounce, surrendered everything I've been carrying, even things I didn't realize had weight, like unarticulated worries, attention on others, memories, thoughts. Being in this nothingness, this all-ness, is effortless, peaceful. A paradox of emptiness and fullness. And now that I'm here, I see how much energy I've wasted in my life, worrying that I didn't have this in me, that it would take more discipline and effort than I was capable of to see truth so purely. I woke up when I had to, when I knew Theo would die, and then everything in me became love.

I hope I don't go back to sleep, but I know it's okay if I do. When I need to, I will awake again. None of our life is truly wasted. We will always land here in the end.

Paul sits with us and says, "You're both profoundly changed forever." His wife, Patty, a former nurse-midwife, can't get over what a beautiful baby Theo is. She says, "If you'd had an amnio, you'd never have had this incredible experience of change."

Dr. Moreno comes in to check on me. She holds my hand and asks how I'm doing. Through choked tears, I tell her how grateful I am that she recommended the C-section, that she got our baby out in time for us to meet him and be with him for those irreplaceable hours. She nods solemnly, her eyes blinking open and shut with emphasis, making me wonder if she is uncomfortable.

Just then, Sam bursts into the room. "Tia! The nurses gave me a quacka!"

Dr. Moreno smiles and tells me, "My nieces and nephews call me Tia." I wonder if she has her own children but don't ask.

Jennifer, the pregnant family doctor, comes in and tells me how sorry she is that she reassured me before the surgery that the baby would be okay. "I've never delivered a trisomy baby," she says.

I tell her I understand and that her words helped calm me down, even though they didn't turn out to be true. I ask when she's due. "Next week," she says. I smile, feeling nothing but sweetness for this kind doctor and her soon-to-be-born baby.

Kathy, the anesthesiologist, comes in and can't speak at first because she is crying. I show her Theo, introduce her to him. I thank her for being so warm, and tell her she made all the difference.

"You can have another one, right?" she asks, her voice thick with emotion.

Without thinking about it, I shake my head. Then I say, "Well, who knows. I guess we'll have to wait and see."

I cry my eyes out all that day but never lose touch with how graced I feel. Looking at Theo's angelic, peaceful face makes me weep, mostly with a sense of awe and gratitude. I'm also aware of a new force pushing up from the depths of me. Gradually, I am starting to feel the longing for what I know I can never have back.

A friend arrives with cups of coffee from Dutch Brothers, and they smell good. My first thought is, *Too bad I can't have any,* because I'm thinking I need to keep my breast milk pure for the baby. When I realize my error, I sob. I don't want the coffee after all.

These two days in the hospital, I almost always burst into tears at the sight of anyone I haven't seen yet. I cry on the phone to my father, my brother, friends. I cry when I see what we have been through reflected in their eyes, their voices. But I'm not just crying from sadness. I am moved by everyone, their love for us, their every gesture. It's like I'm seeing them without any filters, and their beauty is astonishing.

Dicken's mother Caroline arrives. I feel a strange sense of pride as I show her Theo and watch her tenderly take him into her arms. She looks at him, smiling and wiping tears from her face. Then she comments on the light in the room. "The angel of birth is here, and so is the angel of death. No wonder this place feels so heavenly."

We discuss Theo's features, noting the family traits he seems to have inherited. "He's got the Edgecumb hook nose," Caroline says. "A big nose for such a little face." I remember that she said the same thing about Jasper when he was born, and again feel slightly defensive about my baby's looks, even though I know that in Theo's case the size of his nose will not shape his future. *It doesn't matter*, I tell myself. But it does. *This is my baby and he is perfect.*

Karen, who years ago lost her own baby boy to trisomy 18, leads a beautiful blessing ceremony that afternoon. Midwives, friends, nurses, and family crowd into the small room. All the family members dip flannel pieces into rose water and lavender oil and anoint Theo's body.

Grace tries to sing "The Rabbit Song" and keeps bursting into tears. We wait each time and she finally gets the words out in her sweet voice:

> *Oh the racing of the moon and the rising of the sun*
> *These flowers green and tall must go the way of all*
> *And winter comes too soon . . .*
> *Oh the sparrows in the sky and the dragons in the sea*
> *In mad or merry weather we'll take a rest together*
> *Under the apple tree . . .*

Later, Karen sits with us and tells us the story of her son Juniper, who was born with trisomy 18 and lived for a number of days. "What a blessing he was," she says, eyes shining. I can't help but note the strange fact that both Karen and Rhione, whose son Jared died three years before, have lost their third child, like me. *What are the odds? Did everything line up this way so that our birth team could support us through this experience with the most powerful form of compassion?*

Kevin looks at Theo and says, "It's such a shame he didn't stay around longer." Jasper clings to Dicken.

Several members of the Threshold Choir come by. *You are loved*, they sing, and I sob. It feels very odd to be on the receiving side of the choir's offerings.

The Megaritys, very close family friends, arrive at some point. Shannon, Dicken's fishing buddy, is carrying a huge platter of halibut he's cooked. His face is so intense that it touches me, makes me want to reassure him. Angie is wiping away tears. I show her Theo, and she smiles. She takes him and we gaze at him together. Shannon gently cradles Theo in his big arms, looking down at him. Their kids and Courtney's are eager to hold Theo. I'm amazed at their lack of fear.

Throughout our days at the hospital, the handful of children coming in and out flit between crying, laughing, playing, holding Theo, asking the nurses for sweets, and testing various medical devices. Sometimes they fight over whose turn it is to hold Theo. Grace and Rosie agree that he smells like cookies and cream. I think it's the lavender oil we used to anoint him during Karen's ceremony.

Whenever I break down, Dicken rushes to hold me. I feel utterly dependent on him. When he leaves the room to talk to someone on his cell phone, I get agitated and panicky, and wheel my IV machine into the hall to find him.

Holding Theo is bittersweet. I love being able to hold him tight, to feel his comforting weight in my arms, to gaze at his features, which were a mystery for so long. He smells delicious. We dress him in the purple sweater Maud has been knitting for the last month. Some of the time I feel almost normal, as if I'm holding a live baby I've just given birth to, one who will wake up any moment and need to be nursed. But then reality grabs me, and knowing we will have to let him go, watching his lips begin to dry up—it all rips at my heart, and another wave of sobbing begins.

One of the nurses brings us a container of lip salve for Theo, and I put it on his cool, crackly lips. I repeat this every so often. I like being able to take care of him this way. It is one of the only tangible acts of mothering I will get to do.

I don't notice anything about my body or the recovery from

surgery. As the nurses come to check my vitals every few hours, look at my incision, ask about pain levels, put my feet in a strange pulsing machine to increase circulation at night, and so on, I keep thinking they're making an unnecessary fuss. All of my attention is on Theo. The rest of life, even my physical survival, seems completely irrelevant. My pain level is always below five on a scale of one to ten. I get off the opiates the first day, then stop the ibuprofen. Everyone keeps telling me to "keep on top of the pain," meaning I should take a painkiller before things get bad, but I prefer to get off all medication as soon as possible. I want to be pure and clearheaded through all of this. I feel crushed yet at the same time invincible.

And through it all, I am aware of a deep feeling of gratitude to the doctors and nurses for their training and knowledge, to modern medicine for how this birth has unfolded, and to each person for their sensitivity and kindness. It's as if I am above everything, looking down at the thousandfold actions and paths that have led these people here, from their youthful aspirations to become medical professionals to the classes they had to take, to the years of training and licensing requirements, job placement and scheduling, all the way to the moment I checked into the birth center, and then through the surgery and its physical aftermath, all smooth and relatively painless. I am aware of medical progress over decades, research and practice and honing that have led to low-risk surgeries like mine. I know it is a miracle and a luxury that I don't have to suffer physically, that my loved ones don't have to see me in pain or worry about my survival. I know that in many parts of the world today this C-section wouldn't have been possible, and that in other places right now and almost anywhere in relatively recent times, childbirth itself was and is a gamble; in another time or place, I could easily have contracted an infection and died.

Because of my good fortune—not only the modern expertise available to me but also the empathic skills, the presence of these openhearted medical people—we can forget the physical

and pay full attention to Theo, to love, to the cataclysmic events
of the heart.

CHAPTER 15

January 16

Theo was born early Sunday morning. By Monday evening, Dr. Moreno says I am medically stable enough to go home the next day. I don't want to go. I want to stay in this beautiful place with Dicken and our beloved son forever. I can't imagine life anywhere else. I do not know what awaits me beyond here. I don't want to know. I don't care.

Dr. Moreno asks me if we've decided what we are going to do with Theo's body. I sense some pressure, maybe even judgment from her, as if there is something strange about us having Theo's body for so long. I feel rushed. She is urging me to move on, and I don't feel ready.

Someone, Mom I think, makes arrangements with a funeral home to have Theo cremated on Tuesday. Monday night, I don't sleep at all. I just hold Theo and look at him and cry until I'm exhausted. The nurses bring me ice packs to hold over my eyes, which are almost swollen shut. In the morning I will look in the mirror for the first time and hardly recognize myself. I will see red blotches all over a pale face, grossly puffy eyes, and a pair of irises rimmed by rainbow blue-green-gold kaleidoscopes like windows that go on forever, empty and weightless, haunting.

January 17

As the sky grows light Tuesday morning, dread spreads through me. I cry and tell Dicken I can't bear to let Theo's body go. Can't we wait another day? His lips are drying up, but other than that his body doesn't seem to be in bad shape at all. Lots of people, nurses included, comment on how amazing it is that he isn't visibly decomposing. His cheeks are still pink, his skin still cool and soft. I kiss him so much my own lips begin to dry up. It seems unbearable to leave the hospital and go straight to the crematorium.

Dicken consults with Mom and tells me it is fine to keep him at her house for one night, then cremate him on Wednesday. That feels right to me. Big relief.

As we get ready to leave the hospital, I put the maternity clothes I'd worn there back on. The pants are loose now. Maud, who has come to help us, our friend Amy, Dicken, and I hold hands in a circle and close our eyes as Dicken says a prayer of gratitude. He asks for strength as we go forward. We gather our things, mostly cards, flowers, and the box the nurses gave us. I carry Theo bundled in blankets; closest to his body is the white one he has worn since the moment I first held him. Before leaving the ward, I walk down the hall to look into the operating room, now empty.

"That's where you were born," I tell Theo, tears welling.

I say goodbye to the nurses and we head down the hall. Holding my bundle just like any new mother would hold a baby, I hope no well-wishing stranger will come up and want a glimpse of him. No one does.

Halfway down the hallway, Sage, the sweet nurse who checked us in that first night, comes running up behind us. "I just heard you were leaving, and I want to walk you out!"

On the curb, as we wait for Dicken to bring the car around, Sage takes my hands in hers and looks into my eyes. She tells me that her mother died when she was twelve. "I never saw her body, and no one helped me mourn," she says, her eyes filling with tears. "It was amazing to watch you and your family with Theo. It's helped me more than I can say."

Dicken has moved the car seat from the middle seat, where it was strapped in, waiting for the baby, to the rear, where it now lies on its side. We get to Mom's. I climb into bed while Dicken unpacks our things and makes an altar of flowers, candles, cards. I hold Theo's body close to me constantly. I keep looking at his sweet hands, the tiny extra fingers I've grown to adore. I run my fingers over and over the tufts of fine blond hair on his head. I put my face next to his and memorize the feel of his cool cheeks.

Again, I hardly sleep that night, knowing these are our last hours with his body. It is a vigil, like falling into a sea of stars, as wide open as a universe, full of the shards of my heart, full of love and awe and gratitude. I've fallen completely in love, and at the same time the boundaries of my world have been blown off. I am experiencing more emotional intensity than I've ever imagined. I can't contain it: it is containing me, everything I am, have ever been, will ever be. A bursting, painful, ecstatic feeling all at once, and endless.

January 18

The morning of the cremation, Dicken and I decide to unwrap Theo so that we can wash and bless his whole body. Cecily, Maud, and Caroline join us as we bathe him in lavender water. I kiss every part of him, except his diaper-covered bottom and penis, because the diaper is stuck to him and won't come off. I look closely at the marks on the back of his scalp, the slightly misshapen ears, his lovely broad chest, long skinny legs, tiny toes. I apologize to each part for my reluctance to love it at first. I see them all with utter beauty now. I think of Mother Theresa saying she worshipped God in his most wretched disguises. Your wretched body, Theo, is the most splendid temple I have ever beheld.

Dicken kisses Theo tenderly. My tears fall on his little body.

"You don't know what you're missing," I tell Theo, my voice suddenly bitter. "You had such an amazing dad waiting for you."

We pick out an outfit from the diaper bag we took to the hospital—a white baby-grow, an orange wool sweater and matching hat with a velvet ribbon. Tiny white socks. I dress him carefully. I take out the necklace set the nurses gave us, two chains, each with a white ceramic heart. The two hearts fit together, the smaller one resting inside a larger one just like it. I pull the hearts apart, putting the small necklace on Theo, the larger one on myself.

This is surreal, I think as we head down the road into town. *Dicken and I are driving to the funeral home to cremate our son.* I hold Theo's body close, inhale his smell, kiss his cool soft forehead and cheeks again and again, wanting to kiss him a thousand times so that I'll never forget the feel of his skin on my lips. He is wrapped again in the white hospital blanket. We pull into a parking lot that I've seen countless times on our drives through Ashland but never really looked at before.

I force my legs to take one step at a time, and then I find myself inside the funeral home, hearing Cecily and Michal's CD of "Mere Gurudev" playing in the background, seeing family and friends dressed up and looking sweet and solemn. I break down and fall into Mom's embrace, unsure whether I can stand. I let my mother hold me in a way I have not let her since I was a very small child. The muscles in my legs seem to be dissolving, and for a moment I wonder if I will collapse onto the floor. But the kids rally around me, reach up with their soft hands to wipe tears from my face, and I stand firmer.

We sit and wait. Maud holds my hand. Kevin sits with Caroline. Jasper climbs into Dicken's lap. I stare at Theo, touch his skin with my fingers, kiss his head over and over. I think of how long it took to build his body, all those long months of sickness and effort to get the right foods and supplements, enough water and sleep and exercise. Now his form—perfect, even with so many wounds—will go back to ashes, to almost nothing, within hours. It makes me think of those beautiful sand paintings Tibetan monks make and then destroy to remind them of the impermanence of life, of matter.

Lots of tears, then relief: the process is being held up by a last-minute run for our doctor's signature. I hope they can't find the doctor. I would be happy to sit here forever. Then that moment when we hear the call—*It's time*—and the funeral director telling me this—the babies, the children—is the part of his job he dreads the most.

Picking out an urn, choosing the green one because it's one of my favorite colors, because I have to choose something even though it doesn't matter. Putting one foot in front of the other out into the parking lot and to the small cement room out back. A few friends and family following us. The air must be cold but I feel nothing. Jasper bravely carrying his brother's body to the kiln-like, industrial crematorium. Looking at Theo one last time. His face is as smooth, as lovely as ever. Final kiss. Despair. Dicken moving more solidly. His hand opening the door of the stove. Me frozen. Part of me wants to tell him to stop, to slow down, to drag this out. Another part of me is grateful he can move at all, knowing if we slow down, we may not be able to do this, to say goodbye and put our son's body in a furnace. Grace in distress, protesting, "No, they can't put him in there! They can't burn him!" Jasper reassuring her, "Grace, it's okay. It's just like a hot sauna, that's all." Dicken placing Theo's white-wrapped body into the stove, which is just beginning to heat; closing the door, his voice breaking as he says, "Godspeed on your journey, son." The funeral director turns up the furnace. I feel the rush of heat, hear the sound of the heavy door sealing shut. I turn away. It's over.

Dicken breaking down in sobs. Holding his chest. The relief I'd hoped for doesn't come. I look around for something to anchor me, something to focus on so I don't fall. Cecily takes me in her arms and I almost collapse. People are hugging me but I am stiffening. My feet feel like lead. I want desperately to get out of this moment, out of this awful cement building, but how can I move, and where can I go? I look to Dicken but his face is grim, his eyes too dark to connect with. Mom and Ralph begin to chant, "Om." I'm uncomfortable, desperate to move away from all this.

"I need to leave," I tell Dicken.

His face changes, comes into focus again, maybe because I've given him a purpose. He puts his arm around me and guides me out into the parking lot. Our friends Angie and Shannon follow. They are saying things to me but I can't understand their words.

I stand in the parking lot. Changed forever. The sky is gray, the world unfamiliar. He is gone, the body I've been clinging to for three days is burning up in a furnace of flames. The hard part has begun.

Back to Mom's house. Empty and stunned, hardly able to move. Into bed, grasping Theo's purple sweater and the white teddy bear the nurses gave us.

That night, I get up to go to the bathroom and as I stand after peeing, the familiar energy coils up in my spine, about to unleash itself. I take a step and it blasts up my spine in huge shivers.

"Theo, help me!" I cry out. I don't think about it; it's reflexive. The observer part of me smiles, touched that I now have a connection to the other world, someone to pray to.

Dicken rushes in. He gets me into bed and brings extra blankets. I don't feel as terrified this time, now that I know my strength. Or maybe because I sense the opposite—my nothingness, and how quickly I'm able to relocate Theo and reach out for him. I surrender to the process, hoping it will be over quickly.

Maud, who is sleeping in the fold-out bed nearby, hears the commotion and asks Dicken what's happening. I am fully aware of their conversation, though my whole being is absorbed in the intensity of the convulsions.

"She's having another episode," Dicken says.

"Why is she shaking so much?"

"She goes into shock. It usually passes after a few minutes."

"I think she has a breast infection," Maud says with concern. "When I had mine I got chills like that."

My milk came in today, so my breasts are full and achy.

Dicken puts his hand on my forehead. "She doesn't feel hot. I doubt she has a fever."

"I'm freezing, not hot," I manage to say through my chattering teeth. The blankets don't seem to be doing much.

After a while, everything calms down. I can't sleep and find myself sobbing, that strange, throbbing cry I'd never heard before Theo, but now know well. Dicken takes me into his arms.

January 19

In the morning, Maud comes to see how I am. "That was really intense," she says.

It takes me a moment to realize she means the episode in the night.

"Your poor breasts," Maud says, breaking into tears. "It seems so unfair."

I look down at my enormous, bursting chest. I feel a strong, primal desire to feed a baby, and my breasts respond, the milk rushing through the ducts. Some of it begins to leak onto my shirt, creating a round stain. I don't mind it. It is something Theo and I have created together, a physical link. What makes me break down is thinking about the time ahead, when my breasts are empty. I resist wearing the cabbage leaves and tightly bound bandages my midwives have recommended to stop the flow, even though I know I am risking infection. I wish I knew a baby who needed breast milk. I rack my brain for any friend who wouldn't be freaked out by the idea. Maud and I offer Sam my milk, but he shies away. I would happily wet-nurse or even pump for another baby. I come close to asking my midwives but sense that someone would have suggested the idea if it had been appropriate.

My father calls and cries on the phone. "I miss my mum at a time like this," he tells me.

"I know," I say, thinking of my sweet grandmother and the daughter she had, Jill, who died of a heart defect at ten weeks old. "There's so much I wish I could ask her now."

"Please tell me what I can do to help you," Dad says, his voice cracking. "I feel so helpless and far away."

I think for a few moments, *What do I really want?* and then I know.

"Dad, can you organize a memorial fund in Theo's honor? People are asking what they can do, and we really don't need any more flowers."

"Okay, I'd be happy to do that. What kind of fund are you thinking of?"

"Well, when I was in the recovery room, getting the early news about Theo, I knew we'd get the best medical care available. At first we thought it was just a few cosmetic defects, the extra finger, the cleft palate. Dicken assured me the surgeons could fix all that, no problem. So, there we were in the middle of the night, with teams of neonatal specialists ready to go, a helicopter waiting to take him to Portland. I felt the luxury of not having to worry about how we'd afford whatever it would take to help Theo. I had such a sense of massive relief knowing all those surgical teams were at our service. I've never felt so helpless, and so grateful for medicine, for people willing to help my child."

"So, you want the donations to go to a hospital?"

"No, I was thinking about this ad Dicken showed me the other day, about a charity that helps third world children who need cleft surgeries. I just feel so deeply sad for mothers who can't help their children . . ." I start to cry.

"Okay," Dad says. "Consider it done."

At some point that day, Maud comes to me and seems eager to tell me about something.

"It's Laura," she says.

Laura is a midwife and friend of Rhione's who lives close to Ashland Hospital. Maud explains that after Theo died, Rhione wanted to stay nearby and not drive all the way out to her home an hour away. She has an open invitation to stay in Laura's studio in back of her house, so she went there. Laura happened to be sleeping in the studio, and the sound of Rhione opening the door woke her from a dream. In the dream she found herself calling out to a man, a "high soul" who was curled up in the fetal position. The name she was calling was "Theo."

"Theo . . . Theo . . ." Over and over she called to him, telling him to come back to Oregon from New York, but he wouldn't listen. When Rhione woke her up, Laura didn't know I'd had the baby, didn't know whether it was a boy or girl, didn't know anything. And she could not have known that we were considering the name Theo.

I am stunned and thrilled at this news of Laura's dream. Warmth floods me like a sudden recognition. I call Gabriella, who is as moved and astonished as I am.

"It just keeps getting clearer and clearer," she says. "Wait'll you hear what I found on the web. I'll have to read it to you over the phone."

Because of the dream she had before Theo was born, the one about the baby's totem being the black panther, Gabriella did some web research and printed out a two-page synopsis, which she will later bring to us. She reads me the list of qualities attributed to the black panther:

Valor.
Lunar, not solar power.
Transformation through suffering and death.
Solitary creatures drawn to other solitary beings.
Awakens Kundalini energy.
Associated with Jesus (suffering and transformation).

I am in awe. Gabriella's dream seems to have foretold many of the unusual, unexpected aspects of Theo's gestation, birth, and death. *Lunar, not solar power:* he was born on the night of the full moon and never saw the sun. *Solitary:* I felt extremely solitary during my pregnancy. *Awakens Kundalini energy:* I had unmistakable Kundalini experiences during the pregnancy and since the birth. *Suffering, death, transformation.*

Gabriella continues: "The black panther has the greatest mysticism associated with it. It is a symbol of the mother, the dark moon, and the power of the night. The black panther encourages us to understand the shadow powers available to us all, to acknowledge these powers and to eliminate our fears of the darkness."

Gabriella and I cry together.

"Oh my God, he is the most amazing being," she says. "We're so lucky to know him."

Oh, the beauty of having a close friend get this the way I do. I feel full, my chest bursting with a sensation close to bliss. And I am so sad, all at once.

In the afternoon, Cecily tells us she'd like to sing a song she and Michal have written. She explains, "After we heard the news about Theo Sunday morning, we cried and cried, booked our flight here, and then sat in our house and wondered what to do. The thought suddenly came to me: *Let's write Theo a song.* I turned on my computer, planning to pull up the words of the poem 'The One Divine,' which Cinda had sent to me, but when I got into the lyrics file, another poem of Cinda's came on the screen. I'd forgotten about this one, and it blew me away. The music came through quickly, like I was channeling it from somewhere."

She begins to sing. I vaguely remember writing these words in my bedroom back in October, when I was about six months along. A poem about lost love, really, which I probably thought was sappy and thin but worth sending to my talented sister and brother-in-law, who can work wonders bringing words to life with music. The chorus goes through me like ice: *Let go, now, let go, let go, I'm here now and that was that, he was real, he was yours but he isn't coming back.* I weep into Dicken's shoulder.

Let Go

For all those months I'd swim

In the mystery of him
Catching glimpses and signs
But not the whole design
And then there was that moment
That blew everything away
A streak of light through history
A glimpse into the mystery.

(Chorus)

I saw it in his eyes
That look with no disguise
But then I watched it rise
And it vanished in the sky
It's beginning to fade
Like the afternoon shade
Casting shadows on your face
And darkening this place.

(Chorus)

I try to hold on
It's why I sing this song
Hold it to my breast
Let go of all the rest
But now I can see
The way it's meant to be
And my whole life's become
A goodbye to the sun.

Let go let go let go let go
I'm here now and that was that
He is real, he is yours, he is yours
He is always with you, now and evermore.

My spirit is moved, and triumphant. I can already sense the skeptical part of me that lurks under all the openness I feel right now. This skeptic will emerge, I know, questioning my entire experience of Theo, trying to recast the beauty and grace as hallucinations, side effects of the surgery and medications, or at best invented and exaggerated rationalizations that serve to protect me from the random tragedy that has occurred. Right now, I let the words of the song I wrote months ago, before there was any inkling or outward sign that our baby had anything wrong with him, I let these words hammer into me, imprinting my soul over and over with indelible truth. *You see? I knew. This poem, Kevin's voices, Laura's dream, the Kundalini experiences, the black panther imagery—what more proof do you need that Theo's life and death were destined, part of a plan far greater than any of us can imagine?*

That evening, Dicken tells me he's eager to get home. I want to stay longer at Mom's guest house. I'm reluctant to take another step away from Theo, another step toward life beyond him, life without him. But Dicken insists.

"I want to get back to my routine," he says.

I can't imagine what he means, or why he seems so agitated.

"Can we just stay for the day?" I ask. "I'm not quite ready to go."

"Of course."

We pack up our things late that night.

Dicken holds my hand the whole way home, managing the Subaru stick shift one-handed. We are silent, the boys fast asleep in the backseat, the sky dark. We pass a window I can see into—a man walking a baby around a room.

When we get inside I notice that my breasts have soaked my shirt. I begin to cry, clutching my arms around my belly as if trying to staunch blood from an unseen wound.

"Are you okay?" Dicken asks. "Are you hurting? Is it your incision?"

"I just miss him," I cry.

Dicken takes me in his arms. My breasts ache as he presses me to him.

"I miss him too," he whispers. "I was pining for him the whole way home."

Dicken goes back out to the car to carry the sleeping boys inside, while I head to our bedroom. I see the stack of baby clothes waiting on the shelves, neatly folded. The changing table is all set up in the bathroom with flannel wipes and salves sitting next to it. My legs feel weak under me. I head for the bed and fall.

Dicken joins me in bed, turns out the light.

"Everything's okay," he says. "We're home now."

But even in this familiar place, I don't know where I am. As I lie in the dark, my mind is silent, but I have the physical sensation of being tossed in a wild sea. The expected path, the future we assumed we were heading for, keeps crashing into the actual path we've found ourselves on. It is a violent reckoning, filled with shock and denial and resistance and struggle, waves colliding in a furious storm. Far, far below that clashing tsunami is the calm beneath the water, the peaceful, deeply sorrowful aching that is longing, longing for what will never be.

No, I am not home. My bedroom, along with the entire external world, has become an empty, foreign space, my internal world a strange and terrifying ocean of sorrow. The bed spins I experience when I close my eyes take me back to the nausea of the sickly first trimester, and the clear knowing I kept having, odd and random as it seemed at the time: *The earth is not our home.* So where is home? Where is Theo? Where am I? Who am I now that he has come and gone? I cling to Dicken's warm body, feeling such a powerful yearning for him I can hardly breathe.

And suffusing all of this is the sense of peace that has held me throughout these last days, a silent weightless thrumming that soothes every part of me. Only one thing is clear to me right now: everything has changed.

PART 2

CHAPTER 16

January 20

The first night at home is long, with black, dreamless sleep punctuated by bouts of wrenching tears.

At one point I wake up with a desperate feeling. Where is he? I have an overwhelming desire to know the exact nature of death. Is there an afterlife? What is it like? I have pondered these questions at times in my life, but now they are an imperative. I need to know. Someone I was responsible for went over to the other side and I cannot rest until I know where he is, how he is.

We were symbiotic, as close as two human beings get, living on the same blood, the same oxygen, the same nutrients. And suddenly our oneness was cleaved, and he went as far away as it is possible to go. I don't know if I can live in this world without knowing where he is, where he went, where that half of my soul is.

In the morning, I wake to find Dicken sitting by me, dressed and holding my hand.

"You okay?" he asks.

I nod, pulling his hand closer to me.

"Let's change this room around," he says. "I think it would be good to shift the energy."

I don't care one way or the other, so I go along with him, sitting on our soft armchair while he moves the bed to the other side of the room. He works quickly, with a determined look on his face. Soon everything is rearranged, and dust long hidden behind furniture cleared away.

"Okay if I change the sheets too?"

"Sure," I say. "Just stay close to me, that's all I ask."

"Do you want me to wash those clothes you have on while I'm at it?"

I look down at my wooly blue sweater, the one I've had on for days now, except during and just after the surgery. Gabriella gave me this sweater in my second trimester, which seems lifetimes ago. It is thick and warm and has layers and holes designed for discreet, easy-access nursing. I held Theo against this material for the days and nights we had him. I can still smell his cookies-and-cream scent when I bury my face in the softness.

"No," I say firmly. "I'll never wash this sweater."

Dicken nods, looking reflective for a few moments, a faraway look, maybe sad. Then he whips the sheets and pillowcases off the bed and disappears downstairs.

I get up and trudge to the bathroom, splash water on my face, and look in the mirror. My cheeks look swollen, my eyes puffy. My chest aches slightly from my still full breasts.

I'm distraught that I have all this milk and no one to feed. I feel cheated. During all those miserable months of pregnancy, I was so looking forward to the sweetness of nursing: to the lovely hormones, that unmatchable satisfaction of nourishing a baby entirely from my own body, and that ravenous hunger and thirst, all those extra calories flying off. Here I am with my stored fat, wondering if I'll carry it for the rest of my life. Part of me doesn't care, seeing it as a sweet way to accept my imperfections the way I learned to love Theo's, another legacy of his. I would like to be able to wear my clothes again, but it's certainly not the end of the world. How could it be? Not even Theo's death is the end of the world.

Still, when Dicken comes into the bathroom, I ask him, "Am I fat or just swollen from the surgery?"

"Well, if you are fat, you're a beautiful fat woman."

I smile at his answer. He takes me in his arms. I nuzzle his neck and notice how good he smells.

"How long before this 'pelvic rest' is over?" I ask, referring to our doctor's euphemism for no sex until I'm further along in the healing process.

"Five weeks and two days."

"Not likely!" I say.

He squeezes me closer to him.

I have a hard time eating. Whenever I try, I weep, thinking about how Theo never got to eat or even taste my milk. How he couldn't have digested anything, how skinny his legs were.

My full breasts make everyone else sad but I like feeling them, because it's a physical reminder of Theo. I dread them emptying into sagging sacks. I'm happy I'll always have this scar to remind me of Theo.

My dad calls most days. Today he is crying and says, "I miss my mum."

"I know," I say. "I feel Granny close by. I wish she was still alive."

Granny told me about Jill twice, very briefly, saying she thought about her only daughter every day of her life. I listened in silence both times, never knowing what to say, not even an "I'm sorry." How I wish I could go back, sit with my grandmother, take her hand, ask about her lost child.

Cards and flowers are pouring in. E-mails too. The messages mean a lot, no matter how banal or clichéd.

Gabriella only took one or two photographs of Theo while he was alive; she didn't want to use a lot of flash when his eyes were open. She has just e-mailed one to us. It is stunning—a treasure I will never stop feeling grateful for. It is the shot of Dicken holding him, their eyes locked in a loving gaze. Dicken's big hand cradling Theo's tiny head. Theo looking peaceful, relaxed, unbelievably present. Gabriella says it was Theo's grace that got her the shot. She couldn't see through the viewfinder because it was so dark in the room.

Gabriella tells me how improbable it was that she even had the chance to take a photo: She'd been on call to video and photograph the birth when she got the news from Maud, saying the baby had been born and wouldn't live long. As she rushed out the door into the snowy night to drive to the hospital, she happened to notice her camera equipment waiting by the door.

"I thought, there's no point in bringing it now, but then something said, *Take it,* so I did."

I e-mail the photograph to all our friends and family, happy beyond measure that I can share Theo's breathtaking beauty with everyone. I include a long note, explaining Theo's condition, our decision to let him go, and our thoughts on foregoing prenatal testing:

> *I'm glad we didn't test with this pregnancy, because if we had, we might never have met Theo. We are incredibly grateful for our time with him, and for the way the birth unfolded. He would have died during labor if I'd tried to birth vaginally because of the pressure on his skull. We may never understand the mystery of his brief adventure into our lives and we are missing him terribly, but we don't regret the experience. It has changed us and opened our hearts.*

Dicken's cousin Aidan, who we are both very close to, writes from London:

> *I had been really struggling with getting any kind of grip on what you must be going through—partly the distance but also the scale of the situation seems too immense to get any real sense of it. But this picture of Dicken and Theo is so gentle and peaceful. The way Dicken's hand contains his whole little being is suddenly so simple. It's a picture of pure love. So now I think that this must be an extra-extraordinary experience for you: wrenching pain but also a new source and target of love that will be with you for the rest of your lives.*

Judith, a close friend of Maud's who we've met, sends an e-mail from the workshop she's teaching in Portugal:

I was very much involved with thinking about Theodore and all of you when the afternoon class started. We begin the afternoon class with a circle/check-in when we all say how we are. So I spoke about you, and how we met and how we have known each other over the years and of Theodore Simon and read your e-mail and showed the picture. Everyone was moved and affected by his story and that incredible photo of father and son. So he has touched more lives. It feels good.

The photo made me gasp and cry and marvel at the mysterious wonder of life. What a beautiful beautiful baby and being. Who was he and why did he touch your lives—my life!—for such a brief moment. I am still crying but feel somehow filled with joy at the same time. That's all I want to say for now. Thank you for letting me know, thank you for allowing his spirit, and the love and presence and awareness of your whole family, to fill me in this way.

My old friend Vanessa, the one who predicted in my first trimester that Theo would be a mystic, writes from Tuscany:

Theo's eyes are so wide and full of wonder, as though fully drinking in and transmitting the love his life was made for with the intensity of one who must do so with completion in the brief stay allotted. May we all transmit and receive so fully, in our flickering existences. Indeed blessings abound in the reverberations of His gifts. Rest in love, and in nearness. The separation is only acute that we may be driven to union.

As we're getting ready for bed, Jasper says, "I want my brother back." Tears well in his eyes. He says to me, "Do you know how it feels to lose a brother?"

I am reminded that this isn't only my loss, or my and Dicken's loss. This will be a seminal event in Jasper's childhood, something that shapes him. Kevin too, and Grace and Sam.

I ask Jasper about his experience that night. He recalls that Ralph was very sweet to him when he woke the boys. "I got to sit in the front seat on the way to the hospital, so I told Kevin he could sit in the front on the way home. Kevin said he didn't want the front because he wanted to be in the backseat so he could sit next to the baby."

Hearing this, I feel a slight ache in my chest. "What do you remember about the hospital, when you first got there?" I ask.

"I didn't like seeing you in that condition," he says, his voice cracking.

I open my arms, and Jasper falls into them. "I'm okay, sweetie," I say into his ear. He is crying silently.

I feel deeply sad after the lights are out. Jasper, in bed between us, hugs me a lot, and I fall asleep to the sound of him singing made-up songs about the baby: "*I have a little baby brother and we have the same middle name, and he lives up in the sky on a star, and he shines on all of us and he loves me, and he loves my mommy and my daddy too . . .*"

In the night I have a slight fever. I am terrified I will die and be separated from Dicken, even though part of me wishes I could die and end the searing grief, and be with Theo. I ache for Theo. I feel bitter and angry and sorry for myself.

I wonder if I am being punished.

I hate myself because I wasn't brave enough to have another baby sooner and I didn't give Dicken all the babies he deserves. I feel angry at my body for letting us down. I curse that stupid chromosome, that one moment in time that changed our perfect healthy son into an unsustainable life. I feel hot with shame, sure everyone who hears the news will judge us for not having an amnio, for using midwives instead of doctors, for my being too old.

I begin to wonder if the baby would have survived, if we

made the wrong decision, if we'll get terrible news when the chromosome test comes back with proof that he would have been fine, that it was all a mistake, that with a few surgeries we could have made him healthy. I am terrified it was because of my fear of his disability that I denied him life.

January 21

Dicken says he wishes he could give me a perfect baby, that he has a primal urge to get me pregnant again.

Maud is keen to surrogate a child for us. I must say it's kind of tempting even though it won't bring Theo back.

I feel raw. My womb is empty, yet I still refer to my belly and say "this baby" without thinking. I still feel the imprint of his head pushing on the lower right side of my pelvis, where it was the last few weeks.

As I run my hands over my incision and feel the extra layer of fat on my belly, my lifelong habit of pushing perfection on my body rears its familiar head. But a new voice overpowers it instantly, saying, *No, you will not treat the body that bore Theo this way! This body is sacred, a beautiful temple.* As the critical voice is chased away by this fierce new protector, tenderness washes over me. I love my scar, hoping it will always be prominent, always there in its smiling shape to remind me of Theo. I hope the surgeon's knife carved as deep as it could, made this etching dark and permanent. I love my tummy, the roll of fat, and will happily carry it forever. It's Theo's belly now, not mine. It is the mark of greatness, part of something much larger and more enduring than me and my vanity.

Caroline brings me a bowl of soup in bed.

"How is your incision, darling?"

I shrug. "Fine, I think. It burns now and again but I hardly notice it."

"You are brave," Caroline says.

"The physical part is nothing. It's finite. It's the emotions that are hard. They're so huge, endless."

"Yes, I know just what you mean."

Caroline shares some of her experiences of losing close loved ones. Two of her brothers died young, and her husband, Dicken's father, died of kidney failure in his early forties. Her three-year-old nephew died of pneumonia, and a niece, Athena, who I knew in the first years Dicken and I were together, died at age eleven in a car accident. I find Caroline's matter-of-fact, open way of discussing tragedy comforting. She doesn't seem to feel sorry for herself, and she's happy to answer questions and think back on her experiences.

"My mother lost a baby just after birth," she tells me. "His name was Patrick."

I love that name. It's my father's and his father's. Sam's middle name is Patrick. "Did she talk about him much?"

"No, not really. In those days, people didn't talk about anything like that. She was just told to get pregnant again and move on."

"That sounds awful," I say. "I'm so glad people aren't telling me to move on and forget what happened."

"Losing a baby you haven't had a lot of history with is perhaps easier than losing a partner, when there is so much to remind you always."

"It's worse than I imagined in some ways," I tell her. "But I'm amazed by how relaxed I feel about it too. I'm still here; I survived what I thought was unsurvivable. I feel wiped out but also like I'm a lot stronger and braver than I knew, like nothing can really hurt us."

"Yes, that's just what it was like when Simon was given the news that the doctors had run out of options, that he was facing the end. I'll never forget walking into the hospital room after the doctors filled me in, knowing he'd just been told, and thinking he would be desperate, crushed. But he looked more peaceful than I'd ever seen him, and he laughed with happiness, saying he could finally relax. There was nothing more he could do, and he knew all was well."

"Wasn't that his last line in his diaries?"

I've read Simon's diaries a number of times, eager to know the father-in-law I never got to meet because he died so young, when Dicken was twelve. His way with words was beautiful, his writing honest and inspiring. It makes me feel oddly close to him.

"Yes, he quoted Julian of Norwich, *All shall be well, and all shall be well, and all manner of things shall be well.*"

I recall seeing those words in Simon's clear handwriting on the last page of his diary.

"I finally know what that means," I say. "This baby taught me that," I add, putting my hand on my lower belly.

Tonight, in bed, Dicken is holding his chest with both hands, like he's in pain.

I reach out and put my hand on top of his, and he starts to sob.

"I just love him so much, it feels like I've been stabbed in the heart," he says. "What a sweet baby, why did he have to go? We missed out on so much, it's not fair. I just don't understand."

"It went by so fast," I say, "but it was all there. We had the entire parenting experience—all the worry, the panic, the lessons, the joy, the love, the excitement, the stress, the growth— all of it condensed into a few hours. Amazing, really. Maybe that's why I feel okay about it in moments, because I know it was complete, and as it was meant to be."

"And now it's over, and he's gone."

I move as close as I can to Dicken, kissing his cheeks and tasting the tears that spill down his face.

"We'll never lose the sweetness, the perfect innocence we share with Theo," I say. "He doesn't have to suffer the pain of growing up. We'll never be at odds, never be mad at each other. You and I will never have to worry that he's lonely or cold or depressed, we'll never have to see him drafted into war or suffering a heartbreak or an illness, we'll never have to wait up for him late at night. Never have to bail him out of jail or send him to rehab, or let him go on a dangerous trip."

"He's safe where he is," Dicken says. "I know that. I just want to be with him, I want to hold him and see him and take care of him."

"He doesn't need anyone to take care of him anymore."

I hang on to the relief I feel, knowing that nothing can ever hurt our son: none of the harsh realities of life, or the mistakes I would have made as his mother. I recall my stepfather saying that Theo had a perfect life, surrounded by love. What I don't let myself think about are all the positive things he'll miss in life, all the joy he would have experienced, all the wonder, and how much of that he would have brought us. I can't bear that, not yet.

January 22–23

Jasper has a huge eighth birthday and seems to enjoy everything. Grace comes to my bed before the party, brushes my hair and puts it into braids. She hugs me tightly, looks into my eyes. "Do you need anything, Tia?"

I look back into her beautiful green eyes and see her as an equal, with a heart as open and sensitive as the wisest adults I know. Later, when I walk into the main house, I notice that all the girls have their hair braided like mine. Grace grins up at me.

I don't feel as joyful today as I'd hoped I would, given that it is the birthday of our beloved boy, our one living offspring. We watch Jasper's birth video, which has been perhaps my favorite possession these past eight years, a record of my most glorious, joyful experience. I watched it about a month ago, before any of the pregnancy issues were known. That seems lifetimes ago. Today, as I watch the video, it is with new eyes. I mostly think, *That woman (me) didn't appreciate her good fortune. She complained. She took credit for a miracle that had nothing to do with her.*

* * *

Cecily brings Jasper a box at bedtime, and we sit together as he opens it. He pulls out a bunch of papers, looking puzzled. Cecily says with excitement, "I adopted you a gorilla!" The kit comes with adoption papers, a biography and photographs of Charles, the gorilla, and a little stuffed gorilla. As Jasper pulls out the plastic bag containing the stuffed toy, his eyes grow wide and he eagerly rips open the bag, obviously thinking this is a real baby gorilla. He just received live ants in the mail the day before for his ant farm.

After pulling it out, he says flatly, "Oh, it's stuffed."

"I'm sorry, Jasper," Cecily says. "The real gorilla's in Africa."

Grace asks, "Is he coming *here?*"

We try not to laugh in front of the kids, but when they leave, we fall about in near hysterics. The laughing is odd, a great release, like crying but with the flavor of joy instead of sorrow.

I write in my journal:

> *All these things you didn't need:*
> *Your clothes waiting on the shelves Dicken carefully organized.*
> *Your "born at home" shirt (a hand-me-down from Jasper).*
> *The milk filling my breasts.*
> *The empty changing table.*
> *The gentle creams and herbs Dad was going to use on your cord*
> *and on your skin.*
> *The car seat all strapped in the Subaru, in the middle seat so the*
> *boys wouldn't fight over who got to sit next to you.*
> *The body we grew together inside me all those months.*

Jasper makes his own altar for Theo. He puts tiny food offerings on it, like the Eastern tradition of leaving food for ancestors. I come back from brushing my teeth and find him crying and praying by it.

* * *

I can't read or watch movies. In the night I burst into sobs periodically, then lie awake just being with myself, and with the dark. We grieve more at night. Dicken calls it "Theo time." Sometimes I hear him crying in his sleep, and he doesn't remember it in the morning.

A close friend comes to sit with me for a while. She walks in and exclaims, "I love your room this way!"

"Dicken rearranges furniture as therapy."

My friend sits on the bed as I gather up the pile of letters and cards around me. "Wow, look at all of these. There must be a hundred, maybe more!"

"And you should see the e-mails," I say. "They're from just about everyone we know, plus a whole bunch we don't know, a lot of them people who've had a loss and wanted to reach out."

"Is it strange to hear from people you don't know?"

"No. Every single message, banal or brief or corny or run-on or eloquent, means a huge amount."

"Anyone you haven't heard from?"

"Yes, a few; a cousin and a couple of friends from the retreat group I was sure would make contact. I guess you can never tell. But I have to say, people are so generous."

"You must feel loved."

"Oh my gosh, yes. I think it takes something like this for us to know how loved and supported we are. I have the sensation that every thought, every prayer coming our way, is part of a huge number of hands underneath us, carrying us through this."

"I was telling my sister that I'm so glad I know you, because, because . . ." She starts to cry softly. "I told her if I ever go through losing one of my kids, I'll know someone who's survived it. I'm so grateful to be close to you right now, to get to witness you going through this."

I take her hands in mine. Hers are dry and cool, and I can't remember if we've ever held hands before.

"You look so beautiful, so open," she says. "You're like a goddess or something."

"I feel old and disheveled. I can't take a shower for a few more days."

"Well, you have this glow about you. I think you've been graced by this. I'm actually envious of you."

What a bizarre thing to say, yet I understand what she means.

"Hey," she says, "do you remember when you were in England, in your first trimester, and I sent you that e-mail survey—likes, dislikes, favorite color, food, and so on?"

"Vaguely."

"I still have that e-mail. And do you know what you wrote as an answer to *What is your biggest fear?*"

"I hardly recall the e-mail, much less what my answers were. That seems light years ago."

"You put, *Losing a loved one.*"

She mentions her husband. "If one of our kids died, I think it would break us up. I asked him if he would hold me all night if I lost someone close to me. He said, *No, I'm not Dicken. But there are a lot of things you like about me.* And I nodded, crying, and said that was true."

"You have no idea how you or he would be if something like this happened to you. I used to hear about people losing babies and think there was no way I could survive that, and that it would ruin my life if I did survive it. If there's one thing I'm learning in this, it's that anticipating a potential loss ahead of time is pointless. It's not at all what we imagine, and if it does happen, you'll know how to cope in the moment. You don't need to plan ahead."

"So you're not afraid of anything anymore?"

"Oh, I am, but I'm not going to indulge in worrying about anything as much. It really doesn't help, I *know* that now. Plus I know I'm a lot more courageous than I thought I was. We all are."

"You're amazing," she says.

"No, I'm not," I laugh. "At least no more so than anyone else, you included."

CHAPTER 17

'm sleeping better, not so sore. Maud and I take a walk in the warm sunshine. Water fills ponds and streams, spilling over the banks like tears.

As we make our way on the trail above the farm, Maud says, "I'm sad for you because I think Theo was more your child."

"What do you mean?"

"Well, he seemed more like you, whereas Jasper is so clearly Dicken's, the way Grace is Tom's and Sam is mine. Theo is like you. He is so deep and internal, secretive. He's about spirit and symbols and dreams, not so much about the concrete, physical world, or something like that."

I ponder her words for a moment, recalling that when Paul did his first reading of me, he spoke of me as being in the imaginary world a lot, and in the energetic realms.

I tell Maud, "I know what you mean. And I like that, because Theo and I can meet in those places. Maybe that's partly why Dicken's grief came crashing down on him so quickly, how his heart ached so much he kept clutching his chest from the moment we heard Theo would die. He is so physically present, grounded in the world, using touch and physicality to measure reality more than anything. I was heartbroken, but mostly so relieved and grateful and in love and blissed out by Theo's presence that the sorrow and longing for him didn't settle in until later. The dream world, the world of energy—in many ways it's as real to me as physical reality, sometimes more so. I guess part of me knew I wasn't losing him entirely. But I do miss his body. I'll never stop longing for that."

Maud is crying as we climb higher on the trail.

I love that Theo was one of the rare trisomy cases with no signs of a heart defect. His cardiogram test on the ultrasound was perfect; his heart tones were always strong and reactive. "The baby sounds great" they all told me, until the last day. Gabriella points out that Theo's gift seems to be about opening people's hearts. I agree.

January 25–26

We lie awake into the night talking. Jasper is sleeping between us, his breathing rhythmic and heavy.

"I wonder how much longer he'll want to be in our bed," Dicken says. "I'm in no hurry to move him on."

"Dix, do you remember when Jasper was a newborn, and how several times during those first nights, you woke me, asking in a desperate tone, *Where's our baby?*"

"Yes, wow, I haven't thought about that since then."

"I would point to Jasper, sleeping between us, and say, *He's right here. He's fine, look.* And you would say, *No, I mean, where's our other baby?* It would always take you a few minutes to fully wake up and realize that everything was fine, that we only had one baby and he was right there with us."

"Yes, that was really strange. I was convinced we had two babies and one was missing."

"And do you remember how I dreamt of another little baby boy around that time, nine months younger than Jasper in one dream, and how I told you we should be careful about getting pregnant again right away?"

"I don't remember that part."

"I do. It seemed like a presence was making itself known." I pause, then ask, "Do you think it could have been Theo, our little spirit child, already with us eight years ago?"

"I don't know. Anything is possible, I guess."

"I suppose it's a stretch, and there's no way we'll ever know, but I like to think he's been there, showed up for a short time in a body, then went back to being a sort of guardian angel for us."

"That's a lovely thought," Dicken says, and I can tell he's drifting off to sleep. I lie awake for a while longer, thinking of our strange parenting journey.

Maybe Theo's spirit really was with us years ago. I hardly dare even to dream of this, but maybe, just maybe, he chose us because we could give him the chance to be born alive. The vast majority of couples go with traditional medicine for prenatal care, and testing would be recommended for any thirty-five-year-old woman. Most couples would opt for an abortion upon learning the grim odds for a trisomy baby's survival.

Statistically, he should never have lived a moment on earth. How can it be a mere coincidence that Theo was born to two people who believe in trusting the process of birth and the wisdom of the body?

From a friend who visited us the day after the birth: *The radiant beauty I experienced amid the sorrow in that hospital room will be alive in me for a long, long time. I've never seen you more beautiful and powerful. Nor have I experienced a family so richly, consciously, and openly navigating through a birth as you all did.*

From a childhood friend's mother-in-law: *Even at the time we lost our baby daughter, in spite of the trauma, we were so grateful for every moment we shared with her. We owe her so much for the lessons of the heart. We wouldn't choose another way, even if we could. We had children in order to partake in a mystery. And I'll share with you the words of a very wise visiting nurse, who said to me, "Don't think of her as your little tragedy, she doesn't know she's sick. Just love her."*

Jennifer, our midwife friend, tells me she had four clients miscarry in the summer, all due in January or February. Tracy was due in March and miscarried in the first trimester. We turned out to be Rhione's only January birth so far—because her other one went before thirty-seven weeks in late December. And during our entire time in the hospital, there weren't any other women recovering from or giving birth. Odd. It seems like a pattern, like the stars were lined up in a certain way, that there was some sort of blackout in January 2006. January was a Friday-the-thirteenth month, and so was the previous May, the first month of my pregnancy.

I reread my journals, mouth agape at all the references to death in the first trimester of the pregnancy. *I must have known.* I want others to witness this too, to make it more real.

"Dicken, listen to this." I begin to read from my journal: "*June 24, I've been thinking of how this physical debilitation makes me feel so uninvested in being in the world, and how people who are ill must benefit from that in that it makes it easier to let go and die. For me the hardest thing to let go of would be Jasper. I also think it's interesting that I'm feeling this whole lack of draw to being human when this soul is doing the opposite—being drawn into the human realm. Maybe we're meeting at the threshold of life and the other side of life, whatever and wherever that is.*"

We are both silent.

"Isn't that uncanny?"

"It just makes me sad," he says. "You suffered so much then, and now."

I feel disappointed that he isn't as amazed by this as I am. I don't want to be sad all the time. I want to marvel, to celebrate this magnificent mystery, this proof that the universe is intelligent, that every tragedy is in its own way pristine, beautiful. I want to tell everyone I know not to fear loss. I want them to trust that the magic web will catch them, keep them sane and intact.

A close friend says, "I told my mom what happened, and she could only talk about how sad it is, how it's a tragedy, pure and simple."

I cringe at this, and wish I could speak to my friend's mother, to everyone who hears of our "tragedy." I don't want anyone to pity me, to think of me as tragic. I want to reassure the world that all is unfolding according to plan, that suffering has a place, a purpose. I feel evangelical. For the first time in my life, I feel I have something truly important to say.

A woman I know from dance cooks a meal for us, brings it by, settles into the kitchen couch to talk for a while before her long drive home.

"You look beautiful," she says to me. "I've never seen you so open."

"It doesn't make sense, but I really am okay, maybe better than ever."

"You know, my sister doesn't understand the blessing this is for you," she says. "I told her your story, and she said you were crazy not to have an amnio. I tried to explain that you were thrilled to know Theo, but she just didn't get it. She said she pities you."

I know this woman's sister judges me, and I feel defensive, for myself and for Theo. To me, she is negating the meaning of his life, wishing him away. My chest burns as I think of this, of how many people don't understand, will never understand. I so badly want everyone who hears of this to know the truth, to know we are not pitiable, to know we don't regret our choices. I tell myself people like this are the ones to be pitied: they live in their closed worlds of fear, afraid to come into the center of this experience and see it for what it is. They imagine desperate, wretched pain and misery. They imagine how they would feel if this happened to them. I know because I did this myself when I used to hear of a baby dying, or a baby being born with a disability.

I think people look for a reason, an explanation, when they hear about something tragic, so they can hang on to some imaginary sense of control, believing that if they only do A, or don't do B, C will never happen to them. The woman who was raped should never have walked to her car alone. The family that went bankrupt shouldn't have taken on that expensive mortgage. The Weatherbys should have had an amnio. If they can distance themselves from the people these things happen to, they don't have to feel so much. They don't have to live with the reality that at any moment, something catastrophic can slice our lives open. They can judge from the false safety of believing they are different, that they are fully aware of and in control of their choices and what those will result in.

I am deeply grateful that with very few exceptions, my close family and friends are brave and humble people, unafraid to venture with us into the center of this and let the sad and stunning beauty rip their hearts open.

I begin to listen to music again. At first it was too painful; I couldn't stand it. I prefer love songs right now, even though they hurt. Eva Cassidy, Coldplay, John Denver. The notes wash through my body and I am filled with the most powerful emotion imaginable. It is not exactly painful, but in a way it feels unbearable, like I will explode.

I am madly, madly in love with Theo, literally feeling I will go insane from this love, will die from it. I hear the songs and tears of joy fall down my face. I am so in love, I am so happy, I feel intoxicated. It is rapture, it is pure high. It is no doubt fueled by the lactation hormones, the post-birth chemical soup designed to bond a mother with her newborn so strongly she will happily forego sleep and comfort to ensure her baby's survival.

I am filled with this powerful bonding drive, yet there is no object for me to focus the energy on. I can feel some part of my psyche searching, searching, searching for the beloved, desperate to keep him safe and secure, warm and fed. The muscles of my arms ache to hold the weight I expected. The gap expands inside me and makes every part of me sore, especially my chest, my heart area.

Yet even this ache is joy, is love itself.

I sing aloud with "Come What May" from *Moulin Rouge*:

Never knew I could feel like this
It's like I've never seen the sky before . . .

Tears stream down my face, tears of the purest, sweetest longing I've ever known.

I look up and see Maud coming. She registers my wet face and holds her arms out to me.

"I'm so sorry," she says, her voice breaking. "It's so sad, Cinda. It's unbearable."

Yes, it is unbearable, but not in the way she means it. I let her hold me, but I don't know how to explain the joyful bursting I feel. This pure bliss is not reflected back to me by anyone. People look at me expecting pain, shock, sadness. All of that is here, but sometimes it is entirely obliterated by the magnificent white light that explodes through me. I feel invincible. My love has transcended death, survival. How could anything scare me now? The worst has happened, and I am still here, whole and alive like never before. I have a sense of calm I've never experienced, and an overwhelmingly sweet, sad, swelling in-loveness.

I feel strange about it, like there is something wrong with me for my unexpected happiness. For feeling so deeply blessed, the way new couples feel when they listen to sappy songs that must have been written just for them, knowing that all of time has been leading up to this moment, to this burning emotion that makes life clear and beautiful and perfect at last.

How can a mother whose baby was born with a fatal flaw, his organs weak and malformed, a baby who lived only five hours—how can this mother feel so happy, how can she cry with joy? How can this mother rejoice and feel blessed beyond anything she ever imagined? Is this a secret only the deeply bereaved know? Or is it the rare convergence of birth and death that has created this odd mixture of exuberance and extreme sorrow?

Maybe I am just experiencing the side effects of massive hormone swings, endorphin rushes like the ones I had postpartum with Jasper. Then, the newborn high was tempered by the awesome responsibility of caring for a helpless infant around the clock, an infant who could be cold, or hungry, or colicky, or stop breathing at any moment. But with Theo, there is no worry, because the worst has happened, and I am not responsible now, not afraid for his physical well-being. Does this account for the pure exhilaration? Or maybe, just maybe, I am feeling this way because Theo was as extraordinary as I believe he was, and being chosen by such a soul explains this otherwise inexplicable sense of blessing, of grace, this secret sense that I am the luckiest mother who ever lived.

But when the in-love feeling passes, I go back to my usual station these days—bed. Dix works on his laptop on the couch across from me; I need him near me. When he drives Kevin to the bus stop early in the morning, I go with him, even though it's cold and dark. I'm terrified that if he goes out without me, something terrible will happen. I can feel the part of me that is bracing for another loss. I know the ground can open up under my feet at any moment. I know now I can endure more than I ever thought I could. But I pray I won't be tested again anytime soon.

Let me learn the intimacies of this loss first. I am only beginning to know them.

January 27

I wake thinking I'm still pregnant with Theo; then reality reasserts itself with a violent stab. *Can't I just go back to December and be carrying a healthy Theo?* How I longed for the pregnancy to be over. And now I miss having him with me, knowing he's safe as I feel him gently turning in my belly.

Maud used to say, "You're so lucky to have that baby inside you." I never agreed, just complained and said how eager I was to get those months over with. Those midnight snacks he and I shared in the dark kitchen—if only I'd known they were all I would get. I stupidly assumed we'd have decades of meals together. I am left missing what I took for granted, the pregnancy—it's all I got to experience of him, other than the five precious hours. Now my stomach is an empty balloon, my breasts small again.

Today I feel angry at my body for letting us down. Watching Dix with a friend's three-year-old daughter is bittersweet. He is such a natural with kids, it feels wrong to think of him not having another child. It's such a rare man who adores babies. Willing to go all out, change diapers, walk around on a sleepless night, nurse them back to health with exquisite attention when they're sick.

Oh, why did I wait so long? Why did I have that abortion? Fear. Stupid fear. Dicken tells me he mourns for our unborn children. Oh Theo, we wanted more of you on earth. We wanted to hold your warmth, delight in your developing body, snuggle you close.

January 28

I wake in the dark, crying. Jasper hears me from his nearby mattress on the floor and comes right over. He holds me tight for the rest of the night, his warm body grounding me, rooting me to this bed, this room, this life.

In the morning, Dicken is getting dressed and reaches into his shirt pocket. He pulls out something, examines it, and comes over to show me. "Look," he says, "the ultrasound pictures."

I burst into tears and fold my head forward into my lap. Jasper comes over and kisses me and says, "Mom, you have a beautiful body." I'm not exactly sure what he means or why he says this, but it makes me smile.

"I wanna show Grace these pictures of Theo," Jasper says. He takes the prints and runs off into the main house.

Dicken lies down beside me on the bed. "Let's go somewhere, plan a trip."

"I've always wanted to go to Kashmir," I say.

"We could stay in one of those houseboats."

"And I want to go to Tonga and swim with the humpbacks."

"Yes, we'll do that," he says, his eyes glazed as if he can see some distant place. He turns to me, his gaze on me now. "I'm going to take such good care of you."

"You already do. You always have."

"But I mean now, you know, with everything that's happened."

"Don't you wonder what will happen to us? If we'll have another baby one day . . ."

"It'll be wonderful, wonderful either way. If we don't have a baby, we'll have so much time for each other. We'll travel, we'll explore, we'll work together. We'll do everything together."

"We'll love our boys, all three of them, and celebrate each other."

"Even if we don't have a baby, we'll have that. I'd be so happy just to have all that."

"Me too," I say, beaming. "Theo has given us this time together, and all this love and closeness we didn't know was so precious until he showed us. He's so generous." I tear up, seeing happy endings everywhere I look.

Then there is a jarring sensation, like a plane that has been sailing along smoothly suddenly hitting a pocket of turbulence. I grab Dicken's arm and cling to it. As long as he's around, I feel safe. I'm not meant to be attached to him, I know. Everything passes. But how I long to merge my cells into his, take refuge forever in his loving presence.

January 29

My dad flies out to see us. I pick him up at the airport. After twenty minutes of him catching me up on his new girlfriend, silence falls between us. For the rest of the long drive back to the farm, the few conversations we strike up dead-end quickly.

"What are you reading lately?" he asks.

"Mostly poetry, and some spiritual books."

"Oh. Are there any you can recommend? I rarely find anything worthwhile in those religious books. I have nothing against them; they just seem to put me to sleep."

"I read them all the time. Especially when I'm down. I find them comforting."

"Are you down these days? I thought you were feeling better."

"Well, you know, it comes and goes."

"Poor baby, I don't like to think you're down." His face looks pained.

My father has always hated to see me suffer. I don't want him to worry about me, so I think about reassuring him, as I always have, by saying something that minimizes my sadness. But thinking of how I have been able to withstand such deep, desperate, inconsolable feelings lately, I decide to let my dad be where he is right now.

January 30

I'm lying in bed. My incision is burning, and my breasts ache. The milk seems to come and go, swelling and then deflating.

The door to the main house is open, and I can hear voices in the kitchen. My entire family of origin is here today, except for my brother.

Dicken comes in and looks at me. "Do you want something to eat or drink?" he asks.

"I'm not sure."

"Do you want it quieter? I can shut that door. Or I can go get Maud and Cec if you want company."

"I don't know what I want," I say. "I can't figure out if I want people around or not. Sometimes it's incredibly reassuring. Then the next minute, I'm annoyed with everyone and wish they'd all go away."

"Your dad just complained that we never have any milk for his tea. I feel bad."

I roll my eyes. "What does he expect? This isn't a hotel!" I fume for a few moments, then point to my chest and say, "Maybe I should express some of this milk for him, maybe then he'd be satisfied!"

Dicken peers down at the carpet, frowning.

Thinking about milk makes the aching worse. My body doesn't get it; it longs to nurse and care for and hold a warm baby. So much seems wasted—my leaking milk, all this love waiting for the little one. It's a crime that a father as loving and nurturing as Dix is left empty-armed when so many healthy babes are neglected by lame, absent fathers.

"You sure you don't want something to eat?" Dicken asks. "Someone's heating up the lasagna Beth brought over."

"That's another thing. I wish everyone would stop eating all the food people are bringing for us. It's so rude!"

"But you're not eating it," Dicken reminds me.

"I know, but something about seeing them eat what was meant as support for us seems so wrong, like they're taking advantage of our loss."

"I don't feel that way, but I can see why you do."

"Sometimes I can't stand any of them, their nonstop talking and the whining about the no-dogs rule," I say. "Makes me want to scream at them to leave! I just want to be alone with you."

"That sounds good."

But then my mom gets ready to leave, to fly to New York to see my stepbrother's baby, and I cry hard, not wanting her to be so far away. I bring out one of Theo's velvety baby-grows to send along to my new nephew, but Mom bursts into tears and says she can't bear to take it with her.

I wave to her as her car disappears down the driveway.

In bed, Dicken kisses me everywhere, including my scar, my nipples, all so tender and exquisite. I'm so moved I bawl in his arms. In an odd way, these days feel like a honeymoon. We are eager new lovers, attached to each other like limpets again.

January 31

I yearn for a baby, yet I feel so weak. I can't face the thought of another pregnancy, this time without the complete trust in the biological process that I had during Theo's pregnancy (and ironically not with Jasper's). Maud keeps pressing us to consider the idea of her carrying a baby for us. I think she's mourning the third baby she hasn't had. She was counting on Theo.

Sometimes the idea of trying again appeals a whole lot, sometimes not. I do think we'd appreciate and love a baby more than we ever imagined. What a special, adored child it would be, a miracle. At this moment, all the dreams I once used to fill the empty space—like travel, writing, pottery, more time with Dix—seem nothing compared to the joy a real baby in my arms and at my breast would be. But then I remember all the expectations for Theo that turned out so differently from the plans and fantasies. And I can't help wondering if the message I'm supposed to be getting from all this is that yes, you *are* too old, be happy with what you have, don't go for more and end up regretting it. Plus, even raising a perfectly healthy child is a huge commitment—time, energy, resources. Is that our *yes*, or is there something else we're meant to be doing? A baby, a child, expands one's heart and world, but it doesn't solve any problems.

I feel dark, let down. Part of me thinks that since I'm being such a good sport about this—seeing the bigger picture, feeling blessed and grateful, trusting the process—shouldn't I be rewarded? But there is still no baby. There is still this gaping hole, this wasted milk, these empty clothes on our shelf. My useless, scarred body. Fat stored and nowhere to go. Where's the happy ending? Not in another baby—we'd have to let him go eventually as he grows up, just more gradually, like with Jabu. Not all at once, like with Theo.

In the night, I wake with a heavy sadness. I reach out and feel Dix's face in the dark, running my fingers over and over his cheeks, and think, *I don't ever want to let go of this one, why is it set up this way, I can't bear it.* All this letting go. Can't we have something that won't be taken away? Not something intangible—my body wants a real physical thing that will never die. My Dicken, my true love. Funny how I cling to him so much more now than to

Jasper. You'd think after losing a child, one would fear for the surviving children and cling to them.

February 1

People are donating to the Smile Train fund Dad set up in Theo's name, which really lifts my spirits. This little one has made a brighter world in so many ways. Rhione thinks this is "big work" I'm doing, that it's not just dealing with my own stuff. I'm amazed at how many people tell us of significant changes Theo's story has brought them, even people we don't know.

Every place I go on my first town run today marks a new milestone; I walk in and think, *Last time I was here, he was with me.* In the co-op, I run into people I haven't seen yet. Most look at me nervously. I try to reassure them, want to tell them the whole story and insist that I'm fine, that all is well. But we mostly stand in our far corners and look at each other like strangers.

Jeff, father of a boy Jasper's age, is an exception. He walks straight up to me. He looks me in the eye with compassion, never saying a word, and takes me in his arms. I start to cry as he holds me in the middle of the snack food aisle, this sweet man I hardly know.

A few minutes later, as I'm walking out the door, he comes running up to me with a bouquet of flowers. You just made it into my heart forever, Jeff.

Later, standing in the chilly playground waiting for Jasper and Grace to get out of their art program, I see Andy, who attends the same retreats I do. He looks agitated as his eyes register me, but walks over anyway.

"Hi, Andy."

"Hello, Lucinda. I'm so scared to see you because I have no idea what to say, and I don't want to say the wrong thing."

"That was perfect."

"Really?"

"I just want people to be honest, that's all," I tell him.

He smiles, sighing deeply, and gives me a big hug. We talk for a long time.

CHAPTER 18

February 4

Jasper is stuffing jelly beans in his mouth when I walk into the kitchen. A few minutes later, I see him helping himself to ice cream. For the first time in his life, he looks chubby to me.

"Jasper, I don't want you eating any more sugary food. How about an apple?"

"Mom, stop being so mean!"

"But, I'm . . . I'm . . . I'm a little worried about your health."

"Am I too fat?" he asks.

"Well . . . no . . . it's just that . . ." I can see by his face I waited too long to say no.

"You're being too hard on me!" he shouts. "You're always too hard on me. I hate you! Go away!"

I freeze, not knowing if he's right, if I am overreacting; or if he is just pushing me away because like any child, he doesn't want to have limits placed on him. All I know is that I feel horrible. My vision darkens, and I can feel angry tears coming. I run to my room and slam the door. Dicken comes in a few moments after me.

"I don't know how to parent the boys!" I cry to him. "Who are these out-of-control sugar-iPod-video-game addicts who have nothing in common with me? I just want a baby—I know how to parent a baby, it's easy for me. I'm good at nursing, I'm loving to newborns. But with the boys it's getting harder and harder!" I sob and sob, let it all out.

When it passes, I ask Jasper to cuddle with me. He comes and lies next to me on the bed, looking curious and a little guarded. I apologize and try to explain myself. "I love you *so* much. I love your body, everything about you. You're perfect. I wish I could show you how much I love you!"

He listens quietly, his face softening. He lets me take him in my arms.

Jasper and I hold each other all night. I feel the innocent perfect love we share, the newborn closeness.

February 5

Dicken and I go into town for my follow-up appointment with Dr. Moreno. In the waiting room, we sit near an obviously pregnant young woman. Part of me wants to look away and not acknowledge her, but I am also curious about what I feel as I register her and her full belly. I stare at her for a few moments and notice conflicting emotions: envy, pity, happiness, fear.

Another woman, who has just been at the counter talking to the receptionist and appears to be on her way out, glances at me and Dicken and says, "Look how sweet you two are, holding hands. Are you expecting a baby?"

I shake my head nervously.

"Well, it's nice to see a couple hold hands," she says. "How romantic."

I smile but can't think of anything to say. A few minutes later, after she is gone, I begin to have regrets. I wish I had told her why we were there. I want to run out to the parking lot and find her and pour out the whole story of Theo. I want to show her the photograph of Dicken holding him. I look at the pregnant woman and hope she'll initiate a conversation, one in which I can find an opening to tell her everything. I don't want to scare her, especially if this is her first pregnancy, but more than that, I want her, and everyone for that matter, to know Theo's story, to know all we have been through.

A medical assistant takes my blood pressure, weighs me, and asks a few questions. Dr. Moreno comes in later, inspects my incision, says I seem to be healing well. She is unemotional, and I feel no invitation to share anything other than how I'm doing physically.

After the exam, she gets out a file, opens it, and says, "I have the results of the postmortem testing here."

I can't breathe for a moment. Dicken takes my hand.

"The test came back positive for full-blown trisomy 13," she says.

I know this means every cell of his body carried the triple chromosome, caused by an anomaly in either the egg or the sperm. The news is what I've been praying for—nothing ambiguous. If we'd medevacked him to Portland, he would have died on the way or been sent home to die; no medical intervention could have changed the outcome. I have been at times paralyzed with terror that the test results would indicate there'd been a big mistake, that he'd only had a few minor birth defects, or that he'd had the mosaic form of trisomy 13, which is much less severe than the full-blown kind. I don't think I could have borne knowing we could have had him longer after all.

Sitting there in the clinic with the doctor's words still ringing in my ears, I feel big relief, followed by a wave of sadness. Dicken squeezes my hand hard. I want to look in his eyes, share this with him, feel all this and express it, but in the sterile room with a doctor who is all business, I can't relax. I look at my hands and don't say anything.

"Can we get a copy of the report?" Dicken asks.

"Yes, I'll have one ready for you at the front desk," Dr. Moreno says. She looks softer for a moment. Then, out of the blue, she asks, "Do you need a prescription for birth control?"

I feel stunned by her question, or maybe by the insensitive way she says it. I glance down, ashamed, hurt, confused. The suggestion that we should avoid a pregnancy feels like a scolding of some kind. I can't put my finger on it, but I feel like I have done something wrong. I also feel strangely defensive, protective of all our potential children: *How could you have seen that sweet baby we just had and suggest birth control?*

"Do you have a method already?" she asks, when neither of us has said anything for a few moments.

"We, uh, we're not sure, we haven't talked about our plans or anything like that," I stammer, feeling like I did as a teenager when my mom mentioned anything about sex.

"Well, if you're even considering another pregnancy, I would advise a consultation with a genetic counselor first."

"But doesn't the full-blown trisomy diagnosis mean it was a fluke, and that we don't have an increased risk in any future pregnancy?" Dicken asks.

"Yes, but I would still recommend a consultation," Dr. Moreno says gravely.

I am relieved when the conversation ends and the doctor leaves us alone so I can get dressed again.

Later that day, I find the e-mail which Dr. Katz, our kind prenatal geneticist in Eugene, sent me after I sent out the news about Theo's birth and death. He gave his condolences and offered us the services of his genetic counselor free of charge. I find the phone number and call.

The counselor is very sympathetic. She speaks about losing her husband to cancer and her grief process. She tells me what she knows about Theo's diagnosis: how in the full-blown cases, there is a split early on in development that affects every cell.

"It means neither of you carries a faulty gene," she explains. "That would be the case if it were a partial trisomy, a mosaic, they call it."

"So we're not at higher risk of this happening again?"

"No, not any higher than any other couple your age."

"And there's nothing we could have done to prolong his life, no surgeries, nothing like that?"

"No. You did the kind thing in letting him go," she says. "He really couldn't have survived, not without drastic measures."

"That's such a relief."

"You know, if you'd had an amnio, they wouldn't have let

you have a C-section, because of the increased risk to you. That's how the medical experts view trisomy 13, as hopeless."

I feel amazed at this, reassured. I am extremely grateful that we didn't do the amnio, because I feel certain Theo wouldn't have survived a vaginal birth; he was already slowing down that day. If I'd been refused a C-section, I am sure we would never have known him alive in the world. Again, I can't help but wonder: *Did Theo choose us?*

"Do you think he suffered?" I ask.

"No. That part of his brain probably wasn't switched on."

"Does that explain why he didn't struggle? He seemed so peaceful when he died. He just closed his eyes and turned pale."

"Yes, that makes sense."

"Is there any way to know what the specific cause of death was?"

"It was probably cardiopulmonary arrest," she says, explaining that his organs didn't function properly, that his lungs weren't strong enough to carry oxygen to his heart. "You see, every single cell would have been affected. It happened early on. Even his placenta was affected, because placentas have the same DNA. That's why it's so amazing he survived the pregnancy. The odds were really not in his favor."

"What does it mean that the placenta was faulty?"

"Well, the placenta is what gets maternal nutrients to the baby and helps it excrete waste. It's a way for the mother and fetus to share blood, basically. And because your baby's placenta had the trisomy, it was defective and wasn't processing nutrients and waste correctly. That means your blood was basically being poisoned the whole time. You probably had a lot more nausea as a result."

"Wow, that explains it. I really felt sick this time and nothing seemed to help. But I just thought it was because I was older and had an aging liver or something."

Maud is really sweet when I report on the conversation. When I tell her about the faulty placenta, she tears up and says, "Oh, Cinda, I'm so sorry you had to go through all that."

Dicken is so wrapped up in work, he doesn't seem particularly interested when I tell him about the conversation. I can feel that I'm mad at him right now. He has so little to give; he seems to be chasing his tail, never landing in silence and stillness.

That I'm not at a higher risk of trisomy than any other woman my age is a relief, though it's still hard to imagine ever having the courage to try again. Theo's pregnancy seemed long as hell, and I wasn't even very afraid until the last month. So ironic, because I was terrified all through Jasper's pregnancy that something would be wrong with him, that he would die, and with Theo I assumed everything was fine until we had that ultrasound in the final weeks.

I try to take a nap, but for a long time I lie there and wonder when and why that chromosome split. Dicken, in his usual generous way, says it was probably his sperm. But chances are, because of my age, it was my egg that had the problem. I think about how much I traveled in those months leading up to the pregnancy: two trips to Costa Rica, another to England. I recently read that going through airport security systems and being on long plane journeys gives you more than one hundred times the radiation of an X-ray. I also remember how I treated the boys' hair with a pesticide shampoo after discovering nits when I brought Kevin back from Costa Rica. That must have been March, a cycle or two before Theo was conceived.

Though the doctors and the rational part of me are confident that there is no one to blame in this situation, another part of me feels responsible. There must be a reason this happened, someone to blame, and it is my second nature to point that finger at myself. At times I mount a mama-bear protectiveness toward myself, knowing I have been through hell. Chastising myself for something I may or may not have caused is not only pointless but cruel. But the self-recrimination rears its head when my defenses are low, like a predator taking advantage of a wounded or weakened prey.

The paradox is that at the very same time, I am sure in my deepest being that all is well. The self-blame comes when I forget this basic truth for short periods. I doubt; I tell myself what happened is bad luck, or worse: my fault. *I deserve this. I waited too long to have another baby. I was reckless. I brought it on myself.* But I always land in a still certainty, a peaceful awe, a relaxed state that hums *all is well.*

February 6–7

A massage from my friend Amy this afternoon makes me feel raw, on the verge of big grief. Afterward I am exhausted and overwhelmed and feel postpartum darkness descending—very much like what I remember from a few days after Jasper was born.

The boys are being difficult, and I suddenly wonder how I can go on. Sometimes I feel done with parenting, and I long to follow Theo and be in his world.

I've been telling myself I'm a negligent mother. My kids are suffering; I can't take good care of them because a stupid plan to get pregnant has gone horribly wrong. The aftermath threatens to destroy my health and emotional stability, to bankrupt us and ruin our family. All this wasted time. Months of uselessness, being dependent. I've aged a decade. Another disaster I'm trying to justify with New Age teachings by pretending everything happened for a reason and I'm at peace with everything. My skeptical self thinks I'm not doing my time. I'm avoiding the grief. I can't be this okay with it—there's something wrong with me.

Am I gloomy because the old me is reemerging? I don't want to go back; I want to stay open and changed. I want to be special, to have special treatment forever. Maybe I'm afraid of forgetting. I'm afraid things are getting back to normal, that the sacred out-of-time days are over, that my heart is closing again, that Theo's gifts will mean nothing, that we won't be special anymore, that we'll forget him.

In bed, with my feet off solid ground, everything spins. I have the sensation of falling. *How will I ever sleep when I fall and fall endlessly?* To ground myself, I hang onto Dicken's arm. It is my lifeline, solid, warm, alive. I adore everything about it: the size, the shape, the soft skin. I cling to it, trying to remember our first days together, thinking, *Has he always had such an incredible arm?*

The next morning, Mom, home from her trip back east, is standing with me on the playground, watching Jasper run around. She says to me, "When I look at Jabu I can't help wanting you and Dix to have another baby."

"I can't think about that now," I lie.

"No, of course not, you're still grieving. Which of the stages are you in right now, do you think? Depression? Anger?"

"I don't know," I say. "I don't really believe in the stages." I absentmindedly kick at the ground with my foot and the conversation ends.

Later, alone in the car, I think about my mom's question. I studied the "five stages of grief" model in grad school, and I recognize the various aspects in myself now. But what I see is not a linear progression from one stage to the next. There are layers and layers, many different parts, and they are all happening at once: denial, anger, sadness, bargaining, acceptance, and more—peace, resignation, joy, hypervigilance, confusion. What changes is where my attention is, or maybe which one is most prominent at each particular moment. This can change suddenly, making me feel volatile, contradictory, even crazy. One minute, I'm completely identified with the inconsolable me, the me that will never stop yearning for Theo, wishing things had been different, and then the next minute I feel completely okay with everything, convinced it all happened perfectly. And then suddenly I am in denial, pretending nothing happened, or bargaining with God, promising I will be good from now on if only Theo is brought back to me. Sometimes I can feel more than one part at the same time. The part that accepts and the part that will never ever accept. They are both real and true and I imagine will always be parts of me.

February 8

In the parking lot at Kevin's school, I see a beautiful baby—the first one that "gets" me, a bald chubby one like Jasper or Grace or Sam. A woman is holding the baby and others gather around, smiling. I look away.

Time is helping in a way, but it's bittersweet too. Creating a bigger and bigger gulf between those hours with him, and now. The physicality, the memories are fading. His clothes still have his scent, but for how long?

I think of what someone told me once, that for a child to feel loved, he must be held as the center of his mother's or father's universe for a time. When I first heard this, I thought about my own childhood, and guessed that my lifelong self-doubt could be traced to my never having felt cherished this way by my mother or father; both admit they loved me but were preoccupied with many other things when I came along. I tried hard to make Jasper the center of my world during his early years. I would guess he felt that, and he easily made his way to being the heart of Dicken's life. I like to think the confidence and security Jasper exudes reflect this.

And I was preparing to make Theo the center of my universe. I had spent the months of pregnancy clearing out the demands and preoccupations of my life as much as possible to make room for the new heir. Now the center of my universe is gone. I am lost, falling into the void he left in his wake. Everything I see or hear or touch or think is filtered through this center that is Theo. He is the true north, the touchstone, the everything. Without him in this world, there is nowhere to rest. There is only boundless white space echoing into the endless sky all around me.

I hope I land in his universe. I am open to the mystery of the beyond. I am yearning for it, willing to sacrifice whatever I am asked to know where my center is.

Maud comes into my bedroom, smiling. She's holding something behind her back, looking expectant. "I have a surprise for you." She hands me a weighted Waldorf doll. It is about the size of a newborn, made of cloth, with simple features and wearing a sewn-on light-green, velvet baby-grow and hat.

I take the doll into my arms and feel its weight, cradle it to my chest. It takes me right back to holding Theo, and I start to weep. When I can see again, I look up. Maud is crying softly.

"Isn't he sweet?" she says.

I nod. He is so sweet.

At dinner, Jasper says he doesn't want anything to eat. This is not like him at all, my hearty boy with the big appetite. He's never been picky, has rarely turned down food.

"Have some pasta," I say. "It's really good with cheese."

"I don't want any. I'm getting chubby." He looks at the bowl of pasta making its way around the table with big eyes but doesn't take any.

"Please eat something," I plead.

"No!"

"Honey," Dicken says to me, "leave him alone, you're only making it worse."

I have to leave the table. I can't watch Jasper refuse food, or say anything negative about his body, especially now, with my great sorrow about Theo not being able to nurse or digest food. He was so scrawny.

February 9

A neighbor, Tim, e-mails a link to a story that aired on National Public Radio yesterday. His e-mail says, *I assume you heard about this*, but I have not. The story reads:

Some scientists have proposed that when a woman has a baby, she gets not just a son or a daughter, but a gift of cells that stays behind and protects her for the rest of her life. That's because a baby's cells linger in its mom's body for decades and—like stem cells—may help to repair damage when she gets sick. It's such an enticing idea that even the scientists who came up with the idea worry that it may be too beautiful to be true.

I close my eyes and concentrate on every sensation in my body, wondering if there is a way I can tune into Theo's cells, the ones still floating inside me. Theo preserved in me for decades, maybe my whole life. I am one with him. I hear priests reciting prayers in churches from my childhood, *Body of Christ, Blood of Christ.* This is communion.

Later, lying in bed, I again close my eyes and sense in, imagining I can feel Theo's DNA in my bloodstream, alive and even healing my own body at this very moment. As I'm visualizing this, I see the structure of DNA in my mind, and recall that a scientist in a documentary I once saw described the double helix shape as resembling a radio receiver. This scientist hypothesized that something about DNA acts to receive information from an unknown source, maybe an unseen creative force, what some would call God. I can't remember exactly, but it has to do with quantum physics and the way the genetic code translates into life.

I think of all this and wonder if Theo's spirit is sending me information through DNA from wherever he is—the other world, the beyond, the place we all come from and will go back to eventually. Maybe this is why I feel my attention is somewhere else: not in this world, not on my life. This would explain why I am much more interested in where Theo went than in where I am right now. I don't care about my own survival anymore. I don't feel drawn to earthly things, to dramas happening around me.

I just want to lie on my bed and beam myself to Theo. My body is heavy on this bed, my heart is here in my chest, aching and beating, but my soul has gone with Theo; it is flying in some other universe.

February 11

It has been four weeks exactly. I am up much of the night, heat blasting through my body, especially my hands. I think of Theo's body burning in the furnace at the crematorium. *What is this heat? Am I having postpartum hormonal flashes? Or am I burning up in some sort of karmic fire? Is this the part of me that's connected with Theo, the cells he left behind that made an imprint on my own?*

Dix wakes in the night, crying, "I miss our little boy."

February 12–13

Kevin and Jasper are off in town for a night. Dicken and I have a sauna in the moonlight. The first full moon since Theo; I feel heartsick.

We make love in the morning. I am hungry: I want Dicken, all of him, to be inside me. I feel a desperate urge to get pregnant. But Dicken withdraws. I am sad afterward, thinking of all his wasted sperm. Lying there, I suddenly think of Theo's body. I don't remember ever seeing his penis or bottom because they were covered by his diaper. I think of how he'll never get to enjoy those parts, how his balls probably didn't drop, how no lucky woman will ever love his beautiful chest, feel about him the way I do about Dicken.

I am empty, and nothing can fill that place. Not Jasper or Kevin, or songs, or poetry, or travel, or pottery, or music, or movies, or even Dicken.

February 14

I enter the office. Dicken is looking down at a letter on his desk, his forehead in his hands.

"What is it?" I ask.

202 // FIVE HOURS

"It's our hospital bill."

"How much?"

"You sure you want to know?"

"Is it that bad?" I ask.

"Yes."

"Just tell me."

"Fourteen thousand," Dicken says.

"Are you kidding me? What about our insurance?"

"We have a high deductible, you know that."

"I thought it was ten thousand, and the rest gets covered."

"Only at 50 percent for the next ten grand."

"That sucks," I say. Then I feel rage coming on. I run up to our room and grab a pillow and start smacking it against the bed. It feels pitifully weak and unsatisfying. I wish I had a baseball bat and some pumpkins.

Dicken appears in the bedroom, alarmed, then stern. "Don't worry about the money."

"It's not the money," I say bitterly. "I just feel sick. *Cheated.* Here I am, fat and fourteen thousand dollars poorer because of a pregnancy that robbed me of nine months of my life and gave me no baby. I'm sick of all the condolence cards, the flowers. I just want my baby. Stop sending letters and e-mails and enormous hospital bills!"

Dicken sighs, then heads back downstairs. "I'll be earning some of that money if you need me!" he calls up.

I can't stand free time. It makes me anxious. It's what I often wished for when I was pregnant, lots and lots of time to myself for all the things I would enjoy and achieve. Now I have all the space and time I wished for and it feels empty and meaningless, such a waste when I could be loving and nurturing a baby. That was supposed to be my job. I had let everything else go.

My friend Geri calls. She and her husband lost a preterm baby years ago and never had other children.

"I love the e-mails you wrote about Theo," Geri says. "And the picture, oh my God! I printed it out and keep it on my desk and look at it whenever I need perspective."

Her words remind me of a card we got from a woman we know in England, who wrote, *The photograph of Theodore. That's a baby I could pray to.*

"Did you have a picture of your baby taken?" I ask Geri.

"Oh God no, I never even saw the baby, or found out if it was a boy or a girl. They did things so differently back then. It was awful."

"And that wasn't so long ago."

"I tell you what, you're lucky you have so much support."

"I know, Geri. And I'm so sorry you didn't have that when you went through your loss. I really don't know how you survived it."

"Well, I'm so glad I know you because reading what you wrote is healing for me. And it will be for other women."

February 15

There is part of me that accepts this loss, goes on bravely, feels at peace. There's also a part of me that can't fully face it: the magical-thinking part. It's waiting for me to wake up and find myself about to give birth to a healthy Theo. It won't let me put away the baby clothes. It can't bear to give away the front pack and changing pad in the back of the Subaru. I dread the day I can't squeeze any more milk from my breasts.

That part of me is the wailing woman. The hysterical screeching mother clawing at the air, out of her mind with grief.

February 18

It's a tough Saturday morning. Kevin groans and sulks while getting dressed for a ski trip. I try to breathe, telling myself it's not my business how he feels about skiing. But my anger grows with each of Kevin's muttered noises.

* * *

That evening, I head to Rhione's house for dance, my first time back since before the birth. Rhione gives me a big hug and I start crying. She holds me and rubs my front—my belly and scar—as I weep. Her hands and body are so soft and comforting, I feel nurtured in a way I haven't been. Mothered. Dicken has a strong, masculine touch. The way he holds me is amazing; it's gotten me through the hardest days. But Rhione's gentle touch is something I've been missing without knowing it.

I decide to dance the intention-question, *How can I love Kevin more?* Before my turn, I have an inkling that Theo might come dance with me, but I know that's just a romantic feeling, a longing. I don't really believe it's possible.

The music starts, and I close my eyes as my arms reach out. I tilt my head upward, and I feel my hands come down over my ears. Suddenly I am deaf, can't hear the music or anything outside, only inner sounds. I know Theo is with me. I think of his funny crinkled ears, how he may not have been able to hear, because many trisomy 13 babies are deaf. Then I wonder with some alarm: If he was deaf, how could he have heard my heartbeat? Why did he relax so much when they brought him to me and placed him on my left side, where I imagined he could hear my familiar heart? As soon as I think that, I become aware of the vibration of my heart beating—an answer! I know I am being told that he could feel that loud and strong, hearing or no hearing. My hands come down over my throat, and I am thirsty and breathless, thinking of how Theo couldn't take in any nourishment or enough breath through his mouth.

By now I am weeping. I gasp a couple of times, like he did when I first held him. Then my hands come together, and as I feel my fingers entwine, his sixth fingers are with me. I can sense them there, like phantom limbs, and I think of Jasper discovering them and calling them "his lucky fingers." So precious, those tiny boneless appendages, and not repellent or strange, as I would have thought. Just pure sweetness, so adorable. My hands make their way to my breasts, and I think, *Here's the milk we made together, Theo. Our milk.* My hands run over my hair and remind me of his, the downy blond tufts I wept over.

As I dance, the recent NPR story comes back to me, the one about the discovery that a baby's cells stay in the mother's body long after it's born, maybe even helping damaged parts of her body. I dance and know Theo is with me, in me, part of me, right here.

After dancing, I keep my eyes closed and am aware of feeling incredibly blessed, light dancing in my cells. A warmth. For hours and hours, I will be free from the desperate ache of missing him.

When I get home from dance, Dicken tells me Kevin has been acting out.

"He's been extremely rude to Maud. I just don't understand what's going on. Can you help me talk to him about it?"

We find Kevin lying in his bunk bed. Dicken and I ask a few questions. Kevin is silent at first, looking angry, and then he suddenly starts to cry.

"I don't want to be here!" he wails.

"Where, here in Oregon?" Dicken asks.

"No, here in the world," he says. "I feel like a nobody."

He cries and cries, turning his back to us. "Nobody really cares about me, not my parents, not you guys . . ."

"I'm so sorry," I say. My heart feels soft, sad. I think of his birth mother, who beat Kevin and his brothers. Nothing we do for him will fix the past.

Dicken rubs his back softly as he cries.

"I wish I could go back in time," Kevin says. "Then things would be better. Then it wouldn't be like this."

"I know that feeling," Dicken says. "Wanting to go back and do things differently, right?"

Kevin nods, more tears.

"It's okay to feel that," Dicken says. "You can feel all this and know that everything's still okay. It just feels scary when you're in it."

Kevin turns toward us inch by inch, nodding as Dicken talks to him soothingly.

"Kevin, you've been through so many changes, so many hard things already," Dicken says. "We love you. You're part of our family now. We're not going to let you go."

It's amazing to watch this little boy open and soften. By the end, he wants me to read to him, and we laugh together. He lets us both hug and kiss him goodnight. I feel huge love, appreciation, and compassion for him, and I suddenly realize the interaction has addressed my dancing intention—*How can I be more loving with Kevin?*—my goal for the evening which I'd completely forgotten about until now.

February 19

In the night, Dicken and I make love, and it is more intense than ever. It is huge, beautiful and terrifying. Beyond me and my body. I'm sure I am about to dissolve, come apart. Not physically; it isn't intense that way. I feel overcome by emotions and images not personal to me. Very odd. More scary than odd, actually. I don't recognize myself. I am strangely disinterested, not invested in my own pleasure, which is rare.

As we lie in the dark afterward, Dicken says, "Wow, that was crazy! I wanted to devour you. I've never felt so overcome by my love for you."

He runs his hands over me and marvels at the beauty of every curve. His touch is painfully tender. It is an edge for me; I feel close to madness, like I am losing contact with reality. I think of Paul saying it's beauty that can destroy us more than suffering. I feel sorry for Paul when I think of how much he sees. I have the thought, *Why would anyone want to see?* How would I meet that much emotion? That much energy? That much heartbreak? I'd prefer to stay in my safe illusions.

I fall asleep after a long while and dream of a woman pregnant with her fifth child.

* * *

The next day, I am looking at Dicken's body as he gets dressed, thinking about how he's got his new rowing machine and will probably slim down a little. *I hope he doesn't lose his belly entirely; he's already perfect.* I compare that thought to how I used to be: panicked when he gained a few extra pounds, withdrawing my love from him, finding him unattractive, nagging him about it. Now the love feels unconditional—devotional. I worship him and his body, feel enslaved to it, especially that left forearm for some reason; I literally pine for it. Can't imagine ever wanting another man.

I'm intending to translate this to myself, my own body. I'm not as freaked out as I used to be about being five or ten pounds heavier. I go in and out, but I don't feel as stuck in body-hatred vigilance as I used to be. There are moments now when I feel sorry for myself that I can't nurse off this pregnancy weight, that I'm stuck with jiggly thighs and belly and no baby; that I'm so far from the place I was when I was nursing infant Jasper, loving the intense hunger, savoring all the extra calories. Now, I don't have much enthusiasm for food. I wish I could turn off hunger and the need to eat. I open the fridge and nothing appeals. Food tastes strange, dead. I just eat to survive. It's not like me.

February 21

This morning before I get out of bed, I lie there and feel heavy grief, like a stone pulling my chest down into the earth. I sense the shock, the memory of everything in my body. I know there is much more to release.

I'm melted by Jasper, his sweet face. I imagine I see an older Theo in him. Letting go of Jasper—halfway grown-up—is heart-wrenching. "Makes me want to have another baby," said Dix last night, adding, "but eventually we have to face it. They don't belong to us."

I have a session with my therapist. She sent me a lovely card right after Theo died, then the CD recording of the retreat I missed. I felt enraged when I heard people in my group laughing and talking about their petty feelings, when they all knew I'd just lost Theo days before. The only person I heard mentioning Theo in the recording was Maud, who was crying and talking about how she hadn't been taking care of herself since the night of the birth.

I don't mention my feelings about all of this to my therapist, because I tend to avoid anger and confrontation. She asks how I'm doing, and we spend the session focusing on my feelings about Theo and how I've changed.

"I can feel that part of me is afraid of going back to pre-Theo states and preoccupations, like worrying about my weight, or being miserly," I explain. "The heavens opened for Theo's birth and death, and I don't want them to close again. I want to stay in the light, in the purified moment, in the beauty."

"Don't you see, though, how you're rejecting who you were before Theo was born?"

I think about this, and say, "Yes, I guess so. I just like who I am, how I am, better now. I feel like I see things from a much more real place."

"But you can see how you're not leaving room for yourself to be human, to forget truth, which is what life is: knowing truth, forgetting it, remembering, and so on. Can you make room for the part of you that didn't know what you know now, might still not know, might never know?"

"No, I don't want her to waste any of my life being that narrow, that petty, that untrusting."

"That sounds like a high bar to hold yourself to."

"But if I stay vigilant, and make use of all Theo taught me, it's the best way to honor myself and him, right?"

"Is it?"

I feel frustrated. I divert the conversation by bringing up my confusion about whether to try for another baby. I'm hoping my therapist will help me see the right answer here.

"What thoughts and feelings arise when you ask those questions?"

"I just wanted Theo to end all the debate," I say. "I don't want to be in this place. This wasn't the plan."

"You sound angry."

"Well, I am, because it's so bewildering. I mean, my gut response is fear, like, I can't go through another pregnancy, especially not in my fragile state. But another part of me wants to give up everything—all my dreams of travel and writing and projects and accumulating wealth—to have another baby and devote myself to it. Stay on the farm, bask in love for baby and Dix and the boys. And the pressure is on, there's no time to lose! It just doesn't seem fair that I'm in this position."

"What happens in your body when you say all that?"

I close my eyes. "I feel a sense of urgency in my chest, and pushing/pulling sensations like a bunch of hands are inside me, kneading my flesh and fighting for space." Suddenly I am crying hard.

"What's happening?"

I struggle to speak. "I'm remembering the abortion we had right after we got married. *Why? Why did we do that?* I just want to go back in time and warn myself of what's to come, change that decision. Oh, I want another chance so bad!"

My therapist is quiet while I contract over my knees and squeeze my hands into tight fists, willing time to go backward. Then she speaks, her voice steady and firm: "That was a long time ago. You were a different person then."

"I know, but I hate myself for doing it. Maybe that's why Theo died: I deserve it. I've been ambivalent about motherhood all along. That's why this happened. It's my punishment." I am so angry at myself, I feel like I will literally implode.

"Lucinda, you are human, so of course you have been ambivalent about an issue as intense as parenthood. Everyone who's ever thought about becoming a parent goes through that."

"Really?"

My therapist smiles, as if it's humorous that I don't know this.

I can feel a slight softening in my chest.

"You've only mentioned your own ambivalence, but Dicken chose to have that abortion too. And yet I don't hear you blaming him."

I think about this for a few moments. "You're right. Look how I put all this on myself."

"How do you feel when you acknowledge that?"

"I feel a lot less guilty. That's a relief."

I take some deep breaths, closing my eyes, feeling my body relax and expand as I let in the relief. Then there is something sharper, a pang in my throat. I open my eyes and say, "You know, I don't deserve all this blame. I did the best I could. I am the woman who gave birth to beautiful Theo, who wanted him desperately and had him taken away. Theo's mom doesn't deserve to go through any more pain. She has been through enough!" Tears spill down my face. I wipe them away, then let my hands fall to my belly, rubbing it gently.

"You've been through a lot," my therapist says. Her eyes are brimming.

"I'm sad for myself. Sad for Dicken, sad for what we went through years ago, and sad for all we didn't know we were facing."

I cry for all that has been lost, and I become aware of how tired I am from the internal struggle.

The session ends, and I leave with no answers.

February 25

I get to hold a baby, a cute four-month-old boy, the son of a couple who come by to talk to Maud and Tom about farming. It feels good to me—my arms full, my body doing what it has been programmed to do for so long. But he smells funny, not my baby. I only really want my child. My Theo.

My breasts are smaller, but I can still squeeze out some milk. I decide to start a sourdough culture using a few drops. I can keep making new generations of sourdough, diluting the original formula but never losing at least a microscopic amount of milk. I'll make bread from this when I miss him, when it's his birthday, when I need a way to connect with him in the physical realm. I can add to the culture each time, keeping alive the sustenance we created together. For the rest of my life I'll be able to make Theo bread.

As I squeeze my milk into a cup and mix in the ingredients for the culture, I hum the chant we danced to at our last retreat, the words of which pierced me so deeply:

> *Where are you going? and she said, "To that world"*
> *Where do you come from? and she answered, "From that world"*
> *So what are you doing in this world? and she said, "I am sorrowing"*
> *In what way? they asked of her, and Rabia replied,*
> *"I am eating the bread of this world*
> *and doing the work of that world."*

CHAPTER 19

Six weeks today.

This morning I sob and sob, my head in Dicken's lap, Grace holding my hand. "I want him back! When am I going to wake up and have this nightmare be over?" I am hysterical, clawing at the air.

"I want a baby so badly—I want a girl like Grace, I want a girl and I want Theo!"

Dicken says, "You have a girl, Grace, and she's the real thing." Grace smiles with her adorable cheeks bunched up.

Afterward I feel relieved, soft. Dix says, "If you really want another baby, I'll get on board for that."

In the night, I dream that Paul says my body would be fine with another pregnancy. He doesn't seem to recall telling me I was at the end of my reproductive years.

March 1

I go down to the office and find Dicken in tears over the medical bills—"Not the money but the reminder of what we went through—what *you* went through," he says.

Then I see an unopened envelope from Dad on the desk. I know Dad is sending us some money to help with the bills, so I open it. Inside is a check for half our medical costs.

I show Dicken the check, saying, "Look at this and feel how supported we are." We both cry.

March 6

In the co-op today, I see a woman with an infant in a front pack. She's on her cell phone, complaining to someone about how exhausted she is, how she hasn't slept more than a few hours in a row for weeks.

I turn around and walk the other way, though I want to go up to her and say, *Do you have any idea how lucky you are? I haven't slept well in weeks either and I have no baby! It is so much easier to have a baby than to think you are going to have a baby and then not have a baby. If you only knew, you would stop complaining!*

My friend Mary comes over for tea. While we're talking in the kitchen, Kevin walks in and says he's hungry.

"What do you feel like?" I ask.

He shrugs, pouting, his eyes on the floor.

"Toast?"

He shakes his head.

"Eggs?"

Another head shake.

"Well, can't you think of something? Help me out here."

Tears start to slip down his cheeks. As usual, I'm surprised by how suddenly they come on, and how fast they fall.

"What is it?" I say, my tone sharper than I intend.

"I hate the food in this house! I hate the food in this country! And I'm *so* bored!"

I just stare at him.

"I hate my life! I wish I could go back to Costa Rica!" He knows we're taking him there for a visit this summer, but that's not what he's talking about. He's saying he wants to leave us and go back for good. Does he mean it? At nine years old, could he truly know what he wants?

I stare at him some more, then say, "Really? Well, it's your life, Kevin, and if you really think you'd be better off in Costa Rica, I wouldn't stop you just out of selfishness."

He looks up at me, the tears stopped. He eyes me carefully

for a long minute or so; then his face relaxes. He cocks his head and says, "I think I'll stay here for two more years."

"I love you and hope you'll stay with us, but more than that I want the best for you."

Mary, who has been listening this whole time, tells Kevin about her son, who has been agonizing over whether he should be here or in New Orleans.

"Even grown-ups feel confused about where they belong," Mary says.

Kevin is listening intently, and comes closer to me.

"Life decisions are hard, however old you are," I say. "Like how Daddy and I don't know whether to have another baby or not. It's really hard. We go back and forth, and there's no way to know the right answer."

Kevin sits by me on the couch and asks me to make him some toast.

Dicken spends the evening with Kevin while I take Jasper to a birthday party. When I get home, Dicken says Kevin seems to be in a much better place, relaxed and laughing and wanting physical closeness.

Meanwhile, Ben and Paula's pregnancy news is alarming—an ultrasound showed their baby has a single umbilical artery. They're having an amnio tomorrow. Poor Ben was very upset when they got the news. He'd just heard my whole story a few days earlier, including the fact that Theo's single-artery umbilical cord was one of the first signs of possible trouble.

I feel depressed, maybe because of my period. I just can't find much fun in anything, like dinner with friends the other night, or watching the Oscars. I feel relieved and reassured when I'm at my best, distracted at times, and debilitated and half-insane at my worst. I don't fit into my clothes. I don't fit into my life. I can't get to sleep at night; I lie there feeling dizzy, scared. I can't relax: my body is holding on, bracing for another shock. Tired, mostly uninterested in external goings-on, I wander familiar terrain like a visiting zombie.

Outwardly, everything appears as it was before, this house, this husband and children, yet I don't know what I'm doing here and I don't remember the woman who created all of this. Who was she and where did she go? Is she coming back?

March 7

At breakfast I am rushing and knock over the bottle of maple syrup on the counter. I shout, "Goddamn it!" as Dicken swoops in and rights the bottle before all the syrup spills out.

"What's the matter?" he asks. "You seem really tense."

I take a deep breath and close my eyes. "Well, I'm really aware of wanting to check things off my internal to-do list, things of little true consequence, like fixing the car windscreen, getting the paintings out of barn storage to Mom's house, recycling, and so on. I want to finish working on the taxes." As I talk, I have a breathless feeling that I'll never catch up with myself.

"You don't need to do any of that," Dicken says. "I'll take care of the taxes. The rest can wait."

"The last thing you need is another task like taxes. You work way too hard as it is."

"You sound mad about that."

"I guess I am. I judge you for being a workaholic."

"So you want me to be like our guy friends who sit around drinking beer most of the day?"

I think of those friends and feel disgust. "No, I judge them too. No one can get it right."

"Well, maybe you could be more supportive of how hard I work. Or just leave me alone!"

"Why are you being so mean?"

"Daddy!" Jasper, who has been eating pancakes nearby, chimes in. "Don't be mean to Mommy!"

"Oh my God, this family is falling apart," Dicken says, his face red.

"You always say that the moment I show any neediness," I say, my voice becoming loud and firm. "Fine, have it your way. I'll toughen up and sort myself out and get off your back."

Dicken looks at me for a long moment. "You seem so hard and distant when you get that way. I actually prefer you when you're needy. You seem more present."

"What am I supposed to make of that? I'm confused."

"I am too. It's just that I love it when you're sad about Theo and stay in bed writing."

"But you never do that," I point out.

"It's kind of like you're doing that part of the work for us, and I'm doing the active part. Does that make sense?"

I nod. He takes me in his arms.

I guess it's my job to be sad right now, not to distract myself or put pressure on myself to do more than I really feel up to.

I can see that it helps Dicken to be doing as much as he is, to be functioning and bringing in money and writing out the checks and picking up the slack around the house. Letting him take care of me is bringing us closer, so it makes sense that we should just grieve in our own ways. When I fight to overcome my inertia and be more like him, it actually creates distance between us.

But there's no simple solution here. Sometimes being who we are and telling each other the truth only seems to bring more struggle. He's distressed to see my pressured self again.

Hearing his assessment of me as less present makes me sad. It makes me feel I've lost everything Theo gave me. I've forgotten. I might as well not have gone through all that suffering.

March 8

Tonight Kevin won't eat his dinner. He is pouty and sullen.

"What is it?" I ask, hearing the annoyance in my voice.

"I hate the food here," he says, tears beginning to spill over his cheeks. "I miss Costa Rica. I hate my school."

"You have such a good life!" I say. "If you could just shift your terrible attitude and realize how lucky you are, you wouldn't be so angry and unhappy."

"You don't know how I feel," Kevin says.

Anger begins to boil inside me. I go find Maud for some coaching.

"What do you feel in your body right now?" she asks.

I close my eyes and describe the red pulsing rage, the feeling that something is trying to crush me into a small mass.

"I just want to make Kevin small, rub his nose in the dirt," I say.

"Sounds like that's what happening to you inside."

Maud helps me get in touch with the bigger picture, how it's really me I'm mad at; *I'm* the one who has everything and still isn't content. How can I be with Kevin's big feelings if I can't be with my own? I feel compassion for the part of me that wants the world to make me happy, to have everything go my way. *You think you should be happy because you have so much,* I tell myself, *and it's really, really disappointing that you still feel so empty and unsatisfied sometimes.*

As the evening unfolds, I notice myself in the flow of the crazy stream of life at the farm—Maud and all our kids plus a gaggle of friends: noise, mayhem, mess; meltdowns, shrieks, tears, pouts, self-inflicted exiles. At one point I'm making toast and I drop Dicken's butter dish, the second or third one I've broken. I finally got Mom to replace it after two years of trying to make him one myself. Each of my efforts exploded in the kiln, except for the one that disintegrated in my luggage while I carted it across Costa Rica. When the replacement butter dish slips from my grasp and crashes on the floor, all I can do is laugh—not my usual reaction. And the mess doesn't bother me.

Tonight the storms of emotion come and go. I find myself laughing, not resisting.

March 13

I take Kevin to an open house for Boys-to-Men, a weekend of

therapeutic work and initiation which he'll attend next month. Bill, the leader, is very impressed by what Kevin says in the interview, and tells me, "He's a little shaman!" I'm excited for Kevin; I think he'll really get into it.

Meanwhile, he's the fourth in reading in his class—and that includes the grade above his. He says his teacher told the class today, "If Kevin has that many points and has only been speaking English for a year, all of you should be doing better." I am very proud; I even cry a little. I try not to overemphasize the achievement, telling him I'd love him even if he didn't do so well.

In the evening we call Costa Rica. Liliana, Kevin's aunt, who took him in for two years before we adopted him, tells us she's pregnant. A big surprise; she's already a grandmother. I am delighted for her and hear myself say, "You're so lucky!" She says she's not so sure.

And there is good news from Ben: their baby is fine. It turns out the cord is a double, not a single. What a relief. Amnio confirmed that all is well. It's amazing how many people we know who've had false scares. I just wish I could count myself among them.

March 14

We do a tree-planting ceremony today—Theo's ashes; Jasper, Grace, and Sam's placentas, which have been stored all this time in the deep freeze; and a lock of Kevin's hair, all placed under an apple tree, an Orange Pippin cross. It snowed last night, and the moon is full, just like on Theo's birthday.

March 18–21

People have stopped calling as much. No one brings meals by. I get a card or letter or e-mail once in a while, but not daily anymore. I go into the closet and look at the baby clothes on the shelf. *I should put these away, it's time*, I tell myself. But I already know I can't do it.

Instead, I go down to the office and look up WinterSpring, a local grief-support organization several people have mentioned to me. I dial the number and leave a message asking for information about their services. I get a call back later that day. A woman tells me they have an ongoing children's program and an upcoming eight-week support group for bereaved parents.

I ask her to send me the sign-up forms. Then I tell her all about Theo. At one point early on in our conversation, she tells me her daughter died several years ago.

"I'm sorry to hear that," I say. "Is it any easier now?"

"Yes. When it had just happened, I never thought I could feel okay again, but gradually, I did."

I'm afraid she will go on to tell me more about her experience, which I know should interest me but at this moment does not. Luckily, she asks me another question, and I get to jump back in. I talk a lot, feeling an intense desire to share my story, Theo's story. It feels more central and important than anyone else's story right now. As I speak, I feel clear, solid, articulate, and I imagine I must sound impressive to this woman. She must be thinking, *What an evolved person. She's got it all together. She doesn't need our services.* I don't realize how badly I'm trying to convince myself this is true.

A few days later, I'm in the office opening mail and find the sign-up form for WinterSpring. I tell Dicken about the group, adding, "I don't think we really need this. We have so much support."

Dicken is typing on his computer and doesn't look up. "I agree," he says. "I feel like I'm doing okay."

I leave the form on my desk and head up to the bedroom. Lying down, I start to feel dizzy. I think of the boys, Kevin back at school, Jasper playing at a friend's house. I think of Dicken down in the office, working away as if nothing has happened. I try to imagine going down there and sitting across from him, editing one of his articles. I know I can't do it. *What is wrong with me? Everyone else is moving on, but I'm stuck.* I can't move my body, but I don't want to stay here in bed anymore. I make myself move and step by step get back to the office. I sit down and stare at my computer.

"Want me to help you with anything?" I ask Dicken quietly.

He doesn't answer, and I start to feel a falling sensation.

"Dicken!" I wail. "What about me? Can't you see that I'm not doing well? That I need help?"

He looks startled, turns away from his monitor and gives me his full attention. "Yes, I see that," he says. "And I'm sorry. I wish I knew what to do. I guess I'm just moving on, and you're taking a little longer."

"Is there something wrong with me?"

"No, I don't think so."

"Well, why are you able to move on and get back to work, and I still feel like this just happened? It actually feels worse than it did at first, and I'm scared it'll keep getting worse forever."

Crying, I run up to our room. Dicken follows me, sits down on the bed beside me.

"I'm sorry, I don't know how to help you."

"It's just so scary to feel like we're not in the same place anymore. I loved when we were so close, sharing every moment of this. Now, I'm alone, and I *can't stand it!*"

"I'm right here," he says, but he sounds far away, like a voice in a dream.

"When is it going to feel better? When is he coming back? I can't do this anymore, I really *can't!*"

I scream and flail on the bed while Dicken tries to get ahold of me, but I won't let him.

"I hate you for leaving me here!" I yell. "How could you be so cruel?"

"I'm *right here.*"

"What's wrong with me?"

"Shhhhhh. It's okay."

* * *

Later, I go downstairs and see that Dicken has filled out the WinterSpring group form with both of our names.

April 6

It's the first night of our WinterSpring bereaved parents group. We walk in late and join the seven other solemn-faced parents. Dicken immediately begins to cry.

"Sorry we're late," I say.

"No problem, we were just about to start introductions," says a dark-haired woman with an English accent and a soothing voice. "I'm Christine, and I'll be facilitating the group. I'm so glad you're here."

We go around the circle, passing a Native American talking stick, introducing ourselves and our children.

"I'm Jerry and I'm here for my son Brent, who was twenty-five. He died of a heroin overdose last month."

"I'm the mother . . . of . . . Brent," whispers a pale woman. Christine hands her a tissue and tells us all to breathe.

"I'm Scott and I'm here for my son Diego, who was born premature and only lived a week."

"I'm Alice and I'm here for my daughter Sage. She was twenty-two, murdered by the father of her baby girl."

"Everybody breathe," Christine says.

"I'm Lucinda and I'm here for my son Theo."

"I'm Dicken . . . and . . . I'm—" Dicken is sobbing. I haven't seen him cry this hard since the cremation. Other parents hand him tissues.

"Take your time, sweetheart," Christine says.

"I'm . . . here . . . for my . . . for my son . . . Theodore Simon . . ."

"Well done," Christine says. "It's so important to speak the names of our children. To say aloud who we are here for. And it's healthy to cry. Emotion is what I like to call energy in motion. E-motion. Crying, or any form of emoting, lets that energy move through us, which is the work of grief and mourning."

I immediately like Christine; she is warm and reassuring.

She keeps using the word "permission." "We have to give our-selves and each other permission to be where we're at. There are no rules when it comes to grieving. So don't *should* on yourself."

When we go around the circle again, sharing if we choose to, I talk about Theo's birth and death. I notice how I don't share the joy part. I match the rest of what I've heard tonight, the sorrow and the pain. Later I will feel remorse about this and promise myself to honor his whole story in the next meeting.

When it's Dicken's turn, his voice is hoarse. "I just feel so sad," he says, beginning to cry again. "I feel like I did when my dad died . . ."

"Every new grief brings up unresolved grief from our past," Christine says. "It's like we're right back there, in that moment from long ago."

Dicken nods as he blows his nose. Then, breaking down again, he says, "And now my beloved brother-in-law is very ill with cancer, and I'm so scared to lose him. I just don't know how I could face that."

I reach for his hand and hold it as he cries some more. My chest aches, yet I know this crying is a great release for him. He holds it together in our life, maybe to be strong for me and the boys, or maybe to avoid feeling pain or falling apart. I realize now that he might need this group more than I do.

Something about the ninety-minute group, this space that Christine creates, these other parents who join us for the sole purpose of mourning, gives Dicken, and me, an opportunity to let down. Over the next seven weeks, Dicken and I will arrive early for every meeting. We will find it almost amusing that we look forward to grief group so much, that we cheer up the closer it gets, that it's the highlight of our week. It becomes a life raft for us, a place where we can tell our stories, be with people whose lives are also broken open, be reminded we are not alone, and maybe most importantly, be reminded that no, we are not crazy.

CHAPTER 20

April 15

I t has been three months exactly.

A couple that just moved into the area came for dinner tonight, and I found I could not participate in the conversation. It all sounded dead to me; it was like they were from another planet, speaking a bizarre language. I wanted them to know why I was not acting normally, but I couldn't figure out a way to tell them about Theo. There wasn't an opening. It got harder and harder, and I finally left the main house.

I only want to be with people who know about Theo. And with people who are willing to talk about it. I like our grief group for that reason, even though the people and their stories are so sad.

Giles, my brother-in-law in England, isn't doing very well. We'll find out more next week, when he gets an important blood test result.

Poor Becca says she's "preparing herself." Dix says Giles sounded positive on the phone, as always.

April 21–22

Grief group.

The mother of the young man who overdosed a few weeks ago cannot speak. She looks around the room at the others, nodding her head as tears pour down her face. Her husband tells the story of not hearing from their son for days, and then the search for his car, and how a relative eventually found it in a supermarket parking lot.

"He was in there . . ." His voice falters for a moment. "Overdose. Not sure if it was on purpose or not."

His wife is shaking her head now, the tears falling even faster.

Another father, whose premature baby died a month ago, says, "I feel terrible," and begins to weep.

Everyone is looking at him, waiting for him to continue. He is absentmindedly fingering the tattoo of his baby's name on his ankle. He begins to cry harder.

"What is it, sweetheart?" Christine asks.

"I . . . I . . . I used to sell heroin," he chokes out. "For all I know, I contributed to the death of someone's child."

The father of the overdose victim begins to speak in a firm voice: "Listen. We were angry at the dealer who sold our son the heroin, but we know a drug dealer didn't kill our son."

The room is silent except for the sound of sniffling.

Christine puts her hand on the tattooed young man's shoulder. "Did you take that in, sweetheart?"

He nods, wiping tears. Then he looks up at the other father and whispers, "Thank you."

The mother of the heroin victim speaks for the first time this evening: "How could this happen to a boy who grew up so sheltered, living next door to his loving grandparents, adored by his three older sisters? How could God have created a terrible thing like heroin?"

I think to myself, *Look how easy we have it compared to most people who lose children. Thank God we lost Theo to a natural cause, not something self-inflicted like drugs.* But then I look at Dicken and his tear-streaked, stricken face, and I think, *No, we're not lucky, either. I'm angry at God, just like this mother.*

April 23–24

I watch the video–slide show Gabriella has made in honor of Theo, by myself. It is heartbreaking, exquisite. My own beauty surprises me. I mourn that somehow. Mourn for what I don't see now, lament how ready I am to discount myself as old, ugly, chubby, unlovable. In the video footage I look open, radiant,

alive, soft, sweet. And the love that surrounds me! The sweetness of Jasper and Grace, their sorrowful faces, their tenderness,
their concern. Too much to bear.

It blows out such a huge space in me, I hardly sleep. I feel
that everything is passing too fast, I can't grasp anything. The
world of the video: it was all so precious and lovely and doomed.
I look for something solid to hold onto but keep falling into
space. I feel hot, especially in my hands, like I am boiling from
the inside.

I wake crying in the night, my hands searching for something—the baby? Then I realize I am hungry, and I weep for all
those nights when I was pregnant and used to go down to the
kitchen and get a snack. My little midnight feasts with Theo,
our only shared meals as it turned out. And there I was, expecting years of them. It all goes by so fast—whizzing along, everything dying, yet we're lulled to sleep, only to wake and find that
the thing we counted on is gone.

Terrifying to see the truth and not be able to find a place to
rest. Is that even possible? Are we supposed to find rest in the
falling?

April 25

I wake at three and can't get back to sleep, my second wake-
ful night in a row. I have so much emotion and energy cours-
ing through me; not thoughts, really, which is a blessing. Tears,
grief, wonder, passion: a sea of feeling. No time to waste in
sleep! We are dying and it's flying by. I see death everywhere. I
feel it in my cells.

I also see beauty everywhere. Today, I really look at the kids
who come over to play, especially the little ones. I pick them up
and hold them and marvel at them, and they beam it back to me
like flowers opening to the sun.

Dicken is thinking of buying us a new car, and I am filled
with grief. Looking at the Subaru, the one we bought on the day
of Jasper's baby shower when he was still inside me, I weep.

"What's the matter with you?" Dicken asks. "Aren't you happy we have the money to buy a new car?"

"Yes, of course. It's just that I see selling the Subaru as a rejection, another death. I can't handle any more changes right now."

I run outside to the car and sit in the driver's seat. I speak aloud, apologizing to the car, promising we'll keep it, love it, never let it go, the way I want to reassure my body that we still love it, tell it it's not useless even though it's aging and most likely past childbearing.

When I come back inside, I hear Dicken talking to someone at the VW dealership. It feels like a betrayal. I almost start screaming, wanting to sabotage the call by yelling so that the dealer can hear me: *We can't afford car payments! We haven't even paid the electricity bill in months! They're about to shut off our water!* I'm such a wreck, a madwoman, but at least I'm laughing and crying and seeing beauty amid all the death.

Cecily calls, saying she wants me to redo some of the lyrics of "New World," a song I wrote the words to last summer.

"Can you make the line 'I was angry, I was scared' a little less predictable?"

"Sure," I say. "I'll have a look and e-mail you what I come up with."

It doesn't take me long to think up the line, "I would sit in his electric chair." *That should add a little spice. If she wants shock, I'll give her shock, literally.* I e-mail her the revision, feeling confident it's a great improvement.

Cecily calls back a little later, sounding worried. She asks gingerly, "Are you okay, Cinda?"

"Yeah, I'm fine."

"Have you been getting enough sleep?"

"No, but I'm used to that by now. How come?"

"Well, it's just that, you know, the line about the electric chair. It's a little . . . a little alarming. I mean, should I be worried about you?"

Suddenly I see how extreme it must have sounded, and I start to laugh.

We end up in hysterics.

And yet in a way I do feel like I am facing my own execution. Everything is dying—the car, my fertility, these precious days. Jasper and Kevin's childhoods. I feel sad about Dad, how far away he lives, how we don't get to see him regularly. I miss him. I don't want to have him grow old and die and find I haven't cherished him enough.

April 30

I walk around town feeling utterly bewildered. My attention is floating. I don't feel like going to the library, the bookstore, browsing in shops. I almost have a panic attack. I try reaching Dix on his cell and can't get through. My pulse pounds in my ears. Everything seems speeded up to some level of activity I can't relate to at all, like time-lapse photography and those films of commuters getting on and off trains and crossing streets. I feel alienated. Spring is here and people are cheerful and celebrating, and I'm not ready.

Thank heavens Dix is more functional, but how in the world are we going to navigate the near future—the July trip to Costa Rica we've promised Kevin, and after that, our annual trip to England? I'm already dreading Costa Rica, mainly because I don't want to be away from Dix, but I don't have a choice. Kevin badly wants to visit his family, and I'll have to be the one to bring him as well as Jasper; Dix has to stay here and keep working. Thankfully, Mom's coming along so that I don't have to handle both boys by myself.

My scar is throbbing today. I feel great compassion for myself, walking around pretending to be okay when everything in me is dying.

The Theo journey has been intense this week with lots of

tears, but I'm pretty used to all that; and in contrast to human relationships on earth, I prefer the one with him right now. It's so simple and pure, even the broken, desperate longing for him, and I never lose the connection to my loving heart. Part of me just wants the world and its complexities to go away and leave me to lie in bed and close my eyes and be with love.

May 10

I'm in the office, working on ideas for Theo's ceremony. Dicken is on the phone with Giles, who is still very ill with metastasized colon cancer.

"Yes, I really would love to get over there this spring," Dicken says. "We could play golf."

Their conversation goes on for a while, with Dicken moving around the office. He seems a little nervous. "I really miss you, Giles. I, uh, I love you. You're a brother to me, I mean that." There's a pause, and then I hear Dicken talking about golf again, and his hopes to go over there soon.

When he hangs up, he's in tears but smiling. "I did it! I told him I love him. I've never done that before. My men's group gave it to me as a stretch. And he said he loved me too."

"I'm proud of you," I say. "I know it's not the English thing to do."

"I really want to go over and spend some time with him, go on my own. Hang out with him, you know, before it's, before it's too late." His voice breaks.

"Yeah, you really should do that."

I want him to go, but I also hate the idea of him being away from me.

"He's so brave, he really is, but it's not looking too good," Dicken says.

I can't speak because I'm choked up, but I open my arms and he falls against me, holding tight.

May 13–14

We spend the evening at the Megaritys' and watch the Theo video with Angie and Shannon. Dicken cries a lot. Back home, as we get ready for bed, he is still blowing his nose.

"You okay?" I ask.

"No. It was really hard to watch that. It just seems like such a waste."

He says the word "waste" with anger.

In the night, I bleed heavily. I wake feeling sad and tender about today being Mother's Day, remembering how joyful it was that first year when Jasper was a baby. I go to the bathroom to clean up the blood.

When I get back to bed, Dicken stirs and says, "What's going on?"

"Just cleaning up."

"Well, don't bloody these nice sheets."

"Thanks a lot," I whisper. It's not like him to be this way; he's usually very solicitous when I'm having a heavy period. I figure he's still upset from watching the video.

We wake again hours later and he apologizes, teasing himself about how mean he was. Then he says, "When I watched the Theo movie, I asked myself if Theo would want us to have another baby, and the answer was yes, there's room for that."

I nod, looking at him carefully.

He goes on: "It just seems like such a sad thing that two people who love each other so much would have all these pregnancies and only one living birth child."

Something about the way he says this makes me feel flooded with light.

Just then, Jasper bursts in from the garden with a huge bouquet of bright yellow daffodils in a thermos flask.

Dicken: "Did you use scissors?"

Jasper: "Nope, just my hands and my teeth!"

Kevin comes in smiling and gives me a lovely card with three poems he's written about me. I read them and choke up.

What a Mother's Day—a banquet! Dicken makes me decaf and we go for a walk.

I'm thinking we'll give this grief process until January, and after that we'll reassess and either try for another pregnancy or move on from there.

That night, I write:

What do you think, journal? Whoever is listening (witness, reader, me in some future), are you as curious as I am about what will unfold in these pages? Will another Weatherby baby be born? Will we stay on the farm? Will we travel, or will travel become less and less possible as the world changes? I think I'm going to start carrying around a note to myself that says, "You are exactly where you are meant to be. Home."

CHAPTER 21

May 15

I have an appointment with a nurse practitioner I know. I've been having hot flashes and tired spells, making Dicken suspicious about a hormonal imbalance. So I'm coming in to get a check-up, Pap smear, and blood tests. Filling out a form in the waiting room, I get to "age," and as I write 36, tears spring to my eyes.

The nurse measures and weighs me, and says, "Wow, you're light for your height." I shrug, not caring either way at this moment. I wonder if she knows I'm four months post-pregnancy. Has she read my chart? I want her to know everything, without having to tell her. I wish I could wear a sign that explains my story. The urge to have her know increases as she takes my blood pressure, and I wait for her to say something that I can jump on, a segue. I will her to ask me how many children I have, or ask me why I think I'm having hot flashes, anything that could justify mentioning my situation. But she is quiet, concentrating on her tasks. I give up and sigh, an ache inside growing as I sit there.

In the afternoon, Courtney comes over to talk about Theo's memorial celebration, which is just over a week away. She's thrilled that we asked her to be the celebrant.

"I'm afraid I'm going to cry too much and won't be able to get the words out," she says.

"Oh, you'll be fine," I tell her. "What I'm worried about is everything else."

"Like what?"

"Well, for one, the space—outside too loud, inside too small.

I'm also worried people will be uncomfortable and distracted. I'm regretting that we invited kids, imagining they'll be disruptive. People will be too hot. The video footage will be upsetting for some. There won't be enough food. The food we do have will spill and create a big mess."

"Wow, that is a lot to worry about," Courtney says.

"I know. I almost wish we hadn't planned this in the first place. I mean, we already did some ceremonies right after he died."

"But you know you'll regret it if you don't do this. You've said all along you want to share him with the larger community."

"You're right, I do."

"And even if all those things you mention go wrong, which is highly unlikely, people will still be moved, and you'll feel supported."

Later, as I lie in bed by myself, thinking about the ceremony, I can see that what I want is to have everything go perfectly, even though I know that's impossible. I realize I feel extra pressure since this is the only shot we have of celebrating Theo in a big, public way. There will be no plays, no music recitals, no graduations, no weddings, no airport arrivals. I've already written this one chance off as a disaster; I've already blamed it on my bad planning. But really, it's my not accepting the human side of this, and the reality that Theo is gone.

May 18

My blood test results arrive in the mail. Dicken frowns as he looks them over.

"Wow, you are severely anemic—ferritin level at six, should be forty or higher. Red blood cells low too. How are you even able to stand up?"

It's nice to know there's a reason I'm tired. It makes me feel gentler toward myself.

Also in the mail is a card from a childhood friend announcing she is pregnant. Paula, Kelsey, Kate, Tracy, Deb, Melanie,

Elizabeth, and Marianne—friends and relatives—are all pregnant. It is jarring to hear of all these women I know expecting babies this year. I feel left behind, not ready for everyone to move on. I'm not exactly envious; it's more about not wanting to deal with the emotions these births and babies might bring up.

May 24

I spend all morning preparing for Theo's memorial celebration. We get ready to head to town early so we can help set up the room and make sure the audio-visual system works. We take the boys with us.

"Can we listen to that funny guy?" Kevin asks as we set off down the driveway.

"Who?" Dicken asks.

"You know, the guy that tells jokes. Mom knows."

"It's not ringing any bells," Dicken says.

"He means Tony de Mello." I run through the recordings on the family iPod and press play. Soon, Kevin is cracking up at the silly religious jokes, and I am smiling inside, deeply touched that this nine-year-old we adopted from the jungles of Costa Rica appreciates the humor along with me. Jasper listens too, but doesn't laugh out loud.

"Mom, can you put all of this guy's CDs on my iPod?" Kevin asks.

"Of course," I say, trying to sound nonchalant but feeling secretly thrilled.

"I want them too," Jasper chimes in. "But not till I'm nine."

"Okey-dokey."

I am nervous all day, similar to the way I felt at our wedding. Numb, jittery, out of my body. The clock moves slowly, the anticipation growing. Finally, we are at the half-hour-before mark, and people are streaming in. I am grateful beyond words as a friend makes sure the sound system works. Nicoya puts together a beautiful altar with flowers and blown-up photographs of Theo.

Nancy sets up her video recorder on a tripod. As I watch each face that comes through the door to the sanctuary, I am touched in a different way. Many people from our retreat group show up, and two of the nurses from Ashland Hospital.

While we wait to start, the children stay in the outdoor area out front, with its green grass and lily pad pond. Angie has arranged for a babysitter to play games with the kids. I can hear their screams of delight. Beams of sunlight and a light breeze caress them all. I feel tears coming, but I am afraid to let the floodgates open.

After fifty or more people have gathered in the room, including many of the children, Courtney begins the ceremony by welcoming everyone. Her courage, and her ability to speak as tears form in her eyes and her voice breaks, impress and move me. Mom, Jasper, and Grace stand in front of the group and sing "The Rabbit Song," the one Grace sang to me in the hospital room the morning Theo died. *These colors green and tall must go the way of all, and winter comes too soon.*

Dicken stands tall in his dark suit and reads some passages of the poet Rilke's I chose. His voice is strong; I can tell he's trying to be stoic. I almost swoon at the beauty and truth I hear in the words: *We need, in love, only to practice this: letting each other go. For holding on comes easily; we do not need to learn it.*

Maud and Andrew play a song, the readers we've chosen read a selection of quotes from the condolence cards and letters and e-mails, and then we watch the video Gabriella made. Tears, tears, and more tears.

After the video ends, Dicken holds me in his arms, and people flock around us. They tell me:

"You are so beautiful."

"You're so precious."

"Thank you for sharing so much."

"I've never been so moved."

"I will never forget this."

"I can't tell you how grateful I am."

Mom says, "I couldn't help thinking of the Pietà."

The next morning, I feel exhausted in a relaxed, emptied-out kind of way, and lie in bed a long time, replaying the ceremony over and over in my mind. I'm mostly relieved, because more than anything I've been afraid that people wouldn't get it, that how we tried to portray the experience just wouldn't come across right—too intimate, too wordy, too mysterious. But they did get it, all of it. The depth, the beauty, the wonder.

Cecily phones from Boston. "I know it was stunning," she says in her amazed, uplifting voice. "Anne just called me and said it was so beautiful she couldn't speak about it without crying."

Theo has inspired more love. *We did it*, I want to tell him.

June 14

It has been five moons. Almost five months. Paul asks if he can record us talking about Theo, so we spend a few hours with him and Patty. Paul says we are incredibly lucky: Theo was a rare being. His questions are unusual; they bring out things I've never even articulated to myself.

He asks how I feel I've changed. That evokes much pondering, and a few insights, some of which don't occur to me until we are driving home. Here's what seems true: I am more baffled by the existence I find myself in. I don't feel as attracted to drama for drama's sake. I don't feel the need to hear of others' misfortunes to get a vicarious emotional experience. I'm not looking for more openness or motion. I'm not bored and wishing time would pass so something exciting will come sooner. No yearning to travel. I avoid parties. I feel uncomfortable more often. I notice that decisions large and small seem overwhelming. I have a harder time sleeping. I'm clingy toward Dicken and obsessed with his forearm. I enjoy cleaning and organizing. I can't stand accumulating clutter, trash. I think I'm more tolerant of foibles in others. I feel less of a need to seek spiritual answers. I pay closer attention to children and animals. I feel more humble. I cherish my parents more. I'm not obsessed with death—it's only another transition. My heart hurts a lot.

July 5

Today, I rationalize having a baby by arguing that the morning sickness would cure me of my attachments, including my extreme dependence on Dicken. When I was sick last year, I hardly noticed when he was away for ten days, and those were long days.

I'm terrified about my trip to Costa Rica with Kevin. We leave in three weeks. Two and a half weeks apart from Dix—it feels like suicide. Luckily I'll have Jabu, and Mom's help, and lots of sleeping herbs, pills, and tea. But the days will probably seem very long, the nights longer.

Right now, I feel paralyzed by life. I'm not sure what to do that has meaning, not sure which path to take. I want truth. I want needless suffering to end. I hate thinking that life is a banquet (as Tony de Mello says) and that I'm missing all the fun. Yet others say this is a hell realm, in which case I want out.

I'm terrified of losing my reality, my love with Dix—it couldn't just be a mirage, could it? Am I only projecting onto him? When he and I are parted, I wait to be reunited, for life to be sweet and relaxing again. Yet sometimes we're together and there's nothing to say; I watch him give so much of his energy to his computer and his work, and I can't relate. Then when I tune into my heart, he's all there. His devotion floors me. He loves his work but does it so he can support us. And he only goes to Paul because of me. He says he'd never do any "seeking" if it weren't for me.

July 22–23

I tell my therapist, "I'm struggling quite a bit—very in touch with my bewilderment at existence. Also my dependency on Dix, and my inferiority. I often feel unsettled, not at home in my body, not wanting to get out of bed, not knowing what do with myself. And I still can't sleep most nights, not well, anyway."

"Is it getting to sleep that's hard, or staying asleep?"

"Both. I close my eyes and everything seems to spin, and I get hot, especially my hands."

"It must be hard to relax. You're waiting for the next shock, afraid that if you relax, something terrible will happen."

I nod.

"Theo died at night, so you're more likely to be activated at nighttime."

"I think I've always been more restless and anxious at night. But it's really bad now. Is there anything I can do about it? I'd like to be able to sleep. I forgot how long the nights can be."

"You might want to try some compassionate statements, talking gently to the part of you that's scared. It's a way of witnessing what's happening, softening it. You might also try grounding breaths. When you're horizontal, you lose connection to the earth, and that can be unsettling."

"It also takes me back to lying on that operating table," I say.

Later in the session, I bring up the question of another baby, and immediately start sobbing.

"What comes up for you when you think about this?" my therapist asks.

"So much fear, so much pushing away the world, the pain of existence. At night, I think of all the pain and vow to never bring another poor soul to life. And yet I don't know how I'll ever stop yearning for another baby. I want one so badly, but I can't figure out if it's the right thing."

"The question is, is it your dharma to have another baby? And to get any insight on that, first you have to come to terms with what you want, what you think having a baby will get you."

"Well, right now I don't have anything else to fill my time. Of all the things I could throw myself into, it's a baby that appeals the most. And it seems like a good idea because Dicken and I enjoy the adventure of child-rearing. Plus, it would mean so much more to me now after losing Theo."

"Be careful, that could be a real setup," my therapist says. "You'll have ambivalence and doubts with another baby like every mother does, and you shouldn't expect more of yourself. What I'd be more curious about is the question of your life now and the issue of that not being enough. What are you expecting a baby to bring you that you don't have already?"

I shrug and feel blank.

This afternoon, we join some friends by the river in a nearby park. No one says much to me. I think most people know I'm not interested in small talk these days, and this isn't the environment for a deep discussion. Dicken is down in the shallow water, helping the kids find crawdads. I can hear Sam squealing.

Suddenly, I feel a strange agitation growing in my chest. I close my eyes and begin to see a flurry of images: everything speeded up, the kids outgrowing the river and the valley and Dicken growing old and dying. I see police chaplains showing up at doors in the middle of the night and telling grim news. All of these images seem to be flashing in my mind simultaneously. My breath speeds up, the sips of air getting shallow, like the river.

What are we doing, relaxing by the river, as if we don't know we're all going to be dead? We will lose everyone, everything we love, all this! How can anyone enjoy a single moment of life when this is the truth? And why is no one talking about it? What's going on? Are they all crazy? This stupid, pointless gathering by the river? It's a lie!

Gabriella, next to me, shades her eyes with her hand and asks, "You okay?"

I shake my head.

"Oh, sweetie, what can I do?"

"Can you get Dicken?"

She's off, and in a flash Dicken is standing by me, his face creased in concern.

"Will you drive me home?" I say as calmly as I can.

"Of course. Come on."

I start to gather belongings.

"Leave those," Dicken says. "Maud will bring them."

He holds my arm and steers me toward the parking lot. I can hear Jasper protesting that Dicken is leaving: "I just saw the hugest one ever, and I need you to catch him, Daddy!"

Dicken doesn't look back. He drives home faster than usual, eyeing me every few moments but saying nothing as I stare blankly ahead.

We get home and Dicken leads me to bed. He holds me as I begin to shake. Then I am in a rage, screaming, "I don't want to lose you and I'm going to! I can't pretend to sit by the river and enjoy it knowing that that's looming over me!"

Dix just holds me and talks to me soothingly; then we make love, then fall asleep together. From this quiet place, I look at our speeded-up life and think, *What's it all for? Why are we here? What are we doing in these bodies and what does it all mean? We should be clinging to each other all the time.* I feel like a small baby, merged with my mother, held, vulnerable, unknowing.

I see that the upcoming separation from Dix is bringing this up. Two and a half weeks without my lifeline. I feel sandwiched between that and Theo. Pressed up against the void with nowhere to run. I've lost a lot, I realize. Not just Theo and the expectations associated with raising him.

Thinking about the trip, I wonder if it will be good for me to get away, to break out of this downward spiral. Or will it freak me out? Can I hold it together?

Today I reflect on how Theo is always on my mind, never far away, and I apply that to me and Dix being separated. I'll just have to reach deeper to find my connection with Dix, not relying on the physical. I'm trying to minimize the time we'll be apart by thinking of soldiers who leave their partners for months and years at a time. I wish I could go now and get it over with. The anticipation is probably worse than the reality will be.

I try on an old bathing suit, look in the mirror and see dimples of cellulite on my thighs. Panic begins to rise: the familiar fear of aging and the energy I'll have to mobilize to fight the tsunami of decay bearing down on me. But quickly I let it pass through me and it's gone, like I've just done some swift and effective defensive martial arts move. I don't actually think this, but there's a knowing in me that radiates, *There is nothing frightening about cellulite, or aging. You've faced death and come through the other side. This is easy.*

July 25

In a dream, I am holding a baby, pulling it close to me. As I wake, I become aware that I am holding Dicken's arm, and only then do I make the connection between the size of Dicken's arm and the size of a newborn. No wonder I've been literally obsessed! It reminds me of a story I read in the paper when I was young, about the panda in the Washington zoo whose cub died, how for weeks afterward she would take the butter stick from her food tray and hold it and stroke it. That image struck me so hard, it has stayed with me for more than twenty years.

CHAPTER 22

July 26

Mom and I drive the boys to Portland for the flight to Costa Rica. On the way, Jasper sees signs for the amusement park outside of Salem and begs us to stop. "We have plenty of time," Mom says.

I think my mom is a bit of a pushover, but I don't say anything.

"Mom, come on the roller coaster with me!" Jasper shrieks.

I look up at the large wooden structure, not enthused at all.

"C'mon, Mom! You said you used to love rides."

"Okay," I say, and we get tickets and stand in the short line.

I am filled with dread and remorse as the car labors up the steep first hill. *This is fun*, I tell myself. *I love roller coasters, remember?* As we start to drop hundreds of feet at almost ninety degrees, I close my eyes and grip the handle bars with white fists. *What was I thinking? This falling sensation is way too familiar and not something I need to inflict on myself for kicks.*

The ride is mercifully short. I feel a twinging sensation in my back as I step out of the cart onto wobbly legs.

In the car again, Mom says, "You look like you're in pain."

"I think I tweaked a muscle in my back." I turn to make sure Jasper has his headphones on so he doesn't hear me add, "I never should have gone on that roller coaster."

"You loved them when you were young," Mom says, smiling. "You were such a gutsy kid."

"I know. I used to love a lot of things. And now I'd rather be in my bedroom than almost anywhere in the world. I feel like I'm turning into a curmudgeonly recluse. I guess I'm a lot like your mom, with her agoraphobia and dislike of most people. I think she and I were both too sensitive for this world."

"You're not like that. You're just fragile right now."

My eyes prick with tears. "I'm dreading this trip."

"We'll have fun," Mom says, reaching her hand across to touch mine.

"You're right." I force a quick smile. Inside, I am bracing myself each mile we travel farther from home and from Dicken, my home in this world.

In the airport in Costa Rica, Jasper insists on carrying my suitcase. He keeps hugging me, deferring to me.

"You really think we should take buses and not rent a car?" Mom asks me.

"Nana, my mom has been here more than anyone else," Jasper says sternly. "We should do what she says."

Kevin drags his big duffle bag across the airport. It's bursting with gifts he bought for his brothers and cousins.

It's dark when we get in a taxi. I tell the driver to take us to my favorite hotel in San Jose, where we'll spend the night before heading down to the Caribbean coast. After a ten-minute drive to the city, the driver pulls up at a different hotel. I tell him this is the wrong place. He says the one I wanted is full. We both know that he has no idea if the other hotel is full, that he's brought us here because he gets a kickback. I explain what's happening to my mom, and she begins to argue with him in her fluent Spanish. The man raises his voice. Jasper starts to cry.

"Mom, let's just stay here," I say.

Unlike the hotel I wanted, this one is right on a busy street and has no security guard on duty. Jasper is still upset as we check in and make our way to our large room with three beds.

"I miss Daddy!" he wails.

"It'll be okay," I tell him. "Let's just go to sleep, and when we wake up we'll get the bus and go see Liliana and everyone."

As I secure the door to our room, I note how flimsy the lock is. I hear the traffic outside the thin windows, hear voices on the street below.

Just as I'm imagining we'll be robbed or worse, Jasper says, "Mom, what if someone breaks in and steals our things? 'Member when someone stole Nana's wallet? And Daddy's computer?"

"Oh, Jasper, stop it," Mom says. "Everything's fine."

"But I'm scared!" Jasper cries. "I don't like it here."

I take a deep breath, wishing like crazy Dicken were here. "We'll be fine," I say. "We've never been robbed in San Jose. And the door is locked."

"But I don't feel safe. I just want Daddy!"

He must be picking up on my fear, I think, amazed at how he's articulating my own thoughts.

Jasper presses up close to me in bed, his body stiff and tense, and we turn off the light. I lie in the dark, listening to the traffic noises, seeing lights from cars and trucks flashing across the walls of our room. I know I will not sleep.

July 28

We survive San Jose and the long, winding bus ride to the coast the next day. I'm exhausted from no sleep and spend the afternoon holed up in our cramped room. The air conditioner is humming loudly and dripping water every other second—*splat, splat, splat.* I feel like I'm going crazy, like I'm a prisoner in this room, the dripping sound a Central American version of Chinese water torture.

Kevin is staying down the road with his relatives. Mom has taken Jasper to the beach, so I'm alone. In some ways this is a relief; I was growing annoyed by Jasper's whining, his demands that we turn on the TV, his cries of "I'm bored!" I have had enough of *Fat Albert* dubbed in Spanish, though it did drown out the dripping sound.

But being alone is pushing me closer to the edge of the void, and I'm tired of falling over and over myself, head over heels into that sea of blackness. I have lost too much this year. Too much blood. Too much weight. Too much sleep. I had no business coming to this godforsaken place. I hate the tropics. The burning sun, sweat, surfers, skimpily dressed girls. I have no interest in improving my Spanish. I lie on the bed, willing time to pass, thinking of Dicken at home sitting straight-backed in his office chair, working eighteen-hour days because we're not there to remind him to eat and sleep. I should be home with my better half. I have no business grieving here in paradise.

July 29

I've spent all my time here so far in the hotel room, so I decide to venture out to the beach with Jasper today. We run into Kevin, who is staying with his aunt and uncle while we're on this coast. His father has arrived in town because he heard Kevin would be here. Jasper runs straight into the water with the other kids, hollering with glee.

Kevin's father is holding a small boy on his shoulders and watching the other children play in the water. I greet him and smile. He gives me a shy smile back. He has very dark skin, darker than Kevin's, and his eyes look bloodshot and sad. I wonder what he feels about seeing Kevin again, and how he feels about us. I catch Kevin's eye and call out a hello. He doesn't say anything, just scowls at me, then turns his back. He says something to his cousins in Spanish that I can't make out, and then a couple of the kids point at me. *Are they snickering?* I wonder. I'm sure he's saying something terrible about me. I start to feel dark, telling myself Kevin won't want to come back home with us at the end of this trip.

Mom joins us at the beach and strikes up a lively conversation with Kevin's father in Spanish. I am grateful for Mom's optimism and ability to connect. But I compare myself negatively—why do I see life so pessimistically while she stays positive in the face of virtually any challenge? I am exhausted and depressed, while she smiles and spreads her cheer. She has such a *yes* for it all and I am rejecting the world.

"I'm going to head back for a rest, if that's okay," I tell Mom.

"Okay, that's fine. I'll bring Jasper back for lunch later."

August 2

Our last day on this coast.

As we walk back to the hotel, Jasper says, "There's Kevin!" The boy coming from the opposite direction looks at us and smiles. I say, "He looks a little like Kevin, but not really."

It *is* Kevin, on his way back from a trip to see his mom and brothers, including a new baby born in January, just like Theo. Kevin has a very radical haircut with designs shaved into his scalp. The Afro is gone!

"My *tio* cut my hair," he says, rubbing his hand over his head.

"Are you excited to go home and see Daddy?" Jasper asks him.

"Sort of yes, sort of no," Kevin replies. I take this comment and twist it into scary stories, telling myself, *You might be about to lose another son.* Though maybe if Kevin decided to stay here, it wouldn't be so scary. Maybe it would even be better for him.

I look at this boy with his new teenager haircut. His family of origin is still imperfect, and so is his adopted family. He has known pain in both. He is an old soul who was connected to Theo before he was born. If he wants to leave us, I'll have to trust in his wisdom, and in my own ability to let go.

I sleep for three hours in the afternoon. I don't know if it's the humidity, the heat, the stress of traveling, or just plain exhaustion catching up with me, but I feel rock-bottom tired, like I could stay in bed forever.

I wonder if the physical side of the birth and aftermath is finally catching up with me. For so many months, I didn't give it much attention. I toughed it out, forcing myself to exercise, get back to my town days, ignoring the pain in my incision, the bleeding that went on for weeks. Now I'm realizing what trauma my body's been through, how much blood I lost, how much of my vital force has gone into healing up layers of cut skin and tissue. Is this why doctors prefer women with trisomy babies to have vaginal births? Of course I don't regret Theo's birth for a moment, but I'm also realizing the longer-term consequences of a C-section and can see that I'm in no condition to get pregnant again, not now, maybe not ever. We'll see.

August 3–6

The bus ride to San Jose is long. We drive through Limon, the town where Kevin was born. In the fading light, I can see into the hovel-like apartments in the slums. I make out the figure of an elderly woman at a stove, her posture radiating hard labor, defeat, hopelessness.

Jasper complains of a terrible headache. I feel his forehead; it's very hot. We get to the bus station in San Jose and find a taxi. My favorite hotel turns us away, saying they are full. The driver tells us there might not be any hotels with openings.

"I thought you said we wouldn't need a reservation at this time of year," Mom says, clearly irritated.

"Summer is low season here," I say. "I don't understand this."

Jasper is moaning from his headache. "I have chills, Mommy."

I try not to feel the dread spreading through me.

The hotel we eventually find charges three times the normal rate, but we are too tired and discouraged to argue. Even in his feverish state, Jasper insists on dragging my bag for me.

In the musty room, I feel the walls closing in on me. I have to go into the bathroom to cry so I won't upset Jasper, who is lying in bed. I feel terrible for him; he's been dragged along on this trip, and now he's sick. I'm terrified it's malaria or dengue fever or some other nasty tropical disease. Poor sweet Jabu, heart of gold. I'm praying to God to get him over this illness quickly.

I should never have come down here; it was a very unsupportive move. I can't trust myself to make good decisions. I rue the day I came to this hellacious country, wish I'd never played God by interfering in Kevin's life. I look at the story line and convince myself I've ruined my life and Jasper's and Dicken's. Kevin's too. He must be so confused and have no sense of where his real home is.

I'm seriously considering going home as soon as possible. I'd like to take a sleeping pill and knock myself out, but I'm afraid Jasper might need me in the night.

Before he falls asleep, Jasper says, "Mom, remember what Paul says: this will pass."

I've tried to hide my despair from him, but he obviously senses it. From her bed across the room, Mom says, "Sweetie, remember, you've been through a huge loss, and being this vulnerable makes you feel terrible about yourself. Try to be gentle."

Angrily, I respond, "I should never have come! Why didn't someone stop me? I can't make supportive decisions for myself!"

With so much emotion in me, I can't sleep and end up taking half a sleeping pill, my first med so far. I still don't sleep all that well, but I am able to relax. The night is long, Jasper's hot body next to mine, holding me close. I can feel his skin cooling gradually as we approach dawn, and am hugely relieved.

Morning brings the sun and that amazing sense of hope I never expected to feel again. I whisper, "Good job, Jabu, I'm so proud of you for breaking your fever."

He immediately replies, "Good job to you for getting out your anger." And I thought I'd hidden it! Then he says, "Mommy, last night I felt the walls were closing in on me. It was really scary. I decided to think about surfing, and that made me feel better." He breaks into tears.

"What is it, Jabu?"

"I heard someone whispering in the dark and wondered if it was Daddy."

"Maybe it was," I say. "Daddy is thinking about you all the time, I know that."

It amazes me how closely linked Jasper is to Dicken, and also to me; it is astonishing to hear his description of the walls closing in on him, which was exactly how I felt last night. I think a big gift of this trip has been the way it has shown me how incredibly connected Jasper and I are—all that time spent with him when he was little has paid off exponentially. It makes me want another child, even after all the darkness last night.

Kevin meets us at the hotel that evening. He's obviously not too happy to be leaving. He's had a great time.

"Where did you get that bandanna?" Jasper asks him.

"My dad gave it to me," he says. "My dad says I can live with him when I'm eighteen."

Fine, I think bitterly, *that means we only have to put up with you for eight more years.*

"That's a really cool bandanna," Jasper says. "Can I feel it?" As he reaches his hand out, Kevin pushes it away. I feel a stab of protectiveness toward Jasper.

"I'm hungry," Kevin says.

I pull some crackers out of my backpack and hand them to him. He makes a very slight sneer of disapproval, and I want to slap him.

"You're welcome," I spit.

"Thanks," he grunts back, eyes downcast and dark with anger.

I stew in silence until a short time later, when Kevin and Jasper are chatting and playing cards amiably on the bed in our hotel room. *Thank God things shift,* I think, looking at Kevin and feeling a sweetness for him coming to life in my chest.

"My mom's new baby is called Anthony," Kevin tells Jasper. "He can sit up by himself, and he reaches his arms out for people to pick him up. He's really cute!"

"We missed you, Kevin," I say, and mean it. I can now see how confused he must be, how conflicted. His mom had her new baby boy in January, on the twenty-second, Jasper's birthday and Theo's due date. Funny, as Kevin wished for a baby brother all those months ago, I guess he got one, two if you count Theo, which I do. Strange universe . . . It's hard not to wonder why we would get the baby with a terminal condition, when this mother who was unable to raise her oldest child would get another healthy one. Maybe I am being punished for taking away her baby, and her stolen child is being replaced?

Along with the occasional winces in Kevin's direction, I also want to give him a great life, to help him return regularly to Costa Rica so that he can keep up his family ties. It's wonderful that he's maintaining those connections. We met several young men on this trip whose bilingualism has given them a way to make a good living in Costa Rica. We can consider our time with Kevin a loving boarding school. When I think of the incredibly intense time he's had over the last four or five years—being abandoned by his mother; leaving his country for a whole new family, language, culture, and climate; his experiences during my pregnancy with Theo, hearing those voices at the conception and birth; and all the shock of the death, then the grieving and adjustment—I truly admire him. He's got a strong spirit, that's for sure.

August 7

The boys and I fly to Washington, DC, where we'll spend a few days with my dad before heading up to meet Dicken in Boston. On the plane, I ask Kevin how he's feeling, worried that he'll say he's missing Costa Rica. Instead he smiles and says, "I'm excited to see Grandpa Piggy's house, I've never been there!" Then he tells me all about seeing his family in Costa Rica, meeting new cousins and his baby brother. At one point he gets a faraway look in his eyes, a mix of happiness and wistfulness, and says, "Mom, I have so many people all over the world who love me."

I feel safe and quite settled in Dad's house. I love the books piled floor to ceiling and crammed into massive shelves—so many amazing choices, I feel I could live here forever and never run out of reading material. I call Dicken every hour or so, hugely reassured to have this direct connection to him again.

Dicken tells me, "Giles is going downhill. He was in the hospital yesterday, having fluid drained off his abdomen. Becca explained the situation to the kids, who were crushed, having thought he was getting better."

I am unable to say anything, and feel the tears coming.

"I'm on standby to go over," Dicken says. "I want to say goodbye."

"Oh, Dix, what can they be going through?"

That night, lying in bed with my used tissues piled around me, I feel the bigness of what Giles and Becca are facing. I'm afraid of getting my hopes up too much for being reunited with Dix, trying not to buy the illusion that something is missing in me or that my "problems" will be solved when we're back together. I am in touch with a part of me that is strong, that can survive.

August 13

The day I've been waiting for arrives, and I spend the morning counting down the hours till our flight to Boston, though I have so little energy I can't even muster up much more than relief at the idea of seeing Dix. I'm at my wits' end, tired, sick, sick and tired of managing the boys. I keep having bouts of low fever, feeling dizzy and odd and floaty. East Coast humidilty exhausts me.

Dad watches me chase Jasper down before he can unleash a water balloon at Kevin and tells me, "I'm amazed you can keep up with the boys. Jasper seems particularly hyper today."

"He's just keyed up because we're leaving today," I say. "Transitions unsettle him."

"I still think you should consider Ritalin."

"Dad! I hate it when you say that!"

"Don't take it so seriously, you know I'm kidding."

I wish Dad adored the boys the way he openly adores girls, like Grace. People are allowed to have preferences, of course, just as Ben hopes to have a girl, though I can't help taking all of it as a personal affront to Jasper. I can see Dad's comments as an expression of compassion for me, because it is tiring to have these two very full-on, energetic boys. I'm ready for a break. I wish I could go somewhere alone with Dicken, preferably to a monastery. At the same time, Kevin has been close to angelic. I'm grateful for that. He's hardly sulked at all, and he's friendly and cheerful with people. It has been a fine visit to Dad's; I'm very glad we came. I do regret one moment from the trip: when Dad's friend asked me if Jasper had any siblings other than Kevin, and I didn't mention Theo.

I have an exit-row seat and butterflies in my tummy as the engines gear up for takeoff. Paula was due yesterday. No sign so far. My heart aches for some vague reason, something other than Paula's pregnancy. I wonder how Dicken is. Is he excited, nervous?

At baggage claim, I glance up and see Dicken running to meet us, looking incredibly vibrant, with a cheerful orange flower in his hand. I am so struck by his attractiveness, I feel a little shy.

We stop at Cecily and Michal's house in Boston before driving up to our summer home in the Adirondack Mountains. Cecily gives me a huge hug, then gushes about how big and handsome the boys look. As we start to catch up, her phone rings. She glances at the caller ID and says, "Oh, it's Benny! I have to get this!"

Seeing her light up with excitement when she answers the phone makes my chest throb.

"They talk every few minutes," Michal says, smiling.

Cecily hangs up after a minute and says, "Nothing new. Okay. I've got to calm down. Oh my gosh, I'm such a bundle of nerves!"

Later, in the car, Dicken comments, "You seem sad about Benny's baby. Is it hard to see Cecily paying so much attention to them?"

"I guess so. I also get sad thinking of how Theo and this baby would have been friends."

The mountains I've loved my whole life are beautiful, but I feel removed, like the usual openness I experience here isn't close enough to the surface to access. Dicken looks at me and says, "You're not all here, are you?"

"No, I guess not."

"Are you unhappy?"

"No, not unhappy or miserable, just neutral. Lifeless."

"Well, I consider it my mission to bring you back to me, all of you. I've been waiting for you desperately for the last two weeks, and I will find you."

I smile as he takes me in his arms and begins to gently kiss my neck.

August 16

Mom, Ralph, Cecily, and Michal have joined us. This morning in the kitchen was a completely harmonious family scene—no tension, no competitive undertones simmering below the surface like in some years past. Theo's legacy, I would say. Thinking that brings him here, reminds me his stamp on our world will never be erased.

Mom can't stop talking about Ben and Paula's baby, debating with herself aloud about when she should go to New York to stand by for the birth. I share her excitement, but I also feel a dull ache in my heart. I retreat to my room.

Dicken walks into the room in the late afternoon and finds me in tears.

"Oh, darling!" he says, and rushes over to hold me.

"I'm so, so sad."

Later, I ask him, "Is hearing about Ben's baby hard for you?"

He shakes his head. "It doesn't make me think of Theo, I don't know why."

"Will I ever get over this? I mean, I see Theo in everything."

"I don't know," he says, frowning. "I feel normal again, so I don't know what it's like for you, but I can see you're struggling."

"I'll try to get better, like you," I tell him.

We end up making love. I feel more powerful in the throes of desire. I sleep well, dream I am in labor and have gotten to five or six centimeters with no pain. I am excited to tell Dix about how well I'm doing—he is not there yet—but also want to surprise him with the baby. I think this dream is about a baby, not realizing until later it is about wanting to show Dicken that I am able to handle pain by myself.

CHAPTER 23

Today Dicken's stomach hurts and he feels "funky," upset by his computer woes, irritated with Jasper's antics. But I'm feeling relaxed, finally sinking into the beauty of the mountains. Wishing for a rainy day to justify sitting by the fire, reading all the great books I've checked out of the library.

Mom is exhausted in New York, waiting for Ben's baby, who may not appear for a while as the due date seems to have been miscalculated.

Cecily and I take a walk together. Her dogs run ahead, and one of them starts barking at something in the driveway. As we approach, I hear a soft chirping sound.

"Oh no!" Cecily says. "It's a baby bird. It must have fallen out of its nest. Oh my God, I can't look!" She covers her face.

I shout to the dogs to leave the baby bird alone. As I lean down to see if it's okay, it suddenly bursts into action and flies off into the woods, and I hear a much louder chirping. I can't see the bird now, so I turn around.

"I think it's okay," I tell Cecily. "It flew off into the woods, and I'm pretty sure I heard its mother."

"Phew," Cecily says. "Wow, Cinda, you're so brave. I can't handle things like that, you know, injured animals."

Later, I reflect on how I used to react the way Cecily did, how I would flinch and not want to see any blood or pain. My instinct today was to run up to it and offer myself. No fear in that moment, but a new willingness to see beyond blood and injury and threat and look straight into the experience.

The desire for another baby is strong today. I'm imagining

all the attention I'd get and the joy it would bring. I feel like such a victim most the time around the subject of our reproduction, a sense of defeatism. Then the rebel in me gets activated, saying, *You don't have to lie down and take it. You're young; you can still have another one. Just pull yourself up by your bootstraps and go for it! Make your own destiny. Don't pity yourself and forever say, "We ended on such a sad note."*

August 21

Maud and Grace arrive for a few days. And with no imminent birth in sight, Mom and Ralph return from New York, bringing my stepbrother Johnny and his family. Ten-month-old Arthur is adorable, good medicine. Yet every time he smiles, I feel a stab and think, *We missed that one with Theo.* I remember how in the early days after Theo died, I concentrated on all the pain he avoided and the pain he spared us by dying so young. Now my heart begins to let in all the small moments of joy we're missing. How he would have changed before our eyes, growing into himself day by day, a beautiful unfolding. Little Arthur's beaming at me burns its way through me bit by bit.

August 24

I'm drinking hot chocolate with whipped cream when I hear the phone ring. Mom answers it, and I hear her greet Caroline. I go upstairs and get Dicken, telling him it's his mom.

After a ten-minute conversation, Dicken hangs up the phone and shakes his head. "Giles went to a hospice this morning," he tells me. "He was delirious, trying to pull out his drip, and had to be sedated. I'm going down to the library so I can get online and buy us tickets. I need to get over there!"

He grabs the rental car keys and heads out.

Dicken comes back half an hour later. He is distraught.

"I was about to book us tickets when I remembered, I don't have my bloody passport here!"

"Oh my God. Are you sure?"

"I remember putting it back in the drawer at home. I didn't think I'd need it. How could I be so stupid?"

"You're weren't stupid, honey," I say. "We weren't planning to fly internationally. You couldn't have known."

"But I always bring my passport. This is the first time I decided not to, thinking I could get by with my license and not risk losing the passport."

I wonder if he did this subconsciously, if it was his way of not looking reality in the face. But I don't say anything.

Dicken calls Tom back in Oregon and asks him to FedEx his passport so we can all fly over as soon as possible. We'll have to wait at least another day and a half.

In bed, Dicken and I talk late into the night.

"I can't believe Giles is going," I say, "will soon be gone for good."

"It would be nice if he can hold on, but it sounds unlikely," Dicken says.

"Did Becca say how the kids are doing?"

"They said goodbye . . ." Dicken's voice breaks. Then, "They're at the Aldeburgh Festival today. Becca didn't want them to miss it."

"We were all there together last year, remember?"

"Yes, I'm glad we did that with Giles."

"Giles and Theo too."

"Yes, little Theo too. How amazing."

August 25

I toss and turn most of the night. In the wee hours I get up to pee and run into Dicken, who is coming back from the bathroom.

"The baby was born," he whispers. "Your mum just told me."

"Oh my gosh!"

"They had a girl."

We go back to bed for a few hours.

* * *

We wake to the sound of Maud's voice. She's got the phone in her hand. "Dicken, it's Becca for you." My face must register shock and fear, because Maud says to me quietly, "I think everything is okay. She sounds fine."

Dicken pulls his boxers on and goes downstairs. I hear him say, "Oh, Bex," and begin to cry. I rush downstairs, expecting the bad news. But he doesn't signal anything to me, and they keep talking, so I assume Giles is still hanging in there. At one point Dicken says, "That's how it was with Theo." For a split second I wonder if he did die, but I tell myself, *No, Dicken is just talking about the experience of being with someone before they die.* I imagine Giles alive, hanging on, with his friends and family around him, loving him. Tomorrow we will fly there and see him ourselves, and tell him how much we love him.

I go into the living room, crying a little from seeing Dicken so moved. A few minutes later, I enter the kitchen and see Dicken, now off the phone, weeping with Mom and Maud. He looks at me and says, "Giles died last night."

I burst into tears and we hold each other. He recounts what his sister shared with him: "Becca was with him, along with Charles, Giles's father. Giles's breathing changed and Charles told Becca that the end was probably near." Dicken pauses, wipes his nose with his sleeve. Mom, Maud, and I are all huddled close to him, listening intently. "After he died, Becca stayed with his body all night, then helped the nurses wash him, saying it was like washing a gladiator's body, with all the scars and holes from his many surgeries. Becca said in all those years of fighting the cancer, he never, ever complained. A true hero."

In a fog, we gather our belongings, try to eat some breakfast, and set off for Albany, where we rent a car and drive to Boston. Soon we're on the flight to Heathrow via Iceland.

I find myself unable to believe that Giles is really gone for good. It doesn't seem possible, even with the warning of his gradual decline. The end came so fast—merciful for him, I hope.

Just last Monday, he was setting off for their week in Aldeburgh, signing up for the tennis tournament as always. And now he's gone. Utterly gone. No more laughing with him. No more curling up to watch a movie. Just last year, he and I were walking back from lantern night in Aldeburgh, arms around each other, his breath slightly sweet from beer, reminiscing about all of his magical summers there. We said goodbye that night and I never saw him again. I spoke to him on the phone in the spring, talking about Theo. That was our last conversation. I wrote him a goodbye letter in the early summer, then didn't send it because I'd heard from Becca that he wasn't talking about death. I figured he didn't want the bare truth acknowledged so openly.

I'm very sorry I didn't encourage Dicken to go over sooner. He certainly regrets that, and the timing with the passport. But I suppose we have to trust the unfoldment, just as under the grief and anger and stunned shock that he is gone, we have to trust his life *and* his death.

I keep thinking about what Caroline wrote in an e-mail yesterday: *We shouldn't talk about "life and death," but "birth and death," and all of it is life.*

August 26

We finally arrive at Becca's after a five-hour crawl through bank holiday weekend traffic. I am in tears as we get out of the car, and Becca comes out to greet us, waving bravely, the absence of Giles glaring. As we embrace, she says, "We're *okay*," in a very sober voice.

Olivia, Becca and Giles's daughter, comes out looking worried but not in pieces. She points to her head and says, "I have lice, that's why my hair is greasy. It's an herbal oil treatment."

"Come in, come in," Becca says. "I'm just making some pasta for supper." She trips as she climbs the steps into the house.

"You okay?" I ask.

"Oh, fine," Becca says. "It's these moccasins I'm wearing,

they're Giles's. I couldn't find my own shoes. Fergus! Where are you? They've arrived. Come and say hello."

We sit with Becca and the kids as they eat their pasta. After dinner, our boys join their cousins in the TV room while Becca tells us the whole story of Giles's swift decline—his terrible night, sitting on the side of the bed shaking, his arms outstretched, not quite making sense; then on his back tossing and turning, saying, "Jesus!" over and over in a distressing tone.

"I couldn't get cell phone reception in our rental house in Aldeburgh, but I finally went up the road in the early morning and found a spot where I could get through, and I reached my favorite nurse. She told me to get Giles into hospice right away. I called all our close friends, and they came over to say goodbye, one by one, the children too, crying. Giles said to Fergus, *Oh lad, don't cry,* and held him as he wept."

"Oh, Bex," Dicken says, reaching for his sister's hand.

"Later, he was barely conscious, in a lot of discomfort. He didn't speak again until two days later, his last words to a nurse who gave him a shot—*Ow . . . Fuck off!* Great, isn't it? His last words . . ."

We all smile.

"Later, I realized he was uncomfortable for some reason, and I finally figured out it was because he couldn't pee, so I demanded they do something, and they got him sedated and catheterized. He went downhill fast, his eyes fixed. Soon Charles noticed his breathing had changed and told me he thought he'd die that night. Sure enough, he started to struggle for breath, gasping a bit; a little distressing. Then there were long gaps, and he died. I stayed with him for a long time. In the morning it looked like he was smiling. It was amazing, it really was!" Becca gets her cell phone out and shows us a photograph, and it does look like Giles is smiling. "I'm so glad I got to be with him for so long. His body was like a shell and that comforted me, made me certain his spirit was elsewhere."

Becca seems amazing. She breaks into tears occasionally, often when listening to music or talking about Giles's death. She says she's relieved that the pain and suffering are over for him, and that her stress is gone—the illness stress. She speaks of how well he left things, that he said it's like leaving the party on a high note: the kids flowering, the business thriving, their marriage better than ever. "He said he would have loved to stay and find out what happens next, but he had no regrets. He felt fulfilled."

As we go over reading ideas for the funeral, Becca suddenly says to me, "I'll move on, I won't live in the past. Giles and I were never clingy. We could always go out on our own, we were always independent, like that marriage reading from *The Prophet*. I'm just sad that I won't be able to count on seeing him at the end of the day."

At bedtime, I settle Jasper on the floor in Fergus's room. Fergus, about a year older than Jasper, has been upbeat all evening, but moments of dark worry cross his face from time to time. He is chatting now, telling Jasper about some English TV show he loves. I notice the collection of photographs by his bed, and come over to look closer.

"Oh, look at that one!" I gush. "Look how sweet you are, so little in your dad's arms."

Fergus smiles broadly. Then an expression of stunned sadness comes into his eyes, and I wonder if he'll cry, but he quickly turns his attention back to Jasper and asks which Harry Potter recording they should listen to tonight.

August 27

In the early morning, I come out of the bathroom to find Becca standing in the hall, looking upset. "Would you mind getting in bed with me?"

"Not at all." I feel sad and sweet at the same time.

I slide into bed next to her, and we hold hands.

"I can't believe you're sleeping by yourself," I say. "If it were me, I'd have Jasper or one of my sisters in bed with me every night."

"You know me, I'm not like that."

"Are you sleeping okay?"

"For the most part, yes. I'm actually very tired."

"You don't even need sleeping pills or anything like that?"

"No, I'm really okay."

I squeeze her hand and we lie there together for a while. I notice a spy novel sitting on the bed table on Giles's side, a bookmark partway through it.

Then Becca says, "I miss him, I really do. I've had him every day for fifteen years. I hate being on my own."

And for the first time since we arrived, I see my sister-in-law break down.

Becca keeps herself busy in the day, opening cards and letters, organizing the funeral, helping us find photographs for a slide show we're assembling. It's almost uncanny how together she seems. I wonder if she was already coming to terms with the loss—no real surprise, three years to slowly grieve and let go—or if they weren't that dependent on each other emotionally. I know I would be undone, incapacitated. Lost. Desperate. Yet she's almost normal, able to talk about him, look at photographs and videos, receive mail in his name, all without a flinch or tears.

August 28

In the morning, we attend Sunday service at the local church. Becca and I cry through the hymns.

In the communion blessing, the priest says something about eating the body of Christ and drinking his blood. Jasper, who has never been to church, makes a face and says, "That's disgusting!" Becca, eyes still wet, bursts out laughing and later says she could feel Giles roaring with laughter.

E-mail to my brother:

Can't wait to hear all about Maggie. Everyone is moved that she came so soon after Giles left, that they were crossing the veils at the same time. Becca said Giles was very much like a newborn during his last hours, not quite conscious and unable to swallow anything, but extremely thirsty and sucking on a wet sponge like a baby rooting for milk. His father stroked his hair and said to Becca, "This is my baby." He and Becca were with him when he died, telling him it was okay to let go, that he didn't have to fight anymore. They stayed with his body all night, washing it and dressing him in clean pajamas. His midwives, as Caroline said.

It's a relief to be here, I think because we're in the field of all the grace that comes in these seemingly unbearable situations, very much like with Theo. I'm also finding grace in the role of supporter, and I feel all the gifts Theo brought shining through me now, especially the gift of being able to walk through a loss of this magnitude. It makes me feel more deeply grounded than I have in a long time, close to Theo and to Giles, and to myself and the mystery of being alive. I can see why people who've been through these things feel compelled to serve others afterwards. It calls one into the moment like nothing else and brings forward a strong sense of courage and love.

The kids are amazing, all of them. Their beauty blows me away, each one in his or her particular stage. It makes me excited to get to know Maggie and to share moments of life with her. Please give her a big kiss from us.
Love to you all,
Cinda

August 28

E-mails from Ben:

Hi Cinda,
What a beautiful note. I just read it aloud to P.J., who is nursing Maggie on the bed behind me, and I could hardly get through it for sobbing so hard. In our joy and bliss we have been thinking about Giles and Theo a great deal. Regis, Jean, and Michelle were in the hospital room with us on Thursday morning when the call came from Maudie telling us that Giles had gone. We all cried for him, as P.J.

and I have cried for Theo every day, given our now profound sense of how unbearable the grief of losing a child must be.

Hi again Cinda,

    I meant to tell you that had Maggie been a boy, we would have called him George Theodore Miller Macrory. I asked you months ago how you would feel if we used the name, and then we sort of shelved it. But Jasper raised the idea again after you got back from Costa Rica, really cute and so moving. (I had already spoken to him and let him know the names we were planning on—"Oh, Maggie is a nice name!"—and was talking to Kevin when he came back on to suggest that it would be really nice if we used Theodore. What a love!) And we decided it would work out perfectly as above. Alas, we just don't like the female version so much, but please know how much we have been thinking about your beautiful boy . . .

Love,

Ben

August 30

It's the day before the funeral, and we're working on the slide show of Giles's life to show at the reception. Going through Giles's photo albums, Caroline exclaims, "My goodness, Bex, Giles had a girlfriend who looks just like you!"

Becca says, "Mum, that *is* me."

We all laugh.

Becca adds, "It's just like the time we were all watching England play in the World Cup, and Mum said, *That's amazing, that player looks exactly like David Beckham.* Giles rolled his eyes in exasperation—it *was* David Beckham, England's captain."

August 31

Becca asks me to drive with her to the funeral, which is deeply touching to me. On the way she says, "Have you thought about working with bereaved people? You're a natural, you know."

My eyes tear up. "You know, I've been thinking about it lately.

I might call a hospice when I get home, see if I can volunteer."

"The hospice we had was just wonderful." She tells me the story of Giles's last days, which I've already heard once from Dicken and once from her, but I just listen.

We park the car near the church. Becca takes a big breath and says, "Okay, here we go," and opens the car door and steps out. She walks so quickly I can hardly keep up. The yard is thronged with people dressed up and looking somber. We walk in and hear a Cat Stevens song playing through the large church. Every pew is filled, the balcony too.

Dicken, Jasper, Kevin, and I sit in the front pew with Becca, Caroline, Olivia, and Fergus. The service is beautiful. Dicken reads the passage from the Bible about the many rooms in God's house. Before he died, Giles let Becca know he wanted certain people to have roles in the service, and Dicken is one of them, a reader and a pallbearer. I am nervous—aware of being watched, anxious about how our boys will behave in the spotlight. The only moment I break down is seeing Dicken's pained face when he walks up to the coffin with the other pallbearers.

We follow the coffin out of the church, then drive to the village of Aldringham for the burial. Giles was born there, his father was vicar, and his mother's ashes are scattered in a field of daffodils right by Giles's gravesite.

September 3

It is very strange to walk into Caroline's house again and reflect on the last time we were here: last summer, halfway through my pregnancy with Theo. It seems ages ago. A different family, a different life, a different me. But the strong smells take me straight back to that time. Dicken says, "This was your prison for three months." Here I am, no baby, feeling about a decade older than I was last year. Strange.

I sit at the kitchen table in the afternoon, sipping hot Earl Grey tea. Caroline's sister, Dicken's aunt Fania, is slicing some ginger cake.

"Would you like some, darling?" she asks.

"No thanks."

She brings a plate of cake and a cup of tea to the table and sits down.

"I've been thinking of you so much this year," she says.

"I know. I really appreciated your e-mail and your note."

"We don't really know why these things happen, but I do think they happen for a higher purpose," she says, taking a dainty sip of her tea. Fania's son Justin died of pneumonia at the age of three, something she's talked to me about several times in the years I've known her.

"Years after Justin died, I heard from him via a medium, and he thanked me for agreeing to be his mum for the short life his soul needed."

I smile, feeling my emotions stirring.

"You did the same for Theo."

"Thank you," I whisper, near tears.

She takes another sip of her tea.

September 7

Coming out of the bathroom at Heathrow, I see a couple with a Down's baby. He has a shock of blond hair and the unmistakable slanted eyes of people with trisomy 21. I watch him as his mother feeds him ice cream. He is jolly, flapping his arms with delight after each bite. He is absolutely adorable. *I'd love one of those*, I think to myself. As I watch him, I have a strong urge to go up to his mother and comment on his beauty, tell her I had a trisomy baby of my own once. Then I go back to the weeks before Theo's birth and remember how terrified I was to think we might have a baby with Down's, how I didn't think I could love such a child. And here I am, utterly in love with this stranger's child before me, envying his mother for having him. I stare at him so long, I have to run to catch our flight.

* * *

Sitting on the tarmac before takeoff, Jasper points out the window to a 747 and asks me what airline it is.

"It's called Virgin."

"Have you flown on it before?"

"No, but I hear it's amazing. Giles flew on Virgin once, and he told me they have these multichannel personal screens with tons of movie choices. And they serve ice cream!"

"You mean Giles went first class?"

"No, he said they served ice cream to everyone."

"Oh my gosh!"

When we get to Cecily's house for a night, I hear Jasper telling her all about "Yurgin" airlines. I can tell she is trying to take him seriously and not laugh at the mispronunciation, but as soon as we catch eyes, she cracks a big smile. Jasper says, "You want to fly Yurgin too, don't you?"

"Definitely."

CHAPTER 24

September 13

I have pneumonia, plus a big fat cold sore and lice. As I pull a live bug from my head, I dissolve into rage and get in the shower, scrubbing my scalp until it burns. Back in bed, my lungs hurt; I'm full of mucus. I feel defeated, like the plagues have descended.

Just when I'm at my worst, something wonderful comes along: Christine, our grief counselor, calls to ask me to cofacilitate a bereaved-parents group with her, starting in October. Working with death and dying is what I've been thinking I should do for a while now, especially after England, when being with Becca and the kids was the most empowered I've felt in a long time. It's a way to pass along the gifts Theo gave me, a way to make something meaningful come from the experience.

I'm honored. I sign up for a four-day training coming up.

September 16

I discover in the journals of an Irish-American Zen monk that Buddha's *parinirvana*, the day he left his body, is celebrated on January 15! So Theo shares a birthday with MLK and shares the day he died with Buddha. Not bad company.

October 7

In the WinterSpring grief training today, we do an exercise on our earliest loss. Mine was Moose, our family dog who ran away when I was fourteen, the same day my dad moved out. Our front door was open all day as suitcases were carried out, and Moose got loose and never came back. I explore how I never knew what happened to him and never got to say goodbye to his body. I cry for that loss, for how much I went through. I talk about how I was in denial for months, holding out hope that he'd come home, searching for him, checking the papers every morning and going to animal shelters when I read about an unidentified dog that sounded anything like Moose. Waiting. It wasn't until the next fall or even winter that I cried for the first time.

I'm grateful I got to be with Theo when he died, and for all the time we had with his body. What a tremendous gift.

Grief is the price we pay for our attachments.
—WinterSpring training manual

October 12–13

I'm having a bad dream in which a man who looks like the British actor Colin Firth asks Maud out instead of me. I am feeling ugly and rejected, wandering around lost. Suddenly, I turn around and there is Giles, wearing a white suit and literally glowing with benevolent light. His presence completely relaxes and reassures me; it is amazing. I look at him and all my worries about the gritty world no longer matter. He is smiling and I feel complete love and acceptance. Giles is so beautiful, it is dazzling, his aura like an invitation into another world.

I tell him, "I had no idea how much I missed you until just now, seeing you again!" He smiles. His essence shines. It is like one of those black-and-white movies when a person in color is moving through the scene, there but not noticed by anyone else.

I wake with the song from his funeral slide show in my head, The Who's "Real Good Looking Boy," and a deep ache in my heart.

We've decided to go to England for Christmas. I am about to book us a convoluted flight on American Airlines when Dicken checks the Virgin website and finds a very good fare on a direct flight. I have a feeling Giles is helping us: Virgin was his favorite airline. Jasper, obsessed with Virgin since he heard about it, is thrilled.

* * *

In the grief group training manual, I come across something that sharply reminds me of Giles:

> *In the American Indian culture, human life is not seen linearly but rather as a circle that becomes complete at about puberty. From that time on, a person's life is seen as a wholeness that continues to expand outward. Once "the hoop" has formed, any time one dies, one dies in wholeness. As the American Indian sage Crazy Horse commented, "Today is a good day to die, for all the things of my life are present."*

I think often of how Giles told Becca he had no regrets, that everything in his life was better than ever.

In the evening, I start the bereaved-parents group, a big group: three couples plus six other moms, representing nine children who have died, many in accidents, a few from diseases. So much of it hits way too close to home—not about Theo, but my day-to-day life, which feels very fragile from this point of view. A nine-month-old baby boy with pneumonia died as a result of the hospital's negligent treatment—the mother crying, "I never should have taken him to the hospital in the first place!" All I can think at that moment is that Jasper has had pneumonia, Sam a high fever the other day.

Such agonizing stories. I am awake all night, feeling the energy running through me, occasional flashes of the tragic stories playing in my head. But I am gentle, telling myself, *Of course you're awake, you've been through such an intense experience. Don't worry, you can take it easy tomorrow,* which I do. I go slow and easy all day.

October 14

I run into one of the moms from my grief group today. She is on a ladder, stacking boxes in the office supply store where we've always shopped. I greet her, saying, "Oh, you work here?"

"Yeah, I've been here about a year and a half."

"Cool, I've probably seen you before."

"Yeah, it's good to see you." We smile at each other, and then she starts to stack the boxes again, saying, "Catch you in group next week."

As I walk away, I reflect on how this woman's son died less than three months ago. And here she is, working a low-paying job, forced to continue with her routine. I tell myself I will never assume anything about strangers I see every day. We don't know the losses people have been through, how there are incredibly wounded, hurting souls constantly among us, going about their lives.

October 22

Today there is a baby shower for Tracy, our assistant midwife with Theo, who is expecting her first baby soon. In the car on the way, Maud asks me how I'm feeling about going.

"Oh, fine," I say. "I'm just excited for her."

I think to myself, *I'm finally over Theo; I've completed the Winter-Spring training and am now helping other bereaved parents. I think I'm done grieving.*

We arrive, and I see Rhione coming downstairs from the prenatal check-in they've just finished, with her stethoscope and her midwifery bag—so familiar, like I was her client yesterday, but it also feels like a very long time ago.

Then a woman arrives with her baby boy, a bald, Weatherby-like baby. I sit on the couch, trying to suppress my tears. *Don't make this about you, this is Tracy's time.* I pull it together until Maud begins to sing her baby blessing song: *"I've loved you before you were born, I loved you as a baby being born, I loved you as an angel from above, I love you as a child running free . . . you know, I love you . . ."*

I can't stop crying. And I feel so stupid for thinking I can just be done grieving; it's almost humorous. But I am too broken-hearted right now to find anything funny. I wipe the tears from my face as they fall.

October 24

I wake up on my birthday and find a card from Jasper at the foot of the bed. He has drawn the whole family in crayon, everyone named, including Theo in a baby carriage.

"I'm thirty-seven," I tell Dicken, and start to cry as I show him Jasper's drawing.

In the evening I run the grief group, very sweet—the rapport builds: support, articulation, moving moments. Like one of the husbands reaching out to stroke his wife's hand when she tears up.

November 2

Jasper is up coughing half the night. I can't sleep, worrying that he has some dreadful condition—chronic asthma, or an allergy to something he's eating. Every cough raises my level of panic. I think about how neither Jasper nor Kevin is settled in school right now, and of something Courtney said about the effect of competitive games on kids, and my being overwhelmed about the choices we're making for the boys: school, what to feed them, how to manage their social lives, how to meet their physical-activity needs in a healthy way. Ice hockey is Jasper's new favorite sport, about as violent as it gets. We're not done learning how to help them deal with adoption issues, and with their grief.

I recall Dicken saying he thinks Jasper has asthma, influenced by food allergies, which is what Caroline has. I think of how it seriously affects her life, has almost killed her at times. My heart feels like it's cracking in half as I imagine Jasper crying, Dicken explaining that he can't have any wheat or dairy.

Managing the boys feels completely overwhelming right now, and I don't know how to find any answers. I tell myself it's time to throw in the towel on the issue of another baby. The game is up. I don't like either choice in front of me—trying one more time, or not trying. Neither feels entirely right. But I know one of those choices is the reality facing me, and I have to line up with that. All these thoughts crowd my head in the dark night, and I feel like I will explode from the pressure.

Then I feel red rage. Rage so gripping it makes me cry hot tears. I hit my fists against the bed, raging about how impotent I feel as a parent, how angry I am that I can't control anything, how I feel I'm stuck in this game of parenting, of life, and it's not fair because I don't know the rules or who's in charge or what my role is or why we're here and what the point is.

I pound my fists until I am exhausted. A white blankness comes over me, mercifully, like a huge snowstorm that covers everything in sight. I lie in numbness for a long time, savoring the peace of fewer thoughts, and at last fall asleep.

In the kitchen this morning, Maud sees my face and asks, "What's wrong?"

"Terrible night."

She sits down by me and takes my hand, starts to massage it. I tell her about my parenting fears, the raging thoughts.

Maud gently reminds me I'm not responsible for everything that happens, that I just have to deal with what's in front of me, not everything at once, and that these parenting issues are not life or death. "Oh, Cinda, what an intense couple of years you've had. You're really doing well, considering all that."

It's amazing how just a few words of "I get it" can feel so supportive.

I talk to my friend Jenny on the phone. She's had late miscarriages and lost a niece to trisomy 13 last year.

"You know what I see?" she says as we discuss our losses. "Losing a baby is a grief that is compounded by the ever-present question of whether there will be another baby or not."

I am so stunned by how true that statement feels, I'm not sure if I want to cheer or cry. I thank her for articulating what I am living.

This question of baby or not seems harder than anything right now.

November 6–7

We see a new John Lennon documentary—moving, funny, powerful, and disturbing. Dicken cries a bit, especially at the scenes of John with baby Sean. As we drive home, he tells me, "It makes me think of having another baby," and that makes me cry.

The next day, after the reality of several hours with our boys, who are picking fights with each other and being especially demanding, I ask Dicken, "So, you still thinking about another baby?"

"Well, actually, that feeling has shifted a little."

"It has for me too," I say.

"It's actually shifted *a lot* for me."

I smile.

"But it was a sweet moment," he adds.

CHAPTER 25

November 11

Today I am quiet, have been in tears a lot. I feel the familiar turning-in energy of winter, like I'm crawling deep into myself and hunkering down for a while. I think the return of winter is bringing up a lot of last year, and I'm bracing for what feels like a plummet into deep, dark grief.

My mom calls, chattering away about Thanksgiving plans. My brother is coming with Paula and their three-month-old baby girl. "I'm trying to find a crib for Maggie to sleep in while she's here," Mom says, "and a car seat for her to use. Do you have anything?"

I feel like I've been kicked hard in the chest. "Um, I don't know," I stammer. "I'll look in the barn."

Later, I tell Dicken about it. "I don't know why it was so hard to hear her ask that."

"It doesn't seem very sensitive to me," he says.

"No, you're right, it wasn't. And you know what? I'm not going to Thanksgiving this year. Forget it. It's such a setup."

"That's fine with me," Dicken says. "I don't really want to go either."

"Mom won't stand for that," I say. "She's counting on you to cook."

"You're right, I should probably go. And Jasper will want to be there, he loves Thanksgiving. Kevin too."

"Yeah, you three should go. But I don't need to be there."

I've given myself a year of permission to do exactly what I need to take care of myself. I tell myself I've been through such a hard loss, I deserve to support myself even if there's fallout, which there will be if I don't show up at Thanksgiving.

I wish I could sleep through the winter, through Thanksgiving and Christmas and Theo's birthday and all the feelings that will arise. But that doesn't feel right, because I'd wake up in spring. And spring seems ridiculous to me. It felt like a mockery last year when it came, and this dark weather resonates more, makes me feel understood on some primal level. So really, I have a yes for going into this season, even though it's not comfortable.

November 13

In the night, I wake up thinking of Theo and feeling alone, starkly so. Everyone I love is out of reach. So much anger comes up. I want to stop time, but I am impotent. The sky is about to fall on top of me and there's nothing I can do about it. And every year winter will come, with the holidays and Theo's birthday, and I am only now recognizing that I'm alone with this. No one gets it completely, and I'm never going to finish this, whatever "finish" means. It will just keep cycling through.

In the morning, I get a sweet e-mail from Gabriella, saying she woke thinking of me and Theo. Then, just as I'm trying to come up with a soothing person to call, the phone rings, and it's Cecily. I tell her about my immersion in dark grief, and she says I should stop fighting myself. "Don't you realize that this process is really sacred, maybe the biggest work of your life?"

Could this really be "my work," whatever that means? This up-and-down, all-over-the-place, crazy-making existence I'm living? This thing I'm trying to get over as fast as I can? What would it be like to stop fighting it, stop fighting myself?

I lie in bed with my eyes closed, and suddenly I'm thinking about how I got pregnant around the time of our wedding. I remember the abortion. I feel the familiar shame and remorse begin to bury me, the voices demanding, *How could you, you idiot?*

Then the fierce protector intervenes: *You will not talk to Theo's mother this way! I won't have it. She's been through enough, can't you see that?*

In the peaceful white space that has spread before me, I imagine meeting the me from all those years ago, the one who is pregnant, sick, and terrified. I take her soft hands in mine. I talk to her gently, and I give her a chance to voice her feelings. I listen to her fear, can feel the memory of it in my body as I lie there. I realize that all these years later, I am in a way no different—still scared to have a baby, to bring another river of life into the world, scared of what it will demand of me. I decide to stop blaming her and ask instead how the me now can reach out to and comfort the me then, and vice versa. I don't hear a clear answer, but I know my openness to connecting these distant parts of myself is a start.

November 17

Gabriella calls me and says, "Listen to this: In Venezuela, when someone dies, families take two full years to mourn. They put up black curtains, don't socialize, don't leave the house unless necessary."

"Wow, that sounds *so* right to me," I say.

I spend the rest of the afternoon thinking about Venezuela, and how it feels so much more appropriate to have quiet days in the safety and familiarity of our house. Going anywhere almost invariably makes me feel unsupported. I'm amazed—partly appalled, partly impressed—that I've been out and about so much this year, starting my town days again only three weeks after Theo died.

November 24

Dicken has taken the Venezuela thing to heart. Now, whenever he runs into someone who says, "How's Lucinda? I haven't seen her in ages and she doesn't return my phone calls," he says, "Oh don't worry, she's doing fine, and her isolating has nothing to do with her feelings about you. Have you heard about grieving in Venezuela?"

November 27–28

I meet my niece Maggie, three months old, who is at Mom's for a week-long visit. I look at her tiny features, her sweet bald head, and think of how she was born just hours after Giles died. My brother and his wife don't offer her to me, and I don't ask to hold her. But I stare, fascinated by her and the feelings she evokes in me. I feel curious, excited, and numb.

Later, when I hear her crying, I can feel something in my breasts, like letdown. I watch Paula settle Maggie down to sleep. Lying on her belly, Maggie lifts her head one way, then the other, her eyes gently closing. Her back rises and falls with her even breaths, like a soothing wave.

I wake the next morning feeling like a mass of lead that has fallen to the dark ocean floor. *Why didn't I get to lavish attention on Theo the way Ben and Paula get to with Maggie?* There's nothing I love more than that.

Today, thinking about Maggie, and Theo, and whether or not to try again, I notice that letdown feeling again in my breasts, and I am able to squeeze out a drop or two of milk. Sweet. A physical reminder of Theo, that he was real, like finding money from the tooth fairy under my pillow.

December 15

"Can you believe it's been eleven months?" I ask Dicken.

"No, not really. It still seems like it all happened yesterday. Every day I wake up thinking about it, telling myself, yes, it really did happen. And he's still gone."

"Do you have any ideas about what to do on his birthday?"

Dicken shakes his head.

"Well, I guess I can finally stop buying all those heavy Mexican candles," I say. We've kept a memorial candle burning in the bathroom window nook, where his changing table was once set up and waiting for him, ever since we returned from the hospital. The tall, rounded glass-encased candles, which come decorated with images of Mother Mary and Catholic saints, last about three days, longer than any others we've found, and cost only a dollar each. Every time I go to the store, I pick out a few to bring home. I'm proud that we haven't let the light lapse; it's been a continual vigil.

"What do you mean?" Dicken asks, his face creased with concern.

"We talked about letting the candle ritual go after a year." I pause, noticing the sadness in him, adding, "But if you want to keep it going, that's great with me."

"Maybe we should keep it going until you're pregnant again."

Until? I'm stunned. I don't know what to say.

December 24

Dunwich, England. At a lovely carol service, I cry through every hymn. All the words about beautiful babes bringing light remind me of Theo, plus the church is filled with babies. I think of how big I was last year at this time, Theo lying on my right side, a constant companion. I also think of Giles. What a year it's been. A very long year.

I stay up late into the night, stuffing stockings and having a wonderful conversation with Charles, Giles's father, who has joined us for Christmas. Charles, a vicar, is explaining his spiritual philosophy: "We're all on a path of gradual correction, on our way to perfection, some of us slower than others." His eyes twinkle, and it is hard to imagine how he can be so positive after losing his beloved son just four months ago. He amazes me—so wise and articulate and generous in spirit. I can see how Giles got to be the way he was: his ease, his sense of a benevolent universe.

It takes me a long time to fall asleep. When I finally do, Giles comes to me in a dream. He floats down, and I reach out and touch him, feeling his clothes and his flesh. I say, "If I can still touch you and know you are here, why should I fear death at all?" I wake up before he answers.

December 25

I tell Charles about my dream.

"That's marvelous," he beams. "You know, Giles reported a very similar dream about his mother not long after she died, that she came to him and told him not to worry because she was fine and happy."

Christmas Day is hectic and messy. By evening, I'm tired and have a faint headache. I try on the one present I got, a sweater from Caroline, and it doesn't fit me. Dix got me nothing (our agreement, but still disappointing); neither did the boys. I feel teary now, maybe sorry for myself.

I read the card Mom sent me. She tells me to remember that she thinks of me all the time, in case I am up with fear in the night.

December 28

Ardmore, Northern Ireland. I see Sheelagh, our Irish cousin-in-law, today. She is heavily pregnant with twins, and her belly looks like a torpedo. Her babies are arriving tomorrow by induction—or should be, if all goes according to plan.

It's very relaxing here. We take a long walk along the river with Dad and Caroline. It's rainy and gray when we set off, but soon the sun comes out and it is spring-like. Lots of hot chocolate, cozy meals in the kitchen, reading; the boys happy, playing hide-and-seek and football. They play soccer on the lawn in a crushing downpour, then shriek through the house and into the bath together. Full of energy, plans, some bickering, mostly camaraderie. I'm amazed at how they get on with almost any other kids, their many cousins in England and now here in Ireland. The feeling of not relating to them or wanting to be a mother has shifted entirely, just like Irish weather.

December 30

The twins arrived yesterday afternoon—Iona and Rose, lovely

names. Dicken and the boys are over there now at a shoot. I join Dad for a walk on a mountainside, then take a trip into Limavady to shop and drink coffee at Hunters bakery, then head home for lunch and a bath. I'm really enjoying Dad, so engaged and optimistic and energetic and charming. Also smart and hardworking, generous, funny. Not bad for a dad, lucky me! I used to struggle with him sometimes, feeling unappreciated and not listened to. Maybe he's changed somewhat, but I think it's more that I've changed. I'm no longer as closed off as I used to be. I also *know* without a doubt that Dad loves me, and that I know this now is largely because of Theo.

I'm glad I've enjoyed my day away from Dix. It reminds me that I'm independent. So much of this year, I've felt like a tiny, needy child, clinging to him for dear life.

The rooks, crow-like birds that nest in the tree in the lane, the ones I've always loved to hear cawing at daybreak and see darkening the skies with their swarms, haven't been here this year. I knew something was amiss but couldn't put my finger on it at first. I am worried that they're gone for good after all these generations.

"What's happened to the rooks?" I ask Faye, our caretaker.

"Oh, they disappear for a month every December. They should be back any day now."

I feel relieved. I don't want anything to change.

I love the limited daylight. It's a good motivator: every morning I push for a walk "while it's still light." And it's so cozy coming home as the sun fades in the early afternoon, hunkering down by the fire or the kitchen cookstove, drinking cocoa, relaxing for hours that stretch on and on.

"Are you envious of Sheelagh?" Dicken asks me.

I shake my head. "I have no illusions that raising children is anything other than a lot of struggle . . . along with a lot of magic and love, of course."

"That surprises me a little," Dicken says. "You just seem to love kids so much."

"Oh, I do. I love mine, you know that. I also love other people's children; I notice I pay more attention to them since Theo died. I guess I appreciate their preciousness more than I would have otherwise, and plenty of them could use the extra attention. And I yearn for the baby magic, the merging, the closeness to the mystery. But the gritty everyday reality, the meal-making, the decisions—all that is part of the package."

"Except with Theo it wasn't," Dicken says.

"Maybe I wished too hard for an easy-to-raise baby." I pause, recalling the invocation I wrote in my journal the night he was conceived. "He didn't require much raising at all other than nine long months in utero. Oh, I do miss him. Last night I ached for him."

"I did too," Dicken says.

December 31

I can't sleep all night. The chiming of the grandfather clock is a curse: a startling reminder of how late it is, making me panic that I only have an hour to get to sleep before I hear the next ominous gonging. I put in my earplugs; then I can hear the sound of my ticking heart, rising in intensity as the fear of insomnia grows. I try to find my book light to read, but it is nowhere to be seen. Lamp on. Dix moans. Lamp off. I break down in tears. The bravery of the last few days is gone, the dam breaks.

"I miss Theo so much," I say to Dicken. "Why does Sheelagh get two?"

"I know, it's not fair," he says, his voice sleepy and soft. "It's a mystery."

The end of the year is bittersweet: an end to a very sad, long year, but also the end of the year of Theo's birth, the year we knew him, the only year we got to be with him. Time is separating us—an illusion, I suppose, but it feels so real. I'm a good sport a lot of the time, but sometimes I'm overcome by the heartbreak. Our little boy, gone. Can't hold him, can't see him. Can't watch him grow, share this side of life with him. I feel it for Dix. He rolls closer to me and says, "I miss him too." I reach out and feel his hands in the dark, feel how his little boy, *his* beloved baby, is gone for him. Lost in the night.

I watch these other babies arrive and feel cut off, like I'm separated in an entirely different reality, watching something alien unfold. Part of me feels left out, trapped between a lost path we'd set out on when we thought we'd be raising a third child, and the unknown future. Not a strong enough *yes* to pull us into another try for a baby. But nowhere near ready to admit we're done trying. So where are we? Derailed. No energy for a certain path ahead, a definite wanting. No object to pour our present energy into—just the remains of our previous life, so changed now.

In the morning, the rooks have returned; I look out the window and see the trees laden with them, and I can hear their familiar cries.

January 5, 2007

We visit the newborn twins. They are tiny and perfect, but I don't feel broody. It doesn't break my heart to think we're done, the way it did the first six months. I think of how I'm already weary from mothering the boys. I can't see us doing this into our sixties.

On the other hand, Jasper is half-grown—nine years old this month. In another nine years, he'll be eighteen. Such a paradox, wanting him to grow up and *not* wanting him to outgrow us and move on. I look at the package of parenting—the years and years and all the diapers and meals and early mornings and carpools and birthday parties and chaos and sleepless nights. Yet what else is there? What else has as much meaning, fun, laughter? What else can open the heart so wide?

January 6

Dicken is teaching a seminar in London, and I get to be his assistant. The boys are staying with Caroline for the weekend.

After a night in a small hotel on Bond Street, we wake early and walk through the gray streets to a coffee shop.

"What would you like?" Dicken asks me.

"I'll have a *pain au chocolat* and a decaf Americano with whipped cream, please."

Dicken orders and we settle into armchairs in a corner.

"Chocolate for breakfast?" Dicken says. "You never used to get sweets before protein."

I shrug. "We're all gonna die. Might as well have what we want while we can."

"You might want to listen carefully to the lecture on blood sugar dysregulation this morning," Dicken says, smiling.

I laugh.

"I actually think it's great that you're so much more relaxed about food," Dicken says.

"Yeah, my relationship with food has really changed."

"I've noticed you don't carry healthy snacks with you anymore, or water."

"My self-preservation energy is much less activated. I don't think about protein. I can skip meals, though I don't like to. I leave food on my plate—very new for me. I like to taste a bit of everything but don't usually eat a huge amount of anything."

"You look healthy too."

"What do you think it is? Has my stomach shrunk? Did something happen to me physiologically after the surgery? Or did a mental-emotional shift happen as a result of Theo?"

"Gosh, I don't know. What do you think?"

"I have a hunch it's the latter." I sit, musing on all of this. I realize that I've experienced a big change: I no longer see the fight against death as the point of life. I see life as an expression of love, a journey, a chance to create something. Death is inevitable, a mystery we *will* encounter—not something to avoid or try to outrace, not something to put off as long as possible by eating perfectly at every meal. I used to see all death as wrong, an injustice that threatened to make everything else pointless.

Dicken is looking at me, his eyes quizzical. The coffee and *pain au chocolat* arrive, and I can't get over how delicious the first bite of my pastry is.

January 14–15

Back home. It's almost Theo's birthday, and I watch myself functioning and feeling fairly cheerful for the most part.

But all of a sudden, I am leveled. It's as if my body has turned to lead. I'm lying in bed with a huge weight on my chest, pinning me down. I manage to get up but cannot walk without great effort. It is very odd, though not disturbing at first, because my emotions seem to be frozen too. I stay in bed for twenty-four hours, and as the day wears on, I start to feel more and more. It's like my cells are reawakening, and as they do, my mind starts to flash back to last year, reliving each moment of the hours leading up to the birth. I can't sleep; I can't stop the memories, the images, the sense that it's all happening again.

In the morning, Maud and her kids come in. Friends begin to appear, some bringing flowers, cards. The heaviness gradually lifts. I bake some bread with the sourdough culture I started last February. We drive to Gabriella's house for a birthday party the kids have organized.

Cards and cake and presents. I share the bread.

"I made the culture with a tiny bit of breast milk," I say as Andrew puts the bread to his lips. He makes a face and pretends to gag, and I laugh.

"It's delicious," he concedes after swallowing a bite.

Maud gathers us all together. Little Rosie stands close to me, holding the Theo doll. "We have a little surprise for you," Maud says, addressing me and Dicken. "It was Cecily's idea, and I have her on the phone here . . ." Her voice breaks a little. "I'm going to try not to get choked up. Okay, close your eyes."

When we open our eyes, Courtney is standing in front of us holding up a large colorful quilt. As the quilt comes into focus, I see it has an image of me and Theo embroidered onto one of the patches. It also has an elephant, a black panther, a snake, a tree, and roses. It is stunningly beautiful, and both Dicken and I start to cry.

"Where . . . where did you get this?" I stammer.

"We made it!" a bunch of them say in unison.

"Actually, Courtney and Eva did most of it," Maud says.

They turn it around so we can see that the back is stitched with the names of everyone who worked on it: my mom, sisters, Grace, and my closest girlfriends.

Later, as the children play, a circle of us adults sit and remember last year and talk about Theo. It is amazing to recall all of this together.

"I never held him," Andrew shares. "I guess I didn't feel worthy somehow."

"The sadness of losing him was blown away by the beauty he brought," Courtney begins, "but with time passing, it's easy to fall back into the human tragedy and forget the gifts. Let's always remind each other to remember the gifts, and integrate more beauty into the loss."

Maud cries the most; she was more excited than anyone about me having another baby, even more than me. I can understand, because being a live-in aunt is such a wonderful experience—so much of the joy of having a little one with few of the responsibilities.

I tell the group, "I still feel him in my cells, in my heart, and I know I could never really lose him. He's changed everything, so I see the world through a lens that he's part of. But of course I do miss his body, the unfoldment of the babyhood and childhood we were anticipating. It's complex, this loss, this gain. No words can sum it up."

CHAPTER 26

February 5

I'm feeling surer about not having another baby. I still have moments of longing, but the trend is clear. It no longer hurts like hell to think we're done, to remember our abortion. The boys are a lot, in positive and negative ways. Having Sam and Grace for two days and nights reminds me that as much as I love kids, taking care of them is hard, hard work. Fortunately, we have Cecily's baby or babies to look forward to.

Lately, I've been settling on the idea that I'm not a natural enough mother to have any more kids. It's not a judgment, just an observation which I'm surprisingly willing to accept. I loved having the chance to go through a healthy pregnancy and a not-healthy one, and mother Jasper and Kevin and Theo, plus Grace and Sam, all in very different ways. I love it and it's plenty.

And I'm aware that this could all shift, and I could easily line up with a completely different path should one arise.

February 10

In bed with a fever I've had for three days—the first two accompanied by a killer headache. Sitting here for hours, I find myself thinking of Theo a lot. As I swab my own dried-out lips with ointment, I remember how I got to put ointment on Theo's lips after he died to keep them from drying up. It was one of the only maternal acts I could do for him. I can picture his sweet lips still, the shape of his mouth, and how it felt to touch them. Now I'm crying and I'm afraid it will make my head throb again.

March 29

I wake early and drive to Grants Pass, where I speak to a group of nurses about infant loss. It is a stretch for me; I have always avoided public speaking, but I tell myself, *You have gone deep into terror and made it through, this is nothing.*

I start off my talk by sharing that I am nervous. My voice shakes and I can't get any words to come out and think, *Oh shit* . . . then I ease into it, and by the end much of the audience is crying.

As we're leaving, a nurse takes my hands and tells me, "Your story has moved me more than I can say. Thank you."

May 20–22

I'm on a weekend retreat, and the theme is love. My therapist keeps using the actual physiology of the heart as a metaphor. She mentions that in utero, the hands and the heart begin entwined during early development. "So our hands naturally evolve as an expression of our hearts."

All the analogies about the heart invoke Theo for me. He had an uncharacteristically strong heart for a trisomy case, one that always beat strongly and looked great on ultrasounds, fooling us all, including Oregon's most respected prenatal geneticist, into thinking he was healthy. And his gift to me and to many others is about opening hearts. I am not surprised that he comes to me during the meditation Friday evening. He shows up as one of my guides the way I've seen him before, as a boy with a bow and arrow protecting me (from self-criticism as much as anything). When I describe my vision in the group sharing, my therapist says, "That boy archer must be Cupid, the piercer of hearts!"

I smile deeply. "Yes, that's him."

The words that come to mind strongly in the silence this weekend are patience, courage, and fierce compassion for myself. The patience to be with what comes up in me, for however long it's there; the courage to trust myself to be gentle with whatever I'm experiencing. I have shifted a lot in how I talk to myself. At night without Dicken this weekend, when I can't sleep, instead of giving in to the scary stories like, *You're going to be so tired tomorrow, what's wrong with you, you're so screwed up, how are you ever going to survive on your own?* I treat myself like a sweet, scared child, and say, *It's okay, you're fine, nothing bad is happening. You can just be with this awakeness and settle into it, and tomorrow you can take a nap if you need to* . . . I give myself the love and security I have been relying on Dicken for. Lo and behold, I get back to sleep, and in the meantime enjoy this sweetness. I can rely on my inner resources, richer than I knew. The vast desert of solitude is blooming.

During the weekend, I am numb some of the time and can't feel my heart. Instead of wishing I wasn't so resistant, I practice patience and gentleness: *You're numb, that's fine. It'll pass, it's really okay. You're exactly where you're supposed to be.* I enter the numbness, and it morphs into vibrating energy, filling my whole body with joy and power. For the first time, I get that wherever I am is the way in, and I shouldn't try to change where I am. In this place of energy, I can be with all my cynicism and see how flimsy it is compared to the vast beauty inside. I remember that several intuitives have told me that Theo and the Kundalini energy are calling me to "greatness," which my skeptical self completely discounts; but from my expanded place, I can feel that greatness. I feel rich, like I am discovering a gold mine in myself, and that quiets the "get it from the outside before it's too late!" impulse.

On Sunday afternoon, as the group is winding up, I'm asked to read a poem I told my therapist about, one I wrote.

"No," I say, my face turning red. "I'd really rather not."

"Lucinda, it's time for you to read the poem."

"I can't."

The whole group is looking at me, waiting. I feel my heart beating in my ears, a loud drumming. I want to disappear. The attention is unbearable. The pressure inside me threatens to explode. I want to scream, but instead I start to cry.

"Lucinda, we are waiting to hear your poem."

"Why should I read it? It's stupid, I just wish you'd move on." The silence of the group and the feeling of their eyes on me are excruciating. I start to tremble. "I can't read this poem," I say. "My voice is shaking too much."

"When I first started teaching," my therapist says, "my voice shook through every lecture. There's nothing wrong with the shaking. It's a sign that there's a lot of energy in what you're doing. Please don't let this keep you from sharing yourself with the group. We want to hear from you."

Nodding all around.

I cry and tremble some more. I glance around the room and see that no one is going to rescue me from this. I am not going to get out of here without reading the poem.

Then the trembling begins to awaken memories in my cells: *I'm four months pregnant and shivering in the bathroom in Ireland . . . I'm eight months pregnant and seeing brown stains on the toilet paper and beginning to shake . . . I'm on the table in the hospital having the first ultrasound and I'm shaking . . . I'm about to have the C-section and am trying to hold still so the anesthesiologist can get the needle in my spine . . . I'm in the recovery room shivering uncontrollably . . . I am back in the hardest moments, in the hour after, before we know the outcome and get to hold him, and there, in all that, is the strength. I have to journey far, far into the darkness within me and summon the strength to get through this experience, and in this place no one, not even Dicken or my mom, who are there with me physically, no one can get me through the darkest place but me. I have to support myself and be courageous. I do, and I know I am touching a strength I haven't experienced before.*

From this place, I say, "Fuck it, I'll read the stupid poem." I have reached way down deep to a part of me that no one else can touch, a place where I'm beyond caring about what my instincts are telling me, about how what I share is received; beyond anyone's reach or rescue. From that place I can summon the courage to read my words, and I do.

Later, I won't remember reading the poem or how people

responded, but I will remember what it was like to summon my deepest courage, and how I felt Theo's grace, and nothing else, holding me.

June 6

I hear from my dad that a new friend of his, Sally, has a daughter whose baby just died. He had a heart condition they knew of before birth, but he didn't survive the postpartum surgery. I send a condolence e-mail to Sally right away, initiating a lengthy correspondence.

> *About mentioning the baby's name, for me, I wanted people to speak of Theo. It was a way to keep him real then, when I so feared he would be forgotten, his existence pointless. The thing about losing a baby is that you have the joy of meeting him and seeing him for the first time mixed in with the agony of his death. And I think all parents are bursting to share the joy in their hearts that a baby came along to bless them, even if they aren't aware of the joy because the heartbreak overwhelms them at the moment. In a certain way I was like any new parent, wanting to spread the happy news of our baby's birth, yet people for the most part only focused on the death.*
>
> *So maybe look for cues in Frances and her husband, giving them an opening to share the happy parts and show off their beautiful boy without feeling that it's odd or morbid. And at the same time acknowledging the very real pain, of course.*

> *Dear Lucinda,*
>
> *I have read and reread your e-mail countless times over the past few days. There are blessings—and you are one of them. We have made the wonderful discovery that we can speak of our beautiful baby boy Logan without being self-conscious . . . and there have been magical moments when Frances and her husband have been able to see so distinctly her mouth in Logan's—and laugh.*
>
> *I am so very grateful for your words, that you took the time to*

reach out to us. You have made an enormous difference in our ability
and capacity to cope. Thank you.
With love,
Sally

I will have scores of e-mail, phone, and in-person exchanges with women who've lost babies or grandchildren. It becomes one of the most fulfilling aspects of my life.

CHAPTER 27

Dicken and I decide to move to town. It's something we've talked about for months, as we've struggled with the increasingly frequent hour-long drives back and forth for the boys' hockey, soccer, dance lessons, and so on. And we've become convinced that Jasper would be better off in a structured school environment. It's wrenching to think of not living with Maud, Tom, Grace, and Sam anymore, yet it's hard to see continuing to live so far out when there is nothing we need to be there for, and so much in town that fits our changing needs as a family. Contemplating the move brings many intense conversations among the four of us adults, and agonized nights. It will mean more grief, more change. Are we doing the best thing for our boys? What about the dream of communal living? What is life asking of us, and what has to be let go?

It doesn't take long for us to find a house in the neighborhood close to the school we've picked out for the boys. The weekend of the move, Dicken takes Jasper on a fishing trip they've had scheduled for months. Kevin is in Costa Rica, where he's visiting family for part of the summer. I do the majority of the packing, with help from friends like Gabriella. I take as little as possible, especially from the communal areas of the house, not wanting to upset Maud any more than I already have. Sam wants to come with me to town, so he and I spend the first two nights in the new house together.

"Tia, let's follow the big moving truck the whole way!"

I am grateful for his sweet innocence, and for the warmth of his sleeping body next to mine in bed as I reel from the disorientation of such a big change.

September 25

I'm visiting a neighbor who has a one-year-old. Running after her daughter, she looks tired but happy. She tells me about her dream of one day opening a yoga studio.

"It's years away at this point," she sighs, lifting her toddler into her arms. "But I hope it happens."

"Little ones take all our energy for the first few years," I say. "But we get our lives back eventually."

"I feel like my life hasn't started yet."

Without thinking, I say, "I feel like mine is over."

The conversation moves on, but later I think about what I said, about my life being over. Why did I say that? I guess because I've had my kids, and that mystery is ebbing. I'm aging. A patch of my hair is turning white. I've been married for fifteen years. I've traveled the world and feel like my personal allotment of airline fuel is waning. I've earned an advanced degree and worked in an intense psychiatric hospital not far from the one in *One Flew Over the Cuckoo's Nest*. I've been through childbirth, adoption, having my baby die in my arms. I've had wild Kundalini experiences, a bad mushroom trip, unexplainable coincidences. I've seen numerous babies being born. I've seen meteor showers, the Northern Lights, white midnight and pale dawns. Euphoria, despair, night terrors, deep bliss, multiple orgasms, blistering rage.

But to think that at thirty-seven my life is finished? I guess I was always waiting for "real" life to begin, and when I met Dicken it seemed to. Romance, marriage, happy partnership, beautiful baby, needy child rescued, another beautiful baby who broke my heart and opened the sky. What else can happen now? Everything feels anticlimactic. Published writing, more travel? I can work hard to find the mystery through yoga, art, meditation, writing. But to create life with Dicken, to say yes to the mystery of a being entering my body and then our lives, how could anything touch that?

I'm sad it seems to be over. I can embrace other children, my nieces and nephews yet to be born, maybe grandchildren if I'm lucky; but my glory days are behind me. This feels massive to me because I equate it with the "real" part of life, what I wondered about all through childhood and adolescence: *Who will I marry and what children will make up our family?* I'm left with a sense that I'm less worthwhile as a woman with that access to the mystery closed off, the most powerful channel forever blocked.

Am I beginning to die? To accept my mortality, the speed with which life is passing? Am I becoming fatalistic? Or am I being ageist? Some people say life improves after middle age. But I don't buy it. Again, I wonder: *Will I go gracefully or with a struggle?*

October 26

Christine, who runs WinterSpring, calls to tell me she wants me to take the program coordinator position that's open.

"Oh, I don't know, Christine. I'm not very organized. I don't think I'd be that good."

"Oh, sweetheart, you'd be perfect, believe me. We're all hoping you'll accept."

"I'll need a few days to get a résumé together."

"You don't need a résumé. Just tell me you'll take the job, and it's yours. The board has already approved you."

"Wow, that's easy," I say. I've always dreaded job interviews.

"So you'll take it?"

"Well, I'm not sure. I need to think about it. I just don't know if I'm ready to be that busy. What about my writing, my boys?"

"Remember, it's only half-time, and I think you could actually get everything done in a lot less than that."

"So I can do all my hours while the boys are in school?"

"Yes. Why don't you just try it for a month and see how it goes?"

* * *

When I tell Courtney about the new job, she says, "You've been called to this, Cinda. Everything in your life has led up to it, and it's so connected with Theo."

"I do feel lined up with this because it's become my passion to help people who are grieving. It helps me and it's also a way to give back. I feel so blessed with what I've been given, it just feels really right to spend twenty hours a week serving others."

Dicken says, "You've been headhunted."

"And you might have to live with a messier house."

November 28–December 1

I get a call from Jasper's school, saying he's hurt his shoulder in games class.

"Should I come and get him?"

"No, he's had a little rest and says he feels okay enough to go back to the classroom. I just wanted to let you know."

"Does he want to talk to me?"

I hear a muffled conversation.

"No, he's heading back to class. He says he'll walk home on his own."

"Okay, thanks for letting me know."

When Jasper gets home, he looks pale. I inspect his arm. It looks fine on the outside, but he can't move it at all.

"Does it hurt?"

"No. I'm just mad I can't use it. I want to play hockey tomorrow!"

Jasper has been playing hockey since Andrew and Gabriella insisted he start last year, thinking it was the perfect sport for him and would help him with his grief. They drove him to practices and games three times a week for a whole season.

"Sorry, Jasper, but you'll have to miss the game."

"I hate that kid who kicked me!"

"It was an accident, right?"

"Yeah, but I still hate him. He's an idiot!"

When Dicken comes back from work, he checks out Jasper's arm. "It's not swollen, and he doesn't seem to be in pain," he says, puzzled. "Maybe it's just sprained, or badly bruised."

Over the weekend, Jasper takes it easy, watching more movies than usual. At night, he complains of his shoulder aching, so we give him arnica, a homeopathic remedy, and he's able to sleep.

On Monday, Jasper goes to school but still can't move his arm. He comes home with his friend Noa, complaining that he wasn't able to play four square at recess. Something about this is beginning to scare me. I call Dicken, who is on his way to teach a seminar in Portland. When I tell him I'm worried, he suggests taking Jasper to see our chiropractor. I call the office and they say to come right over. Dr. Matt has a few minutes between appointments.

After a physical exam, Dr. Matt mentions possible dislocation. "You know, it doesn't seem that serious to me," he says, "but I am concerned that he can't lift the arm at all. I'd like to get it X-rayed, just to be on the safe side."

He tells me to take Jasper to the emergency room for the X-ray; otherwise, we'll have to wait weeks.

I call Maud, who is in town today, watching a friend's children. I explain the situation and ask her if she can meet me here at Dr. Matt's office and take Noa home, then pick up Kevin from basketball practice.

"You mean you have to go to the emergency room?" she says, upset. "That's going to be intense for you. You haven't been back since Theo, right? Someone should go with you."

I'm touched by her concern, though I don't think I need someone with me. "It's not like it's a real emergency. I'll be fine."

"No, Cinda. Sorry, but I'm not letting you go alone. Listen, I'll come get Noa, take him home, get Kevin, then meet you at the hospital."

The emergency room is quiet. I check in, fill out initial paperwork, and then we sit in the waiting room. Maud and the other kids arrive. She hugs me, talks to Jasper sweetly, offers him some corn chips. Jasper says he isn't hungry.

A nurse comes out, and Jasper and I are shown to a small examination room.

A doctor comes in, asks a few questions as he studies a chart, then does an exam. Jasper is chatty, asking his own questions, talking about how much he loves ice hockey. The doctor says he suspects a rotator cuff tear, which would require major surgery.

Hearing this, a dark shadow comes over me. I can't bear the idea of Jasper having anesthesia, going under, being cut open. I try not to think of our friends whose son recently underwent a routine appendectomy and almost died from postsurgical complications.

"Let's get an X-ray now," the doctor says. "I doubt the arm is broken. He'd be in a lot more pain, but we'll check just in case."

After the X-ray, the doctor comes back and says to Jasper, "You are one brave young man."

I feel a strange mixture of concern and pride.

The doctor turns to me and says, "You sure you haven't given him anything for pain, not a single aspirin?"

"No, just arnica. Why, what is it?"

"He has a break all the way through the shoulder bone."

"Oh my gosh!" I gasp.

Jasper's eyes are wide. "Will I get a cast?"

I ask the doctor, "Does this mean no surgery?"

"I'm going to get the other doctor on call to take a look at the X-ray," the doctor explains. "He's an orthopedic surgeon."

I take big breaths, then go into the hall and ask the nurse if I can use the phone to call Dicken. I give him the update.

"Wow, what a brave boy," he says, his voice cracking. "Tell him I'm so sorry I'm not there."

"He's being a real trouper," I say.

The orthopedic surgeon shows me the X-ray. I can see the clean, straight white line across Jasper's bone.

"But look at this," the doctor says, pointing to a dark mass below the white line. "This is a cyst, a long one."

"What? I don't understand. How did he get a cyst from being kicked in the shoulder?"

"Oh, he didn't get the cyst suddenly. If it is a cyst, it grew there over time, and it might be what weakened the bone and made it prone to a fracture."

I hate the word *cyst*. I hear *tumor, cancer*. The doctor is acting casual, like there is nothing terrible going on, like a mother isn't standing in front of him hearing terrible news that will turn her life upside down. I am in shock, terror. I feel the ground being pulled out from under me. *Why, oh why, is Dicken out of town?*

We get a sling for Jasper's arm and the name of a surgeon to follow up with the next day. When I see Maud's concerned face, I'm too numb to do anything but grunt, "I need to get home."

Maud calls all our close friends. Courtney drops everything and comes over, rubs my feet, says she'll spend the night and make sure the boys are taken care of. Thank God she is there because I feel paralyzed, and collapse into bed with an excruciating headache. Another friend brings me an herbal migraine remedy, but my head pounds through the night, so loudly I can't hear any thoughts, which is a kind of blessing. My knees ache for the first time in years; I have terrible neck pain. My body seems to be seizing up, refusing to move forward, using every bit of life force to grind everything that's happening to a halt, willing time to stop. I do not want to find out what dreadful thing will happen next.

December 2

The next day, we see an orthopedic surgeon who a doctor friend recommends. He X-rays the shoulder again. The wait feels endless, the exam room claustrophobic; my breathing is shallow. I feel cold and shaky.

The surgeon comes back in, smiling. When he says, "From what I can tell, it's a unicameral bone cyst, seven centimeters long, benign, and in the best-case scenario something he might outgrow," I don't trust his words, or his calm demeanor. My head starts to pound. Then the doctor says, "On the other hand, this kind of thing might require bone graft surgery, I'm not sure. I'd like to get a second opinion from a colleague down at Stanford."

A second opinion. That's what Rhione said after our first ultrasound with Theo. She said the odds were on our side, she just wanted to make sure. And now this doctor is saying the same thing.

"So we have to go down to Stanford?" I ask.

"Oh no, sorry if I didn't make that clear. I can send him these X-rays and get his opinion over the phone. He's probably seen hundreds of cases like this."

"And you haven't?"

He shakes his head, smiling again. "But from what I know, it's not a serious condition, and often reverses as the bone grows."

This pleasant doctor is acting nonchalant, and in the past I would have relaxed and taken his words at face value, but I don't trust him. I am back in the Theo pregnancy, hearing doctors and midwives give me hopeful odds, reassure me that we have very little reason to fear a serious problem.

I am trying hard not to cry in front of Jasper. He looks worried, asks the doctor, "Can I still play hockey?"

"We'll see," the doctor replies. "Let's find out how you heal this up over the next few weeks."

I am not worried about whether he can play ice hockey or not. I just want him to survive this. *Please God. I'll do anything. Just let Jasper be okay.*

Dicken will not be back until tomorrow, so Gabriella comes over and spends the night. My head pounds for hours. I can feel my whole body bracing, waiting for a terrible blow.

Over the next weeks, Jasper's fracture will heal well, and he will play hockey again. Every six months we will re-X-ray the shoulder to check the status of the cyst. The shock and worry will fade, but the underlying terror that something will happen to Jasper comes from the part of me that no longer trusts doctors or fortune or statistics or life. That part of me will remain.

CHAPTER 28

Group e-mail to women friends:

I have been doing a lot of soul searching and processing about the baby question. I got some powerful insight over the weekend, mostly in favor. I just can't seem to rest in the "we're done" place, as hard as I try, and I don't think it's my biology talking (as my sister-in-law warned me it would as I approached forty, saying I shouldn't fall for it). I told a couple of you that I'm in this place where not trying again is starting to seem scarier than trying again, even though on a core level I am utterly petrified of what will come up if we go for it.

Meanwhile, Dicken is now pretty keen to try, so we are contemplating an attempt next cycle (gulp!). I'm scared to even write that. It makes me cringe with fears of going back on my word to people and feeling completely flaky if I lose my nerve again—like backing up from the end of a diving board and climbing down the ladder, the walk of shame. But I have to say, right now it seems that everything is leading me to this, and of course it seems natural that in the process all my fears and reasons not to are screaming at me (including, oh my God, the economy is tanking, this would be a terrible time to bring a child into the world! And Dicken's back is in bad shape, he won't even be able to lift the baby, and all my friends are turning into potheads—they'll flake out on you when you need them! And Dicken will have to go on the rafting trip without me, and he'll fall for one of the girl guides!). Etc., etc. It's actually pretty amusing when I stop believing all this.

The good thing is that I'm in this place where if it does happen, I'll know it's my path, meant to be, an evolution in the long preg-

nancy story of my life so far. And if it doesn't, I feel absolutely fine
about that. From all this work and processing, I've come to a place
where I feel really happy with my life, and having a baby feels more
about sharing all the love rather than filling an empty place.

April 2008

Dicken and I make love several times during my most fertile
week. One time, we are lying in bed afterward, and I hear something across the room fall. When I get up a short while later, I
see that it's the small plastic statue of an archer, a knickknack
I found that reminds me of Theo because of his resemblance to
Cupid in my mythology. Of course I take this as a sign.

About two weeks later, I find my period is a few days late,
so I take a test. It doesn't come out one way or the other, but
looks like a funny hybrid of yes and no. I call my midwife friend,
Jennifer.

"If it's showing any color at all, that means there's hCG in
your system. So I would say you are pregnant. But take another
test first thing tomorrow morning to make sure."

"Looks like I might be pregnant," I tell Dicken.

His eyes are big.

When we realize it's April, the month we conceived both
Jasper and Theo, we laugh.

In the morning, the test is negative. I call Jennifer again.

"Probably a very early miscarriage," she says.

I'm not too surprised or disappointed. But I cry a little that
day, feeling compassion for myself and my body, thinking I
deserve an easy, straightforward road from here on out, not a
bumpy one.

June 2008

I am pregnant again. Weeks pass, and the dollar store tests I
keep taking continue to come out clearly positive.

During these weeks, I am content but not excited. Dicken

and I rarely speak of my state; we only tell my workmates so they understand why I'm a little distracted. I feel well physically, which is suspicious. But I am not worried. I stay very much in each moment, convinced that whatever is happening, or not happening, is perfect.

"Will you want to do prenatal testing?" Dicken asks me.

I shake my head. "I can't see how it would help. I trust this pregnancy. If we have a baby with problems, then we have a baby with problems. Testing ahead of time won't change anything. I love and want this baby, whoever it is."

When I start to bleed, first dark brown spotting, then bright red clots, I cry a lot. But I don't resist my feelings, and I am proud of myself for being able to stay with what was and is happening, proud that I didn't get caught in fearful stories.

I bleed heavily for days. Dicken says, "I'm not putting you through this again. It's too much."

"I guess we're not supposed to have another baby," I agree. "We've given the universe a chance, and the answer seems to be no."

October 2008

Just before my thirty-ninth birthday, Dicken gets carried away during lovemaking.

"Oh boy," he says. "Where are you in your cycle?"

"I think it's too late this cycle for me to get pregnant. And I'm obviously not as fertile as I used to be."

Later in October, I spend two weeks in Ireland with my father and Maud. While we're there, I tell Maud my period is a few days late.

"Could you be pregnant?"

I shake my head, then stop. "Actually, we did have a little unplanned ending a couple of weeks ago."

"Oh my gosh, take a test!" Maud says.

In town that day, I go into a chemist's, but the tests cost ten times what I pay for them in the States.

Maud laughs when I report back to her. "I can't believe you'd be so cheap at a time like this!"

"Wouldn't it be amazing," I say to Maud. "I mean, I asked the universe to tell me what to do. I didn't want to have to make the decision myself to try or not try, and so on. If I am pregnant, and it was unplanned, it just seems like such a perfect cosmic joke or something."

"Oh, I really, really hope you're pregnant!" she says. "I would be so happy."

Maud comes back from a morning bread run and hands me a brown paper bag. I look inside and see a pregnancy test. "You may be too cheap," she says, "but I need to know!"

I do the test, and it is positive. I take a photograph of the test with my new iPhone and e-mail it to Dicken.

I think of the international flights and the X-ray machines, but I quickly let that go. I'm determined not to worry, not to get ahead of myself. I will just take this moment by moment.

It's Election Day in the US. Maud and I stay up through the night to watch the returns. We scream and cheer when Pennsylvania goes to Obama, ensuring his victory. Life feels both safe and exciting in every way.

I fly home and try not to think about being pregnant. Again, I feel well physically, so I am doubtful. I take a pregnancy test every day for weeks. It comes out strongly positive time after time.

December 2008

In week nine, I notice some spotting. Within a few days, the spotting turns to heavy, bright red blood, and I know it is a miscarriage.

I cry. I also feel blessed, because I've been able to have the experience of being pregnant again, and I've witnessed my own courage in the face of that. I know now that I'm strong enough and trusting enough to believe that whatever happens is for the best. I was pregnant and not terrified, not eager to get testing and find out as much as I could. I slept well, I stayed calm, I stayed with the moment day after day. That is a huge blessing in itself, and a testament to how much I have moved through in the past few years.

CHAPTER 29

January 23, 2009

I am with my sister Cecily, who is one week shy of eight years younger than me, which is the exact same age difference between Jasper and Theo, as she gives birth to her first baby in the hospital where Theo was born. It is just past midnight, so my niece is five minutes too late to share Jasper's birthday. Cecily calls her baby girl Lucia, a name that came to her in two dreams, and which, like my name, means light.

The anesthesiologist who took such good care of me the night of Theo's birth is part of Lucia's birth, and a hero to Cecily, giving her an epidural after thirty hours of labor.

Our mom asks the nursing staff if Cecily can have the room we had when Theo was born. No, there is a couple in there already; they have just given birth to a baby boy.

My mother goes into that couple's room, greets the family, and announces, "I want you to know how lucky you are to have this room. My grandson Theo was born here and died in this room. It's a very special place."

August 2009

I'm reading in bed at our house in the Adirondack Mountains. We're spending a whole month here. This morning, we looked at a nearby boarding school that has a renowned ice hockey program. Jasper, three years away from ninth grade, the earliest he could enroll, is eager to attend this school, saying he'd sign up this year if he could. His greatest passion in life is hockey, has been since he started skating soon after Theo was born and died.

Dicken comes in from putting the boys to bed and starts to undress. "It's raining," he tells me.

I look up from my book and discern the sound of light rain outside. The door to the sleeping porch is open and I can feel the fresh air blowing in, a nice relief from the humidity.

Dicken climbs in bed beside me. He doesn't grab his crossword book as usual.

"You okay?" I ask.

"Yeah, I'm fine. I was just thinking, though, about having another baby."

Now? After all I've been through the last couple of years? I want to tell him he's a little late, but I don't. I take a big breath.

"Is this about Jasper wanting to go to boarding school?"

He nods.

"It is crazy to think of Jasper being gone so soon."

"I don't even like it when he's having a sleepover at a friend's house," he says. "I miss him so much."

"He's the center of our lives."

I look over at Dicken and see that tears are spilling silently down his face. I move closer to him and try to put my arms around him. It's awkward in this bed. The mattress is hard and Dicken is a lot bigger than me.

"Why didn't we have more when we were younger?" he says.

"You mean why did we have that abortion?"

"Yes. What was wrong with me? Why was I so scared?"

"Honey, we were young, just married, on the road, about to start a new life three thousand miles away from home. We didn't know anyone, we were both about to start school. We had no community, no place to live, no income other than Dad's allowance."

He nods, but his face looks hard, grim.

"Do you remember that horrible fleabag motel we stayed in, the one in Daly City? The scratchy blankets, the dripping shower, the horrible wasteland outside. I was feeling sick, scared out of my mind."

"I know," he says. "It was awful."

"Of course we didn't feel ready or excited to have a baby. It was terrible timing."

"But we could have done it. We would have been okay. We had each other."

"It would have been really, really hard. We might not have made it as a couple. We were a lot younger, remember?"

"Twenty-two."

"We had no support." I can't tell if Dicken is taking any of this in, but it's helping me to hear it. "We can look back from where we are now and project our current maturity and stability onto our situation then, but honestly, we were completely different. And even when we had Jasper six years later, it was hard. Raising children isn't easy."

"I know, but it's the best thing there is, and I wish we had more than one birth child. We threw away what was probably our only other chance. I just can't forgive myself for that. What was I thinking?" He's clenching his fists, squeezing his eyes shut like he's trying not to see what's hurting him.

"It's easy to see it that way in hindsight," I say. "If we knew what lay ahead, of course we would have reconsidered."

"The thing is, it's my one big regret in life. If I could go back and redo it, I would. But I can't."

"No, we can't. We just have to grieve all that, and be grateful for what we do have."

"But maybe I'm not supposed to just accept it. Maybe the regret is telling me something about our present situation."

"What do you mean?" I ask.

"It's just that I could see myself in twenty years, looking back on us now and having the same regret. Asking myself why we didn't try harder, have another baby when it was still possible."

I take that in and am silent for a while. "I hear what you're saying," I tell him after a minute or so. "But I don't think fear of future regret is enough of a reason to try to have a baby."

"I know. But it's not the only reason. I love being a father. I love having kids around. The way I feel about Jasper is like nothing I've ever experienced."

You're selfish for not giving this great man more children.

Then I think of Theo. He was supposed to be the answer, the joyful exclamation mark at the end of our family, the child who wrapped up our parenting experience in a pretty package and completed the "house full of children" Dicken talks about.

"We tried," I say.

"I know." I can tell Dicken is thinking of Theo too. "We got robbed."

I want to say that we still have Theo, that he'll always be our son, but it feels like a cheap rationalization right now.

The rain picks up. The sound of the drops hitting the roof becomes loud, mercifully drowning out thoughts.

September 24

I'm having a cup of tea with Cecily, and she's telling me about her time with Jasper and Kevin the other day.

"Those boys are so hilarious," she says. "And handsome. My gosh, you are going to have girls knocking down the door any day now. Just make sure the boys know about birth control."

"Oh, we're not worried about that. Dicken and I want grand-children as soon as possible."

Cecily's eyes widen for a moment, and then she bursts out laughing.

I go on: "You know, we'll tell them, *Boys, don't bother with con-doms, they're so uncomfortable . . .*"

I am joking, of course, but I send out a prayer to whoever is listening, to let me experience the closeness and mystery of babies in some form or other again in my life. Maybe a baby who needs a mother, or a caretaker, will come my way. Maybe a future grandchild or niece or nephew will have a deep con-nection to me. I think of Sam and Maggie and Lucia, already so woven into my heart. And I think of Adam, the son of Jasper's hockey coach, not much older than Theo would have been, who plays with me at the rink while the older boys skate, how the other day he looked up at me and said, "I wish you were my mom."

December 2009

I'm sitting in the freezing-cold stands at the rink, watching Jasper play in his weekly hockey game. It's sunny and warm outside, but you can't tell that in this windowless indoor arena. I know about this by now, so I'm wearing a large down parka, a wooly hat, and a scarf. I have a decaf latte in my hands, and when I'm not screaming and cheering or slapping Dicken a high five, I take warm sips of the sweet, creamy drink.

Suddenly, I hear a voice in my head say, *Remember*. I step outside myself for a moment and see a happy, healthy, pink-cheeked woman lost in the excitement of a sporting event, enjoying the unmatched thrill of watching her child follow his passion with every cell of his eleven-year-old body.

The voice takes me right back to the summer of 2005, four years before, when I was pregnant with Theo. How for all those sunny months, I was immobilized by horrific morning sickness, essentially poisoned by the faulty genes that made up each cell of the growing baby and placenta. For weeks, I lay on the couch, barely able to eat or move. I remember how reading made me sicker, but watching TV was doable, so I attempted to forget the deathly nausea by watching Wimbledon. Match after match, I tried to focus, but not even my favorite sporting event of the year could distract me. The hours felt like days, a vicious hangover that would not relent. I prayed for relief, thinking, *If I knew I'd always feel this bad, I'd rather be dead.* This is what strikes me now, how I watched the tennis and envied the spectators as they smiled, cheered, and took sips from paper cups, so remote from my reality it was like looking down the wrong end of a telescope at impossibly small versions of my own species. I fantasized that one day in the distant future, I might feel well enough to venture out into the world again, sip a cup of coffee or tea, and enjoy myself. It seemed like a far-off paradise.

And now, here I am at the rink, feeling fine, my mouth savoring the bittersweet coffee, my spirit soaring on the ice with my strong, healthy son. I thank that voice for reminding me of where I've been, of what came and went. I know if I hadn't gone through that pregnancy and felt that deep yearning to know health and life again, I might take this seemingly ordinary moment for granted, this routine Saturday-morning hockey game with a warm drink in my hands and a beautiful boy sweating his heart out on the ice. Millions of American parents are watching their children in sporting events as we sit here. Millions of healthy, fortunate people with healthy, active kids.

Jasper lives for hockey. His nighttime prayer is, "God, let me be in the NHL." My prayer is simply, "God, let him be." Let him breathe and skate and chase his dreams, but most of all, let him be. Let him outlive me. This miracle child, the only one of my handful of pregnancies to make it to birth and survive into childhood.

I still look back on myself in that sickbed of pregnancy. As I lay there patiently, unknowingly poisoned by a faulty placenta, willing to do whatever it took to carry that new life in me for nine months, I would hear through the open window the loud cries of my then-seven-year-old playing soccer on the lawn with his cousins, his robust lungs taking in the fresh summer air. *Brave woman, lying in misery, puzzled by dreams of death each night, by strange-seeming images on TV each day, willing herself to focus on life and the living: I will never forget you, or the child you carried and lost, the one whose damaged lungs only lasted for four hours and forty-four minutes and then gave out as you held him in your arms. And I will never take this living son for granted. Nor will I take our other beautiful boy, Kevin, for granted. How incredibly fortunate we are to get to raise these two children.*

Of course I will forget how fortunate I am. I will lose my temper with Jasper in the car on the way home from the rink because he left his stick in the locker room again. My body will brace in despair as he shouts back at me, and I will think something defeatist: *I hate being a mother, I'm no good at it!* But I know something now that I didn't before Theo came along. I know all of us will die, just as we were born. I don't mean I just know it, I *really* know it. I can feel it in my deepest being. And I'm okay with not being able to fully understand why we are here, why we get the hours or days or years we do, and where we are going after we die. In the face of this, all I can do is accept my humanness and love as much as I can in every situation, including myself and others when we forget to be loving, when we break our promises, when we fail each other, when we do things we swore we would never do, when we expect too much of ourselves, each other, when we forget we're only human, when we forget how lucky we are to be alive.

Official mourning periods vary widely, from thirteen days in the Hindu tradition to a year in Judaism to two years in Venezuela. In Edwardian and Victorian England, family members were expected to wear black for months or years, depending on the loss. The guideline for the death of a child was "as long as one feels disposed."

By the time three years have passed since Theo's birth and death, I will notice a significant shift. I will still think about him frequently, but it is as if a veil has been lifted, and I no longer filter everything through the lens of that experience. For those first three years, I saw, heard, felt, dreamed, and processed everything from the vantage point of, *How do I relate to this given what I've been through, given that my beloved child has come and gone?* I won't really notice the veil lifting, but at some point I realize it's not there anymore. I will start to think of the whole experience as something that happened to me, not something that defines me. While I can easily talk about it when asked, I will no longer feel compelled to; I've told the story so many times it's almost as if it belongs to somebody else now, a younger version of me. Finally, after all these months, I will feel that I'm back in the land of the living, my feet firmly planted on the ground again.

When I turn forty, almost four years after Theo, I will wake up on my birthday and cry my eyes out, not for any specific reason, more for the passage of time, and a vague sense that something in my life is ending. I will say a prayer, asking the universe to bring me more life. I'm no longer afraid of deep emotion, of intensity. I don't want to continue navigating my life by trying to avoid mistakes and hurts. I tell whoever is listening to bring it on, to fill the rest of my days not with safety and comfort but with adventure and edge, the experiences that make me feel most alive, and have the power to change me.

Einstein wrote: "There are only two ways to live your life. One is as though nothing is a miracle. The other is as though everything is a miracle."

I think about the first time I saw a baby being born, several years before I became a mother myself, and how I was seized by the undeniable evidence in front of me that being able to reproduce and end up with a real, live human baby is an absolutely astonishing miracle.

But I can see that it's not just the healthy baby outcome that is miraculous. The body's ability to know that something is wrong early on in embryonic development (the blighted ovum) is arguably as wondrous as the birth of a perfectly formed baby. Most women experiencing such an event, usually in the form of a first-trimester miscarriage, would probably think of it as a tragedy, or at least a disappointment. But it is a miracle, one that keeps the majority of parents from having to cope with a stillbirth or raising a severely handicapped child.

So what do you call it when an embryo that should have been detected as improperly formed beats the odds by fooling the body? What do you call it when that embryo becomes a fetus that defies the high probability of miscarriage and stillbirth and is born full-term? The chances of a thirty-five-year-old woman conceiving, gestating, and giving birth to a live baby with trisomy 13 are much, much lower than the odds of her delivering a healthy baby. Human biology's fantastically intricate checks and balances have fallen short. Are these facts just tragic anomalies, or do they point to something greater?

And what about the circumstances that lined up just so, giving Theo the chance to be born alive? He was conceived by parents who chose to forgo prenatal testing, who were never urged to consider abortion. If we'd known about his condition and had not opted for an abortion, a stillbirth would probably have resulted because a C-section would have been considered too dangerous for me, and Theo's chances of surviving a vaginal delivery were almost nil. If I'd insisted on a home birth even after the ultrasounds, or changed my mind at zthe last minute and gotten to the hospital too late, or refused the C-section, we would not have met Theo alive.

Had Theo been conceived by another couple, anywhere in the world, he probably wouldn't have lived outside the womb. The vast majority of American women use an OB/GYN for prenatal care, and most European women see nurse-midwives. In both cases, testing is standard. So a Western woman would likely have known the baby's condition, and would have either opted for an abortion or had a stillbirth by vaginal delivery. If carried by a poor woman in a third world country where the rates of miscarriage and maternal deaths in childbirth are much higher, it's even less likely Theo would have made it through the pregnancy and birth, and that mother's life could also have been in danger.

Theo's brief life on earth should not have happened. But it happened to us. We were the tiny pinprick in the fabric of the universe through which Theo entered this world. He passed obstacle after obstacle, and came to a family and a community where his gifts of joy and wonder would not be wasted.

Is this simply an extraordinary set of coincidences, and nothing more? Or could it be that as a soul waiting to be born, Theo sought us out? Did he line up with the whole universe in some sort of perfect order our minds can't fully fathom? Did he know his mother was born under Black Moon Lilith, and would be open to the powerful confluence of mothering and death? Did he know his dad had the chart of a benevolent king with boundless love for children, a father who would love him fully and endlessly whether he lived for one minute or a hundred years? Did he trust we would make that series of crucial choices during the pregnancy and just before the birth, the very choices which gave him life?

When I think that Theo might have chosen us, it's not because Dicken and I, our friends and our family, are such exceptional people—how well I know our flaws, especially my own! We are ordinary people who are open to the mystery of birth and death. We did not look away from Theo. We took in his beauty forever. Maybe that's all he wanted.

The amazing systems of our human biology and of modern medical marvels like amniocentesis did not prevent Theo's birth. So is this occurrence a miracle, or does it justify Einstein's first option, that nothing is a miracle, that everything is flawed?

All I know is that the odds of it happening to us were minuscule, and that some days I'm convinced that we had terrible, terrible luck. Yet there are moments when I think of Theo, the astonishing being he was and all the light he brought people and continues to bring in odd yet undeniable ways, how Paul said he saw Theo's life as the "only perfect life" he's ever seen, and I harbor a secret, bubbling notion that we hit the jackpot. In those moments I call it an extraordinary, once-in-a-lifetime miracle.

Acknowledgments

I am deeply grateful to everyone who has helped me with this book, especially:

Marcia Trahan, dream editor, whose enthusiasm and patience never waned. I could not have done this without her.

Johnny Temple, my hero.

Dad, my lifelong writing champion—yes, from before I could even hold a pencil.

Dicken.

Maud, who insisted I expand the birth story and share it.

Uncle Henry.

Mom.

Mark.

Ben & Cecily.

Gabriella.

Readers along the way: Mary Makenna, Petranka Palzewicz, Khaliqa, Grace Powell, Caroline Weatherby, Katie Sloan, Mary Moeglein, Kara Gilmour, Kathy Temple, Wendy Kline, Natalie Tyler, Vanessa Albrecht, Sarah Rutledge, Pam Colloff.

Guidance: Melissa Coleman, Glenda Burgess, Elizabeth Heineman, Sophie Burnham, Tom McCarthy, Roanna Rosewood.

Jasper, who told me years ago, as I scribbled away, "Mom, when I make it to the NHL, I'm gonna get that book published for you."

CPSIA information can be obtained at www.ICGtesting.com
Printed in the USA
LVOW11s1952250915

455558LV00002BA/6/P

9 781617 754333